The Urban Life and Urban Landscape Series

New York City
An Outsider's Inside View

Mario Maffi

The Ohio State University Press

Columbus

Library of Congress Cataloging-in-Publication Data

Maffi, Mario, 1947–
  [Sotto le torri di Manhattan English]
  New York City : an outsider's inside view / Mario Maffi.
    p. cm. — (Urban life and urban landscape series)
Includes bibliographical references and index.
  ISBN 0-8142-0957-2 (hardcover : alk. paper) — ISBN 0-8142-5123-4
(pbk. : alk. paper) — ISBN 0-8142-9033-7 (cd-rom)
  1. New York (N.Y.)—Description and travel. 2. New York
(N.Y.)—History. 3. New York (N.Y.)—Social life and customs. 4.
Manhattan (New York, N.Y.)—Description and travel. 5. Manhattan (New
York, N.Y.)—History. 6. Manhattan (New York, N.Y.)—Social life and
customs. 7. City and town life—New York (State)—New York. 8. Maffi,
Mario, 1947—Travel—New York (State)—New York. 9. Maffi, Mario,
1947—Homes and haunts—New York (State)—New York. 10.
Italians—New York (State)—New York—Biography. I. Title. II. Series.
  F128.55 .M34 2004
  917.47'10443—dc22
                                        2003025431
Cover design by Dan O'Dair.
Type set in Goudy.
Printed by Thomson-Shore, Inc.

9 8 7 6 5 4 3 2 1

The translation from the Italian (by Derek Allen, with the assistance of the
author) was made possible by funds provided by the Università degli Studi
di Milano, Italy.

A tricky business, that of understanding New York. The city is always on the move, forever shifting. You leave it one day and you come back the next to find that it has changed mood and countenance.

Observing it from afar, as the immigrants must have done more than a century ago, it comes across as a solid, immovable construction in granite—a splendid, impregnable fortress. And yet, maybe even more than Hemingway's Paris, it is a *moveable feast,* spinning, throbbing, and changing, swirling and elusive. That is its charm, that is its curse. And yet, like all metropolises, New York, too, has its own deep-seated nucleus: a solid, fixed kingpin that alone allows it to spin, throb, and change.

Contents

Foreword

By George J. Lankevich

I n *New York City: An Outsider's Inside View* Mario Maffi reveals that two
of his favorite Manhattan structures are the Chrysler Building and Grand
Central Terminal, a combination not altogether surprising since one illus-
trates the verve of a metropolis that reaches for the sky and the other is
forever a place where "something is about to happen." The sites reflect the
allure and tumult of a city whose only constancy is change, a venue which
radically reshapes places and people. If real New Yorkers are produced only
when they share memories of former city realities then Maffi, an Italian
professor whose research has illuminated the history of the Lower East Side,
qualifies as a true resident of his adopted city.

It is difficult to fit Mario Maffi into the architecture of scholarship. The
son of a translator, his graduate work analyzed the dynamic youth culture
of the 1960s, a fluid and kaleidoscopic movement that introduced him to
the complexities and contradictions of Manhattan's lifestyle. His award-
winning *La Cultura Underground* appeared in 1972, beginning an enormously
varied academic output. As Professor of American Literature at the State
University of Milan, Maffi has produced—in both English and Italian—
monographs, articles, translations, lectures, maps and even audiovisual aids.
His *oeuvre* encompasses leftist parliamentary politics, the Lower East Side
of Manhattan island, American authors as varied as James Fenimore
Cooper and Upton Sinclair, contemporary Nuyorican and Chinese poets,
the librettos of George Gershwin and Stephen Sondheim, personal rumi-
nations, and even a foray into the neighborhoods of London. Though his
writings range across a wide spectrum, this book makes clear that his heart
belongs to New York, the capital of the world.

Maffi first came to New York in 1975—he remembers the day was bright
and sunny—and discovered the subject that has beguiled him ever since.
After immersing himself in the "shocking and fascinating" culture of the
Lower East Side, he has spent the last quarter century attempting to "get
a grasp" on the metropolis whose essence is change. In academic terms, Maffi

examines the forces of ethnicity, multiculturalism, Americanization, class
and gender relations, "high" and "low" cultures—influences that immigrants
encountered as they went through the acculturation process. But in
human terms Maffi also passed through the polyglot, "self-centered" world
of America's most famous ghetto and fell in love with the greater metropolis surrounding it.

If "Americanization is an alchemic process," the Lower East Side was a
laboratory where fundamental changes occurred. Maffi, who appears to have
read every book and memoir from its "golden age" of development
(1880–1930), was first attracted by its proletarian culture and published
Gateway to the Promised Land in 1995. *Gateway*, the English version of *Nel
mosaico della città*, analyzed the interaction between immigrants and
American society, a transforming dialectic he calls the "very heart of cultural production." Successive waves of Jews, Italians, Chinese and Puerto
Ricans experienced such give-and-take in the streets of "Alphabet City."
The dynamism of the process was brilliantly summed up by Waldo Frank
decades ago: "We go forth all to seek America. And in the seeking we create her." The laboratory results continue to amaze Maffi and he is clearly
reluctant to see his "alternate city" fade.

Paradoxically, the joy of a community that succeeds in joining mainstream society is always tempered by sadness for cultural loss. Maffi is deeply
aware of the tensions created as immigrant waves interact with modernism,
but he now understands that in Manhattan nothing remains unaltered for
very long. Even raucous Times Square could be "anesthetized by Disney"
and Maffi knows intellectually that the still underdeveloped Lower East
Side surely faces gentrification. His mind tells him change is inevitable but
his passion refuses to admit it. Manhattan's process of continual becoming
eminently suits the talents of a gifted storyteller and Maffi's *New York: L'isola
delle colline* (*New York: Island of Hills*) and *Sotto le torri di Manhattan* (*Under
the Towers of Manhattan*, of which the present book is a translation) adopted
a more personal tone; they ignore the dry statistics of cliometricians and
examine the rich life of real people. Maffi's latest volume also revels in the
moods of Manhattan recording "obstinate wanderings" in search of
Americanization.

An Outsider's Inside View is a wonderful tour through Manhattan taken
with a knowledgeable friend. Maffi knows many pathways into the heart
of the city: names that recall its past; maps that chart its complexities; villages that house its varied folk; images implanted in the mind's eye by the
media. Our walkers together examine the "deep seated and privileged" relationship between New York and the wider world, wonder at metropolitan
tolerance, enjoy a glimpse of the theater that fuels its energy and infuses
its spirit. And with every step Maffi displays an advocate's love for a city

that belongs to the world as much as to the United States. Like a true Manhattanite, he finds it almost unnecessary to discuss the four "outer boroughs" where the vast bulk of New Yorkers live; he even throws a few darts at those neighborhoods. New York may boast three other Chinatowns and Dominicans may dominate its Latin community, but Maffi's heart remains in "Loisaida" and on Avenue C where he became a New Yorker. He, like the acculturated second generation that returns only for weekends, now sees a different East Side but one which retains its pulsating life force. Maffi's Manhattan has a "jealous, exclusive will to capture and possess those who set foot" within its precincts, and those who travel with him benefit from a tour that is both nostalgic and forward looking. *An Outsider's View* is not scholarly, but true New Yorkers like Maffi know they will never fully understand the city he calls a "sphinx." Although this fine volume presents Maffi as only an observer, it really proves he is no longer an "outsider."

Preface: Time and the City

W hen I reread this book for its U.S. edition, I felt that a chapter was missing, and acutely so: indeed, no book on a metropolis (and on New York City in particular) can do without a chapter on "Time." Because time is different in a metropolis: its pace is different, as are its rhythms, its moments and the way they speed up and slow down; so too is the temporal span between sunrise and sunset, between sunset and sunrise, and all the segments contained therein—the way they follow after each other and together constitute such a different timetable. Above all, time is change, and change is what makes a metropolis (any metropolis, but—again—New York City in particular) a living organism, subject to an ongoing cycle of birth, growth, decay, and rebirth—not the frozen exhibit of lines and volumes, shapes and profiles, lifeless artifacts and empty proclamations, which all too often passes itself off as a "metropolis" on the pages of glossy magazines. How, then, to reckon with time and change in New York City? This book was written in 1997, published in Italy in 1998, and translated into English in 2003, and so many things have since changed: how to take them into account? How to recover them and place them within the context of a book whose purpose, from the beginning—from its very inception—was to avoid as far as possible a flat and stiff image of the city?

A chapter on "Time" (I told myself) would have to embrace micro— as well as macro—phenomena. For instance: murals and gardens have been disappearing, or continue to disappear, all over the city, especially on the Lower East Side, where merciless property developers relentlessly throw their weight around; Charas/El Bohio, the huge community center on East 9th Street that served the needs of one of the most depressed (and simultaneously creative) areas of the city for decades, was scandalously served an eviction order to make room for what will probably become a big luxury condo; the tiny Vejigante Café, replaced by a hairdresser, is no longer there to brighten up El Barrio's sunny afternoons; people have moved from one job to another, or left the city, disappeared; friends and acquaintances have sadly passed away; love's labors were lost; other books were written, movies shot, paintings painted, theatricals acted; Petrella Point itself remained a riddle up until a couple of years ago, when the curiosity of an Italian reader of this book helped me solve it . . . Time ran in the streets of New York.

And then, of course, the most dramatic change of all occurred—9/11/2001. I was in Memphis, Tennessee, driving north to gather material for a new book on the Mississippi River, when everything happened—when the New York skyline exploded before my eyes on the TV screen. Someone in the motel lobby had told me that a hijacking was taking place over New York, and I had gone back to my room and turned on the TV set, just in time to see one of the Twin Towers in flames, and the almost surreal scene of a second airplane crashing into the other tower, and both of them finally collapsing in a silent apocalypse of thick, swollen, rolling white-grey clouds. I remember spending most of the morning in my motel room, between the TV set and the telephone, trying to reach New York and Milan, anxious to learn and understand more of what was happening.

Whether one liked them or not (and frankly I did not), the Twin Towers *were* a New York icon. The tragedy consumed within and without them, the lives of thousands entrapped in their crumbling walls, not only changed the city's skyline (that would be a purely aesthetical—and rather cynical—consideration) but also our perception of the city, and the city's perception of itself—as a world-city, yes, but in a peculiar way also detached from the world: an impregnable fortress, around which the world revolved, yes, but almost without touching it . . . Now, every time I think (or read) of the Twin Towers, or glance at one of those by now tragically familiar photos, an image comes to my mind, conjured up with a strange force of suggestion by so many evocations and connections: the last sequence of Franklyn J. Schaffner's *Planet of the Apes* (1968, a movie that is also, so to speak, about New York, and disturbingly so)—the sequence that comes as a shocking revelation to Charlton Heston and his handful of fugitives. And, invariably, in my mind, that sequence is accompanied by the resonating words from one of Henry James's most prescient books, *The American Scene* (1907), where he compares New York's skyline to "some colossal hair-comb turned upward and so deprived of half its teeth that the others, at their uneven intervals, count doubly as sharp spikes." But of course the issue is a large and complex one, and one that would inevitably take us far from New York, and it cannot be dealt with at length here.

Anyway, how to account for all these changes—the large and the small, the collective and the personal, the soft, inevitable change, and that which is sudden and dramatic? An extremely interesting book edited by Michael Sorkin and Sharon Zukin, *After the World Trade Center: Rethinking New York City* (2002), manages to analyze the 9/11 events and their aftermath also by exploring (or by unearthing, so to speak) what was there *before* the WTC—that is, by exploring time and change in New York City, by giving back to the city its status of a living organism, with an all too often forgotten (even hidden) past. But what to do with a book written *before* such momentous (or, as the case may be, seemingly insignificant) changes? How to introduce the continuous flow of time in the fixed format of a printed book? I resolved to modify the text slightly here and there, in order to acknowledge and incorporate the most significant transformations. I rewrote some passages in order to introduce a kind of perspective, a sort of time distancing. I used parentheses and past tenses. I mentioned tragedies great and small. But even so, the fact remains that a chapter on "Time" *is* missing from this book. And maybe—just think for a moment—it is quite appropriate that it be missing. Perhaps it would have been impossible to write it—an endeavor comparable to that of Achilles racing with the turtle. Maybe I would have ended up in a *Tristram Shandy* situation—trying to tell the life of a city and always being left behind by that very life. Maybe it would have been a useless attempt to freeze "Time," thus denying it. Maybe the book as it is, written *then*, read *now*, is itself a testimony to time and change in New York City.

So, perhaps the best way to "write" it is to leave the reader with the task of writing his or her own chapter: his or her own perception of the rhythms of the city, of its ever-changing face, pace, and nature. Perhaps the real, most appropriate chapter on "Time" starts unfolding when a reader opens the book and starts turning its pages. And this, on the part of its author, is surely a wish.

Mario Maffi
Milan, Italy
23 February 2004

1

Names

At the northern tip of Manhattan, where the waters of the Hudson divide to form the Harlem River and, running eastward, separate the island from the Bronx before joining up with the East River and flowing into New York Bay—it is here, well off the traditional tourist circuit, that Inwood Hill Park lies. A little-known spot, it has a certain bearing on the city's topography, and it is symbolic of the intertwining of past and present at the heart of New York's history.

Lapping the soft stern of Manhattan, this particular section of the Harlem River is actually artificial. Originally it flowed more to the north, around Marble Hill, and formed a winding bend, further bedeviling efforts at navigation among the maze of straits, bays, islands, promontories, and secondary branches that unravel their way east and southeast of Manhattan. In 1895 a decision was made to open a new waterway in that section of the river: the original bed was filled and a softer bend was created a few miles to the south. So, on paper at least, Marble Hill passed over to the Bronx, but such was the outcry among its inhabitants that the jurisdiction of this tiny stretch of hilly terrain was soon returned to Manhattan. Yet another strange and fascinating chapter in the local history of the metropolis.

But the reason I've ventured all the way up here to these river banks is another. Set somewhere in a rock along one of the paths weaving their way through the park, there should be a plaque reminding visitors that one of the island's biggest native villages once stood nearby: Shorakkopoch, inhabited by the Weckweesgeek Indians (or, according to some, by the Reckgawancs), a subtribe of the Wappingers. The plaque should also remind onlookers that it was precisely here, in 1626, that the colonial governor of Nieuw Amsterdam, Peter Minuit, was supposed to have purchased the entire island of Manhattan from this tribe for the equivalent of sixty guilders (twenty-four dollars) in beads and trinkets.

I say "supposed" because some measure of doubt persists. Indeed, another version of the event assuredly recounts that the meeting took place between the Dutch and the native Manate Indians, a subtribe of the Matouacs, this time at

*the opposite end of Manhattan, near Battery Park and the present-day site of
the U.S. Custom House—in other words, just a few blocks away from Wall
Street. And I must admit that this second version carries greater conviction: first,
because it is more plausible (in 1626 the northern area of Manhattan was practically terra incognita), and second, because it is more suggestive (where else
could such a bargain have been more appropriately struck if not in the area that,
two and a half centuries later, would become the "business district"?).
However, I still prefer to imagine the episode having taken place here, among
the last remaining woods of Manhattan's primeval forests—somewhere in the
watery, leafy silence of these paths and hills (Minuit forging along the path at
the head of his men in baggy puffed trousers and broad-brimmed hats; the
Weckweesgeeks lined up in front of the village with their canoes ditched along
the shore just a few yards off)—and not amidst the frenetic cacophony of narrow canyons downtown.*

*Whatever the truth of the matter, it is from here, from this past, that we must
first set off to discover Manhattan: by piecing together its history through an
understanding of names.*

So, the Weckweesgeeks or the Reckgawancs (or the Manates, if the other
version is to be believed . . .)—the opening phase of Manhattan's history is far from simple. The tribes and subtribes are numerous, the relation-
ships complex, the trails beset with traps, the settlements clouded in mist,
and any single interpretation is necessarily subject to revision. (There is
even an all-American version that claims that Manhattan was "sold" by
Chief Tammany, whose name is thought by some to loom behind
"Tammany Hall," the palm-greasing political machine of the Democratic
Party in New York; but the truth is that the chief's real name was
Tammanend, and he "sold" *Philadelphia* to the English in 1682.)

What *is* certain is that this island, with its mild climate, its abundantly
fertile soil, and its nourishing profusion of natural fruits, was inhabited by
certain tribes and subtribes belonging to the great Algonquin family.
Members of these tribes called themselves Lenapes ("native men"), but the
Europeans called them "Delawares" after the bay to the north of
Jamestown, which took its name from the first governor of Virginia, Sir
Thomas West, the third Duke *de la Warr*. The island was also inhabited by
Wappinger, Matouac, and Mohican tribes and subtribes (again, belonging
to the Algonquin family), as well as by certain tribes and subtribes (like
the Mohawks) of the great rival family, the Iroquois of the Five Nations.
Thus it was that the first European explorers of Manhattan island
(Giovanni da Verrazzano, Henry Hudson, and the fur merchants of the

Dutch East India Company) came face to face with the Weckweesgeeks and the Manates, as well as the Canarsies, the Matinecocs, the Rockaways, the Nechtancs, the Tenkenas, the Paperimemins, and plenty of others besides—about twenty villages in all, linked together by trails. The most important of these was the so-called Weckweesgeek Trail that cut its way through Manhattan from top to bottom, a kind of latter-day Broadway running east (and not west) of what is today Central Park. (Evan T. Pritchard's *Native New Yorkers* [2002] is a fascinating account of this complex history.)

The Lenape and other Algonquin Indians were hunters and fishermen. They lived in longhouses capable of hosting several families, and they built highly maneuverable canoes out of tree trunks; they cultivated corn, beans, pumpkins, and tobacco, cooked hominy and succotash in terracotta pots, and ate out of wooden plates decorated with animal designs. They were also great oyster lovers: discarded shells littered their settlements and adorned the banks of the two rivers. Their matriarchal form of social organization related to a "primitive communism" that gave short shrift to any ideas of private ownership of the earth (the Great Mother) or animals, both of which were possessed on a collective basis and were there to be enjoyed by present and future generations. Hence the wide-eyed indifference with which the natives greeted unfavorable "transfers of property" and, afterward, their obstinate refusal to recognize and uphold such transactions. The very idea of *buying land and animals* was something completely outside their conceptual mindset—an instance of sheer folly. The treaties were perceived by the natives as agreements of mutual enjoyment: hence, the instances of "trespassing" and "larceny" that so outraged Europeans and sparked a viciously spiraling routine of reprisal, revenge, punishment, and plunder.

Relations between Europeans and natives on the island were not, then, exactly idyllic, especially when William Kieft, the hawkish governor of the Nieuw Amsterdam settlement (and author of a horrific massacre in 1643), was in power. But today this is of less concern to us than the question of what actually remains of the native communities in New York. Very little, to tell the truth: a few arrow- and spearheads in stone (called "Clovis heads") that turned up mainly on Staten Island and around Canarsie and Queens; shell deposits along the riverbanks; the very fine National Museum of the American Indian at One Bowling Green; and, more than anything else, certain *names*. For example, Rockaway ("Sandy Land") and Jamaica ("Home of the Beavers"), which are now neighborhoods in Queens; or Canarsie ("At the Fenced-in Place") and Nayack ("headland"), present-day neighborhoods of Brooklyn. Or, less directly perhaps, the name given by the Dutch to a road that, on the southernmost tip of the island, wound its way alongside the East River: smothered in mother-of-pearl oyster shells, Pearle Straet now goes under the name of Pearl Street.

And then, obviously, there is Mana-hatta, Manhattan, whose meaning and origins are still subject to debate: "a place for general inebriation"? "the place for gathering bow wood"? "the hilly island"? "small island"? "rocky island" (or "rocky founded island," as Walt Whitman translated it)? from the name of the Manates (= "island inhabitants")? In Washington Irving's 1809 work *Diedrich Knickerbocker's History of New York*, a comic-opera blend of history and fantasy, America's first professional author treated his readers to an amusing explanation of the name. It derived, he wrote, from the native women's custom of putting on men's headgear: "Man Hat On"! Meanings and origins are, then, plagued by uncertainty. Nonetheless, the sheer musicality of the name possesses a mythical force and conjures up images of a controversial past shrouded in mystery. And a feeling of guilt that has yet to be fully dealt with.

Very little otherwise remains of the Native American presence in New York: the odd archaeological find coming to light during excavation work for a new skyscraper; long stretches of roads like the Bowery or Broadway actually retracing ancient trails atop the summit of hills (later leveled out in the wake of property speculation), over water meadows and marshlands. Or—perhaps—a sudden revelation while investigating the city's social history: take, for example, two photographs by Danish immigrant Jacob Riis. Working as a journalist for the central police station in the immigrant neighborhood of the Lower East Side at the end of the nineteenth century, Riis was the inspiration behind the very first socially oriented investigations and laid down the roots of American social photography with his extraordinary documentation of urban poverty. The first of the two photographs is titled *Old Mrs Benoir, an Indian woman, in her attic on Hudson Street*. We get a glimpse of a tiny room, a skylight, a pallet, the odd piece of furniture, two trunks, a mirror, and a wood-burning stove; and, sitting astride a chair, a plump old woman, hair tied up with a handkerchief, intent on her crochet work: drawing on her white pipe, she concentrates hard on her task, a lorgnette slipping down to the tip of her nose. The title of the second photograph is *Aquila Montana and her Iroquois Indian family*. It features an elderly man and two women with splendidly sculpted faces, seated around a table to the side of a sash window with a half-drawn blind; the table is strewn with piecework and, beside a trunk, a young man sits devotedly playing a violin, his chair tilted slightly backward. Strange, uncustomary views of urbanized Native Americans.

Native New Yorkers. It is almost impossible not to think of *Apologies to the Iroquois* (1962) by Edmund Wilson (an attentive observer of culture and society, and one of the founding fathers of American literary criticism)—a book that describes the contribution made by this other native family to the building of New York, of its bridges, office complexes, and skyscrapers: the George Washington Bridge, the Triborough Bridge, the Henry Hudson Bridge, the Waldorf-Astoria, the Knickerbocker Village, the Rockefeller Center, the Empire State Building (who can forget Lewis Hine's celebrated photograph of workers eating astride an iron girder suspended in midair during work on the new skyscraper? I wonder how many of them were Iroquois . . .). Neither is it possible not to think of the pow-wows that were still taking place during the 1950s right here in Inwood Hill Park, or of the tiny Iroquois community in Gowanus, Brooklyn, which used to meet up near Nevins Bar & Grill (nicknamed "Indianopolis") between the 1920s and 1960s. (Joseph Mitchell writes of this in his fine tale-cum-reportage, *The Mohawks in High Steel*, now collected in *Up in the Old Hotel*.) And I personally can never forget what poet-activist Bimbo Rivas, a dear departed friend of mine, once told me. On arriving from Puerto Rico, his family settled on the Lower East Side, a neighborhood of German, Irish, Chinese, Italian, and Jewish immigrants. Still living there, among the sweatshops and tenements, were some native families: "one of my friends was an American Indian. It was called the Eagle Family: Dancing Eagle, Swift Eagle. And they used to do the Indian ceremonies in the back yard, I mean they would have their *powwows* in there. We were right there, next to their culture all the time, you know. . . ."

Then it was the turn of the Dutch fur merchants, the East India Company, and, later, the West India Company. The island became Nieuw Nederland, and Nieuw Amsterdam came into being. Judging from the maps and prints of the era, it must have been a small farm-trading village that strove to resemble its namesake city as best it could: the narrow, winding streets, the characteristic houses with sloping roofs, garret windows, and high entrance steps, the numerous taverns where beer, rum, and *genèvre* were imbibed, the star-shaped fort, the windmills, and even two canals (Heere Gracht and Begun Gracht) that wound their way from the East River to what is today Broad Street. The Heerewegh ("the long, main street") announced the arrival of Broadway, and beyond Het Cingle ("the wall") stood broad expanses of farms and fields, orchards and meadows, hills, rivulets, and small lakes.

The Dutch lasted about fifty years (from 1610 to 1664), and their survival was always in the balance. The growing sense of disintegration was countered (sometimes autocratically) by governors like Kieft and Peter Stuyvesant who vainly sought to impose some semblance of order. Everything considered, much still remains of this Dutch past in New York. Not just the poems of Nieuw Amsterdam's first poet, Jacob Steendam, who

lived on the very tip of the island ("See! Two streams my garden bind, /
From the East and North they wind, / Rivers pouring in the sea, / Rich in
fish, beyond degree. // Milk and butter; fruits to eat / No one can enumer-
ate; / Ev'ry vegetable known; / Grain the best that e'er was grown"). Not
just the stories and legends re-created with extravagant irony by
Washington Irving in his *History* (or, in the case of the upper reaches of
the Hudson, in the tales *Rip Van Winkle* and *The Legend of Sleepy Hollow*,
where the slow, dreamy pace of pipe-smoking Dutch farmers and tavern
raconteurs is contrasted with the greedy acquisitiveness and frenzy of the
Yankees). And not just the densely contorted maze of streets in the southern part of Manhattan—so different from the regular geometries that characterize the rest of the city (again, with his usual perspicacity, Irving
hazards an interesting explanation in his *History:* "The sage council . . . ,
not being able to determine upon any plan for the building of their city—
the cows, in a laudable fit of patriotism, took it under their peculiar charge,
and as they went to and from pasture, established paths through the bushes, on each side of which the good folks built their houses; which is one
cause of the rambling and picturesque turns and labyrinths, which distin-
guish certain streets of New-York at this very day").

The chief surviving relics of the Dutch past are the often unimagined
names and words of a genuine social, cultural, architectonic, and linguistic map that unfolds before one's eyes during the journey of discovery in
New York. First and foremost, and in no uncertain manner, comes
Harlem, where, in 1637, the De Forest brothers settled and brought into
being the first nucleus of what would become, over the course of the next
twenty years, the village of Nieuw Haarlem (so called after its Dutch
namesake). Then Brooklyn and the Bronx, the first taking its name from
the village of Breuckelen, situated just to the south of Amsterdam, the second from a certain Mr. Bronck, a Swedish or Danish captain on the payroll of the Dutch who later became an important landowner. Not to forget
Corlaer, van Cortland, Schuyler, and Brevoort, all names of farmers and
landowners linked in some way to the West India Company, all having
some bearing on the city's geography. But the most familiar name of all
remains that of Peter Stuyvesant. Immortalized in many a painting and
book, the choleric wooden-legged governor owned at least half of the
southern part of Manhattan and a generous slice of the present-day Lower
East Side: buried in the tiny cemetery of the St. Mark's-in-the-Bouwerie
church, his name lives on today in a square and a block of buildings.

Neither must we forget Gansevoort, the name of an important family
whose descendants include the mother of Herman Melville—and a name
that is still on the map of Manhattan to define that maze of streets, alleys,
storehouses, and sheds next to the Hudson called the "meat market." And

what of Duyckingh? In its slightly modified form, it was also the name of New York's first great literary critic, Evert Duyckink, renowned for his *Cyclopedia of American Literature*, his magnificent personal library, his pioneering role in discovering and encouraging new authors, and his "soirées" at 20 Clinton Place, his home in Greenwich Village. (Living outside the city, Melville would write in 1851: "I suppose the Knights of the Round Table still assemble over their cigars and punch. . . . I should like to hear again the old tinkle of glasses in your basement, and may do so, before many months"). And lastly, there is that Knickerbocker fellow who, thanks to Irving, would become synonymous with the archetypal New Yorker and, metaphorically speaking, with the metropolis as a whole in its continuum of past and present.

Yet there is more to all this than just the names of the most important Dutch families. If you stroll down Cherry Street, remember that it was once the site of David Provoost's enormous cherry orchard. Or if you take a trip to Coney Island and have a look around what is left of one of the biggest amusement parks built between the late nineteenth and early twentieth centuries, bear in mind that this peculiarly long, thin slice of island-peninsula was so densely populated with rabbits in the seventeenth century that the Dutch called it *Conyné Eylant* (the "island of rabbits"). If you pop into one of New York's most celebrated department stores, Bloomingdale's, don't forget that the origin of the name goes back to a lovely spot on the Upper West Side called "blooming dale" (*Bloemendael* in Dutch). Again, if you gaze across the Harlem River at the northernmost point of Manhattan (where our etymological journey began), the place staring back at you from the other side of the river, immediately west of Marble Hill, is called Spuyten Duyvil. This name is probably a corruption of the Dutch *spuit den duyvil* ("cheat the devil"), which speaks volumes about the difficulties of navigation in that part of the river. And if, when observing a detailed map of Manhattan and surrounding areas, you are taken aback by the number of names indicated with the term *kill*, quake not: it has nothing to do with bloodcurdling mysteries and everything to do with the Dutch name (*kil*) for "strait" or "inlet." If you venture as far as Red Hook (maybe in search of the disquieting events recounted by H. P. Lovecraft in his *The Horror at Red Hook*), or if you happen to be at Corlear's Hook or Sandy Hook, remember that *hook* derives from the Dutch word used to indicate a curving strip of land that runs into the sea: *hoeck*. When strolling along the Bowery, remember that it is named after the road that linked up the main farms (*bouwerie* in Dutch) located outside the urban settlement of Nieuw Amsterdam. And lastly, when wandering around in the rarefied peace of Gramercy Park, the most exclusive park in Manhattan (only those living in the wealthy abodes directly overlooking the park possess a key giving them access), remember that there once used to be a *Krom Moerasje* here (tricks of the city's history!), a "small crooked morass"—from which the English got Gramercy.

Then there are other types of linguistic leftovers. For example, *boss,* which sounds quintessentially American, comes from the Dutch word *baas,* meaning "master" and, earlier still, "uncle." Likewise, *stoop,* the word used to describe the high entrance steps that almost give the old New York houses the appearance of small castles. In the ghetto neighborhoods especially, stoops served many different functions: projected outward into the great theater of the street, these elevated platforms were ideal for observation, courting, a chat, or gossip. And here we must pause and think for a moment. *Stoop* actually comes from the Dutch *stoep,* and linguistic considerations aside, this fact also has important implications in terms of architecture and town planning. Indeed, the first builders in the city (including the celebrated Crijn Fredericsz, who landed in Nieuw Amsterdam in 1625) brought with them their customs of erecting buildings that were elevated (as protection against the havoc wreaked by North Sea floods) and flush to the street (to make up for the lack of space in a canal-dominated city like Amsterdam). The early village of New York thus assumed an identity that, three centuries later, it still retains—and charmingly so along certain streets and in certain neighborhoods.

But let's get back to history. With very few blows being exchanged, the English took over from the Dutch in 1664. Disorganized, forsaken by all, and unsure of its capacity to resist and survive in the New World, Nieuw Amsterdam quietly agreed to become New York. Other immigrants had been filling its streets in the meantime: Huguenots and Sephardic Jews escaping from the clutches of Europe, slaves from Africa and the East Indies "imported" to build the new town. All of them left their mark. Peter Minuit was a Huguenot, as indeed was the merchant and landowner Stephen de Lancey, whose name is inextricably linked to Delancey Street. (Perhaps the strongest linguistic reminder of the passing French presence belongs, however, to the world of gastronomy: the *chaudron,* or cauldron, bastardized definitively as *chowder,* as all those familiar with the characteristic Manhattan clam chowder will no doubt recall.) The first Jewish congregation on American soil ("Shearith Israel") dates back to 1654, and in 1730 New York's first synagogue was built a stone's throw from Wall Street. In 1712 and 1741, the first black slave revolts took place; the second of these, with the aid of some whites, culminated in a public execution just outside the perimeter wall, in the vicinity of present-day Wall Street and City Hall, and just a few yards away from the "African Cemetery" that came to light during excavations undertaken for the construction of a new building in the area between Broadway and Duane Street. Even the celebrated Fraunces Tavern (now a historical landmark), on the corner of Pearl and Broad Streets, where George Washington established his headquarters during the American Revolution, is linked to the black history of New York: the host and owner of the tavern, Samuel Fraunces, once Washington's aide, happened to be from the West Indies.

Other names—perhaps more obvious and less evocative than their native and Dutch counterparts—remain to signal the English presence in New York: Chelsea (site of a Dutch farm purchased in 1750 by a retired English captain, and baptized anew in memory of the district in London) and Queens (the first Dutch settlement, occupied by the English at the end of the seventeenth century, and so called after Catherine of Braganza, the wife of King Charles II). And then, of course, like Mana-hatta for the natives, *New York*, from the Duke of York, owner of the city at the time of English domination and the future King James II: more than anything else, the name reminds me of the *Shambles*, the medieval maze of alleyways and shops in the English city of York, which was perhaps the closest thing resembling the southern tip of Manhattan at the time.

Lastly, two names (among the many) that no longer refer to certain places in New York but which have become symbols of the city as a whole. In 1807 Washington Irving was the first to refer to the city as "Gotham" in the magazine *Salmagundi*: its origins derive from the English town of the same name near Nottingham, whose inhabitants had become legendary folk heroes for having foiled King James's plans to tax them by pretending to be mad or stupid. (The implications of all this are complex and ambiguous, and indeed, "Gotham" has always maintained a certain aura of mystery about it, as anyone familiar with the lengthy saga of Batman and Robin will tell you.) Then, in the 1930s and 1940s, a new term with which we are all too familiar today became common coinage among those jazz musicians who saw New York as a kind of glittering Mecca or a land of promise: "the Big Apple" (whose slang origins came from afar and which, metaphorically speaking, ultimately came to stand for the metropolis itself) was used to indicate the big deals that could be struck in the city.

In the midst of all this—the wealth of things that have disappeared and the little (or much) that has survived (names, memories, signs)—one presence has survived down the centuries and millennia to the present day. A silent, stern witness to events, it can be touched with the hand. Erupting from the deep, dark heart of the earth, the black, shale rocks that sprout from the green knolls of Central Park, and the clear dolomitic rocks that rub shoulders in the primeval forests at the northernmost extremity of the island, have always been here: they preceded and accompanied the recent history of natives, the Dutch, the Huguenots, the Africans, the Jews, the English, and the Americans. *Manhattan shale* and *Inwood dolomite*: a living testament to the past in the present.

I took a good look around Inwood Hill Park. I got off the subway at the end of the A line, at Broadway and 207th Street, strolled up Isham Street and crossed Seaman Avenue. Then I set off into the park. It is a thick and hilly wood, a forest of century-old trees, an intricate network of roads and trails, rising and falling then meeting before departing again, squirrels poking about the bushes and scattering up the trees. Yet it is in a sorrowful mess: the brush is littered with wizened branches, leaves, and fallen trees, bottles and wastepaper are scattered here and there, and not one of the street lamps has been left intact—some of them have even been torn out of the ground, and now lie there like cast-iron trunks uprooted during a storm. There are no signs to tell you where you are, and it's easy to get lost and you just have to trust your luck in finding the odd passerby who can put you back on the right track.

But then, just there, right beneath the pale blue span of the Hudson River Bridge, you come to a point where the waters of the Hudson divide to form the side arm that later becomes the Harlem River, and the view is fascinating. Opposite, perched atop the artificially cut overhanging rock, stand the buildings of Marble Hill; to the left, the immense, grey, and solemn expanse of the Hudson; to the right, a broad cove dotted with seagulls. Behind me, clambering up the hillside, stand what to all appearances are the "Indian caves," the hotly disputed site of Native American settlement prior to the establishment of the villages: oblique, jutting rocks offering shelter. And below, at the bottom of the descending path, a spacious green clearing.

And right there, in the middle of the path (one of the friends accompanying me on this expedition points it out), is the rock I was looking for, and the plaque that reads:

SHORAKKOPOCH
According to legend, on this site of the
principal Manhattan Indian village, Peter Minuit
in 1626, purchased Manhattan Island for trinkets
and beads then worth about 60 guilders.
This boulder also marks the spot where
a tulip tree (*Liriodendron Tulipifera*) grew to a height
of 165 feet and a girth of 20 feet. It was, until
its death in 1938 at the age of 280 years, the

last living link with the Reckgawanc Indians
who lived here

Reading the plaque after two mazelike hours meandering about the hills of Inwood Park, with its blocks of shale and dolomite, its oaks and nut trees, makes an odd impression. No matter how doubtful the legend might be, you feel as if you are in the native place of Manhattan. And the state of abandon into which the park has been allowed to sink is a laconic comment on that transaction (if it ever really came to pass, and on this spot) 350 years ago.

2

Maps

I was worried I'd never find it again. I'd passed in front of it several times before, I'd stopped to look at it and read the scrawly handwriting in capital letters, and it had always made me smile: such a fine example of urban, material culture, I had told myself. But I'd never thought about photographing it or taking down precise details, and now that I'd decided to use it for this book I was really concerned that I'd never find it again.

But it was still there. Another example of permanence in a city whose ruthless pace of change arouses suspicions that nothing can remain true to itself over time. Right there, on the corner of Canal Street and the Bowery—one of the busiest intersections in Manhattan, between teeming Chinatown (the jewelry shops, the tiny restaurants displaying lacquered ducks, the little stores, sunglasses at five dollars a pair, Cartier watches at ten) and the northward-bound traffic, moving along this weird, downgraded thoroughfare (with wholesale discount stores selling implements for restaurants and the kitchen, shopwindows filled with improbable lamps and shades, dormitories for the aged and homeless).

What I was looking for this morning, just a few hours after my arrival in New York, was a small, anonymous newspaper stand, a now-disused kiosk (I had never seen anyone inside it) that could just about hold one person and two or three piles of newspapers. The pull-down shutter was firmly closed, but there on the shutter was the very handwriting I had been seeking.

It read: "Petrella Point. Pointin' Away Since MCMLXXV." Underneath, more or less in columns, were the directions:

Nearest Subway, 2 Blocks North, 1 East
UPTOWN BUSSTOP, 1 BLOCK Other Side of the Street
DELANCEY—4 BLOCKS
GRAND ST.—2 BLOCKS

Orchard St., 5 Blocks East

Ludlow St., 6 Blocks East
Essex St. . . . Where Jewish People Used To Be . . . 7 Blocks East
Allen St., 4 Blocks East
Forsyth St. . . . Where Puerto Ricans Used To Be . . . 2
"Little Italy" . . . Where Italians Used To Be . . . 1 Block North + 2 West

The directions are grouped together in cardinal points, and each group is preceded by a stylized picture of a hand with its forefinger pointing the direction. Just underneath, the writing concludes: "This Public Service Courtesy of Your Favorite Newstand. If you don't see Your Needs Here Just [a Chinese ideogram follows, which I shall have to get translated]." And again: "Closest Good 'Stick-to-the-Rib' Food . . . Right Behind You . . . Jewelers' Café 72 Bowery— 1 Flight Up . . . Ax for Vinnie." Then, right at the bottom, almost flush with the sidewalk, in red against a white background, "North, East, West, South," each cardinal point preceded by a small arrow indicating the direction, and each of the initial letters forming the acronym "NEWS"—an exquisitely American touch (the obsession with acronyms), but not the only one. In fact, when viewed as a whole, the design on the shutter of Mr. (or Mrs.) Petrella becomes an American flag with plenty of pop art appeal. The white handwriting on a blue background replaces the stars and, to the side, those alternating red and white stripes . . .

The crowds around me don't bother to check out "Petrella Point"; they know exactly where they are going. But this handwriting seems to be an artfully contrived lifejacket thrown in the vortex of currents battling their way about this particular corner: an act of simple kindness to tell you where you are, how you can get to the place you're going to, what used to be there before, and even where you can take a breather and freshen up a bit—a shrewd micromap of how to survive the city. Very New Yorkish, too, and one on the mark for those who are forever lamenting the city's anonymous and tentacular nature. It may be that, with all the detailed maps and overly thorough guides at our disposal, we don't need Mr. or Mrs. Petrella's four directions, but it's almost a relief to see that the "Point" is still there (and that it has lasted all these years). Walter Benjamin once wrote that we need to learn how to get lost in a city as in a forest. But, as in a forest, it is also nice to learn how to find ourselves, how to find the paths and trails that cross the city.

The moment you decide to go in search of a city is fraught with difficulties. Magical, yes, but also very tricky, because it is precisely in that moment that you determine your relationship with it: where and how to begin. Unlike other cities, New York won't hang about for you to solve these problems: immediately around and on top of you, it pounces and grabs you haughtily by the scruff of the neck, and that moment of sus-pended time during which you warily size each other up immediately takes on all the connotations of a challenge, a tug-of-war, from which you all too often emerge drained and resigned to putting up the least line of resistance. Hence the need for maps. And special maps at that, because you are on an island and, inevitably, the island (another problem that cannot be underestimated) teases forth any number of special associa-tions, each with its own unique appeal and charm: Atlantis, Prospero and Caliban, Robinson Crusoe and Friday, Long John Silver's treasure, Huckleberry Finn, the island that never was . . .

And so there you are with your map of New York spread out on the table. You've opened the guide, you've started circling your destinations, and you've worked out a couple of itineraries around Manhattan. You've tried to draw a map. There is a risky side to this, however, because instead of obeying your curiosity and thirst for discovery, this map may end up sim-ply reinforcing an idea of New York that has been created by almost daily, involuntary visits: in other words, nothing more than a pedestrian series of places whose "must-see" status can be attributed essentially to their presence on the silver screen and TV, in advertising, newspapers, and magazines.

All told, it is a prepackaged map. It features a visit to the Empire State Building (to see the city from on high), a long stroll down Fifth Avenue, Broadway, or Madison Avenue (to visit glittering stores like Tiffany's, Bloomingdale's, or Saks), ritualized trips to the Museum of Modern Art (the MoMA), the Metropolitan Museum, the Guggenheim, the Frick Collection, and the Whitney (because you can't *not* see them), a foray into Little Italy (in search of "local color" twice over: American and Italian), a pilgrimage to the Statue of Liberty, a leisurely afternoon pottering around at Rockefeller Center or Central Park, an evening at the Lincoln Center perhaps, or in one of Broadway's theaters, the thrills and spills of flagging down a taxi with a flailing arm, and maybe even a spine-tingling nighttime ride on the subway . . . The evocative grip of all those images bound up with the city is such that you convince yourself that simply by unfolding and scrupulously following such a map (allowing those images to fill the voids, join up the circles, and open up the trails) you will somehow achieve an understanding of New York's overall complexity and variety.

Instead, it is precisely for this reason that it is so difficult to grasp New York. Through movies, television, advertising, newspapers, and maga-zines, our eyes and ears have taken it in to such an extent that when we actually go there we end up absorbing far less than we normally do when visiting other metropolises. For this reason, perhaps we should be less ill disposed to the urgings of curiosity and the thirst for discovery, and more willing to draw other maps, circle other destinations. (Not that the drawing of new maps is without its risks, as the characters in Defoe's, Stevenson's, or Barrie's works knew only too well.)

For example, to begin with, why not divide the city "American-style" into its three constituent parts—*downtown, midtown,* and *uptown*—and savor it accordingly? Already we are faced with an opportunity to make some useful cultural considerations. Until medieval times European cities were circular structures arranged around a center, while American cities are mostly linear structures built along an axis. European cities tend to be closed while American cities tend toward a more open structure: this is true at least in the sense that city roads in Europe are centripetal/centrifugal while in the United States they tend to run and cut across. The typical European city is dominated by the square, but in America this role is taken by the "Main Street" that begins in the no-man's-land preceding the city, runs its course through the city, and peters out in the no-man's-land at the other end. In this way, instead of widening out in concentric circles, American cities "rise" from their original nucleus. Hence the reasoning behind the tripartite division: *downtown, midtown, uptown.*

This is true, at least in theory, for Manhattan, although the fact that it is an island tends to complicate things (the sense of "cutting across" is, in fact, somewhat hampered). Roughly speaking, *downtown* occupies the area from the southernmost tip of the island to 14th Street, *midtown* runs from 14th Street to the southern edge of Central Park, and *uptown* accounts for the rest. What is true of other cities from a historical and cultural point of view also holds for Manhattan: *downtown* forms the original nucleus, *midtown* represents the phase of transition, and *uptown* that of consolidation. Or, if we want to use other descriptive criteria, *downtown* is the area of finance, *midtown* is the site of commerce, amusements, and important hotels, and *uptown* is where residential building takes priority. But there are many important exceptions to this, as we shall see.

In Manhattan, *downtown* may still remind us of its original nucleus: the maze of narrow, winding streets, the occasional eighteenth-century building, the tumult of peoples, business deals being struck within and without the noisy chambers of the Stock Exchange, the selfsame street names (as early as the mid-nineteenth century a Russian visitor noted that the roads cutting through Broadway down to Washington Square bore historical names, while those beyond were numbered, as if history had dried up and stopped nurturing imagination). This was the site first of the old Dutch city, and then of the English. Here, until well into the twentieth century, was the port of New York. From here branched out the roads directed north and west. Here merged the lines of communication from the rest of the country. And the settlements established in this area (the immigrant and working-class neighborhoods) were either excluded from the world of big business (despite their being its primary moving force), or liaised with it indirectly through the provision of more or less equivocal forms of entertainment. It used to be the throbbing hub of the city, a vortex of contradictions and wonders, and, on closer inspection, so has it remained: Wall Street, residential architecture, the sprawling mass of tenements, the prism of avant-garde cultures.

An informed visit to the *downtown* area implies, therefore, a journey through time to the very heart of New York. It implies an understanding of its economic, social, and cultural stratifications. It means, for example, observing what is probably one of the oldest buildings in Manhattan, on the corner of the Bowery and Pell Street. Or admiring the cast-iron arabesque of the Houghwout Building on the corner of Broadway and Broome Street. Or walking beneath menacing tenement buildings embroidered with ethereal fire escapes. Or following Ariadne's thread of early-nineteenth-century literature, art, and theater in the tiny streets of Greenwich Village. Or steeping oneself in the atmosphere of other times and places along East Broadway with its tiny synagogues and congregations of Orthodox Jews. And it implies understanding the constant blending, overlapping, and intermingling of all this with the rest of the city and the rest of time and places: Eastern Europe and the Caribbean, the Far East and the Mediterranean, blue chips, trash bonds, techno-trading, glittering skyscrapers, the illegal sweatshops of Chinatown and Division Street, the great SoHo art market, the hotchpotch of students milling about the lovely New York University campus, and gardens conjured up from the crumbling edifices of Alphabet City . . .

In the midst of all these chronological-topographical meanderings you might end up in Union Square, halfway down 14th Street. This marks the boundary with *midtown,* and you immediately notice some changes: the roads straighten out (the only exception being Broadway), the sidewalks are wider, the turbulent contradictions of *downtown* seem to bottom out (at least for the moment), and solid buildings stretch out solemnly along forty-nine blocks that almost irresistibly suck you down Fifth Avenue, Avenue of the Americas, and Broadway in the direction of Central Park.

Here a complex clockwork mechanism is hidden. The bus and train stations with their millions of commuters and visitors and the iron and concrete roller coasters of their entrance ramps. The commanding head offices of the big newspapers, the big banks, the big multinationals, the big hotels, the big department stores. The frantic quadrilateral of the Garment District, situated between Seventh and Ninth Avenues, with its wholesale stores, its workshops on the upper floors, and its racks overflowing with coat hangers gliding in and out of doorways. The Public Library with its stairway guarded by two pink Tennessee marble lions, the high vaults of its reading room illumined by the glow of table lamps. The "classic" skyscrapers of Manhattan (the Empire State Building, the Chrysler Building, the MetLife Building, the Citicorp Center, the General Electric Building, the Trump Tower . . .), their skyward projection dictated by the lack of space (and the prospect of generous land rents). The *Blade Runner* kaleidoscope of a Times Square horribly spruced up and disinfected by Disney. The overbearing, rhetorical pomp of the UN Building. The ever-recurring charm of the Grand Central Terminal and its towering vault complete with painted zodiac constellations. The exclusive wealth-ridden recesses of Gramercy Park, Sutton Place, and Tudor City. And then the other main cog in the machinery of New York: the museums and art galleries, Rockefeller Center, the cinemas and theaters. Altogether, a breathtaking coral reef that spreads out, vertically and horizontally, in the form of terraces, blocks, and stems, with arches, vaults, and projections—a Grand Canyon in treated stone that casts square, rectangular, triangular, and rhomboidal shadows onto spacious sidewalks animated by a ceaseless ebb and flow of people.

By now you've reached the green lung of New York. Maybe you are standing outside the Plaza Hotel: Central Park stretches off into the distance in front of you and, with it, *uptown*. In a certain sense, *uptown* proposes anew the composite and contradictory character of *downtown*. No doubt about it: all around you stand the tangible symbols of established wealth, the crowning achievement of that irresistible progression that you could not help but see and feel during your journey through the rising city—the Plaza and the Pierre, the Sheraton and the Barbizon. And then, skirting the west side of the park, the string of palaces and castles whose unique exclusivity is bespoken by the towers and pinnacles concealed among the treetops. On the east side of the park is *Museum Mile*, the string of museums that have made (and continue to make) New York the world's art market capital (the Guggenheim, the Whitney, the Metropolitan, etc.). And finally, everywhere, the high and mighty houses dotted along Park Avenue, Madison Avenue, and Fifth Avenue, and between Central Park West, West End Avenue, and Riverside Drive—the topography of money and success. And in the middle, this astonishing metropolitan clearing, Central Park: almost to proclaim all the more strongly the sheer tranquility and leisure of economic power.

But then, just a few steps away from the dignified, sophisticated halls of Columbia University, *uptown* also means Harlem with its broad no-man's-land avenues, its side streets blinded with boarded-up windows and hulking buildings inundated with debris and scrap—the long, tragic, never-ending story of the world's most famous black ghetto. And it means East Harlem, "El Barrio," the most recent yet equally trouble-ridden Puerto Rican ghetto, *la isla en la urbe* of immigrants forever to-ing and fro-ing between Caribbean palms and New York concrete, both in their reality and in their memory. No wall separates these two worlds of *uptown* (just as *downtown* there is no wall separating the Lower East Side from Wall Street). These two worlds are the *same* world. One implies the other, and New York acknowledges these things openly, shamelessly, even if you are not always willing to actually see them or believe them.

But what if this south-north guideline were something of a set course, too? At a certain point you might like to jettison it in order to savor Manhattan *crosstown*, or horizontally. One morning, with the sun at your back illuminating everything in front of you, you might, then, take 14th or 23rd or 42nd or 57th on the eastern side of the island and walk toward the Hudson River in the extreme west. Your steps will follow another map, and this will allow you to cut across the metropolis transversely— thus sharpening your perception of the city-island that openly proclaims, on the one hand, its monumental immensity, and on the other, at the same time, its insurmountable limits. From river to river and from port to port, from fish market (Fulton Fish Market) to meat market (Gansevoort Street), you can experience an aspect of Manhattan that prepackaged maps can never give you.

Or you might choose to work through the quadrilaterals of New York, scrutinizing on opposite sides of the squares (Washington Square, Tompkins Square, or Marcus Garvey Square) the contrasts in time and style, in spatial dimensions and architectural solutions, in social classes and relationship with the rest of the city: an open book, solid and palpable, whose subject is urban history, and the history of culture and society.

Or again, you might want a completely different experience. New York is overwhelmingly square, regular, and right-angled, so why not take advantage of those rare oblique views where roads seem to diverge almost on the spur of the moment, affording you glimpses of an unwonted three-dimensional nature—unconventional cut-and-thrusts indeed. Or you could turn to good account those "wheel hubs" where, in the space of a few hundred yards, the city seems to interrupt its linear flow and spin itself around, in a joyful, unceasing ring-around-a-rosy or in a dramatic star collapse. At Bowling Green, for example, almost at the southernmost tip of the island: where getting lost is child's play, where the roads become anonymous, directions are almost nonexistent, the small garden becomes a mirage, and mighty buildings (colonnades, roof gardens, spires, entablatures, friezes) explode with architectures that seem Assyro-Babylonian, removed from any time and space, or a dreamlike distillation of the subconscious. Or again, a little farther to the north, at Astor Place, where the city suddenly plunges headlong toward *Alamo* (the cubic sculpture by Bernard Rosenthal) and all about you your bearings are thrown to the four winds among the volumes of massive century-old buildings, flights of perspective toward *midtown*, and unexpected diagonals that are the joy of avid skateboarders.

In accomplishing this, you will have experienced an out-of-the-ordinary journey through geometries and scaled-down urban plans, a necessary journey that will help you redraw your map, placing at its center (and thus overturning another commonplace) New York's architecture, with all the cultural and social implications such a process involves. The city's stony countenance must be discovered first, well before the concrete-glass-steel one: walking around absentmindedly, taking in all the various colors, perspectives, materials, and volumes and then (and only then) dipping into fascinating books like *New York: A Guide to the Metropolis: Walking Tours of Architecture and History*, by Gerard R. Wolfe, or *The City Observed, New York: A Guide to the Architecture of Manhattan*, by Paul Goldberger.

And you could do more: you could look at Manhattan from other observation points. For example, observe the island (measuring it, superimposing one view over another, following its contours) from *other* islands: from Staten Island (a romantic boat trip away), from a hackneyed Liberty Island (whose monument needs no introduction), from Ellis Island (whose museum is dedicated to what constitutes the *real* history of America and New York: immigration), or, sailing up the East River as the Dutch explorers and fur merchants must have done so many times in days of yore, observe Manhattan from Governor's Island, Roosevelt Island, Randall's Island. Or you could do the same from other *boroughs*: from Brooklyn, Queens, the Bronx (or even from New Jersey, in that fleeting moment when the road cut out of the rock opens miragelike onto the New York skyline before disappearing into the neon unreality of the Lincoln Tunnel).

There are thus several ways to feel it as a living organism, pulsing, an organism that is not simply cloned from media images. Discovering *this* New York, *this* Manhattan, also means that we can feel different about a metropolis that is striking and, at times, overwhelming.

For example, cocooned in the choice territory of the big skyscrapers, hotels, or museums, and aloof from nontouristy neighborhoods like Harlem, the Bronx, and the Lower East Side, it might escape you that New York has also been—and indeed *is*—a working-class city: another stereotype that bites the dust. Traces of working-class New York have remained, strewn about here and there but still visible in its living tissue.

The building from which 146 Italian and Jewish working girls threw themselves to their death on 25 March 1911, in order to flee the lethal fire that had broken out in their clothing workshop (the doors having been bolted to prevent leaving work early and the unwelcome entry of militant unionists), looms large and awesome on the corner of Greene Street and Washington Place. And the block on East 4th Street between the Bowery and Second Avenue is a kind of compendium of New York's social and political history: from the building that once hosted the head-quarters of the Industrial Workers of the World to that which was the site of the first Yiddish performance on American soil. And so on—an unsus-pected wealth of signs and relics.

The New York Labor History Association is currently trying to piece together the puzzle of *this* New York's past and present. In addition to its *Work History News* bulletin, the collective has also produced an intro-ductory map (which can be integrated perfectly with Toby and Gene Glickman's nice booklet, *The New York Red Pages*), featuring 105 evoca-tive proletarian historic locations scattered about the city in Manhattan (which contains more than half of them, thus making a lie of the idea that the island is simply a happy hunting ground for financiers and tourists), Brooklyn, Queens, and the Bronx: from the first known strike (1667, when carters refused to transport loads of firewood and stones) to more recent conflicts (1994, when the waiters, cooks, and staff at the Silver Palace Hotel in Chinatown were involved in a prolonged struggle).

Tompkins Square, for instance, is just a stone's throw from where I'm writing at the moment, on a beautiful mid-September morning that promises another day of transparency and brilliancy. Together with Union Square, it was one of the places most closely tied to the complex and ever-changing history of the American working-class movement. And even today, the neighborhood displays in all manner of political and cultural expression (posters, drawings, recollections, and the experiences of its older and more aware inhabitants) the pride of such a past and such a pre-sent. And another thing: Absorbed and stunned as you are by the awful might of Manhattan's buildings, by all the concrete and glass blocks that have been poured onto the island, with all their ripplings and surgings, and by its skyward-heaving masses, you may have neglected the fact that this is a very green city. Of course, there is Central Park, suspended in time and space, an interruption in the whirlwind of urban rhythms, an Arcadia carved out of the heart of the metropolis. But it would be wrong to think Central Park is the be-all and end-all: again, it is time to discover other maps, to tread different paths.

First, any old map will do. Including the long strip of Riverside Park that presses its way northward as far as Inwood Hill Park from West 72nd

Street (halfway up, the delightful Boat Basin, where you can sit along the banks of the Hudson, face-to-face with New Jersey, in front of the moored houseboats, and have a serene chat in the peace washed by the waves), there are about thirty green areas marked out for Manhattan: parks, squares, recesses, and niches complete with oaks, elms, basswoods, sycamores, ashes, false acacias, planes, tulip trees, and gingkoes—dense forests or leisurely gardens for quick-paced and ever curious squirrels. But even that number, deduced from a cursory glance at the map, is inexact, for if you venture a little farther into certain quarters you will be met with unexpected views, utter surprises.

Take the Lower East Side. With its century-old buildings, rubbing shoulders with the debris and rubble of its urban offspring (and vulgar rats in place of sophisticated squirrels), it is one of the most degraded areas on the island. Well, for about the last twenty years the Lower East Side has provided the focus for a grassroots movement intent on snatching the streets back from the jaws of metropolitan desolation and desperation. Once the debris-lined cemeteries of pushers, several abandoned lots have been transformed into marvelous gardens of the imagination, an incessant dissemination of tropical landscapes beneath the towers of Manhattan. If you take the Lower East Side in its *entirety*, you will count more than eighty gardens (out of a total of four hundred for the whole of New York!), with the sweetest names: the Parque de la Tranquilidad is right beneath where I'm staying, and then there are El Sol Brillante, Brises del Caribe, Serenity Garden, Jardin de la Esperanza, Dias y Flores, All People's Garden, Jardin de los Amigos, Hope Garden, Miracle Garden, Magical Children's Garden, Siempre Verde . . .

Michela Pasquali, an Italian landscape architect who has worked in the streets of the Lower East Side for years, has recorded the experiences of those responsible for this incredible outburst of imagination and taken a wonderful series of slides to show for it. She has also drawn up a map of about sixty gardens that exist in the northern section of the Lower East Side alone, for the most part concentrated in the area between East Houston Street and East 14th Street, the river and the Bowery. The exact number is variable, because the survival of these gardens is precariously akin to that of life in the neighborhoods itself: between removals and evictions people come and go, abandoned lots are reclaimed by the city or by real-estate owners, bulldozers suddenly turn up to flatten everything in sight and make way for new apartment blocks, or railings suddenly spring up to assist in the "gentrification" and "privatization" of areas that had been earmarked for collective experience, and the garden simply becomes an appendix to the building next door. The story of these Lower East Side gardens is a unique one: at once strangely fascinating and dramatic, it explicitly reveals tensions that exist within the city—and never disappear even in the beautiful "fantasia" of these places.

At this point, if you take a map of working-class New York and another detailing the areas of greenery, and you connect up all the places you have newly circled, you will find yourself confronted with a texture of "other" trails. Not only will they assist you in becoming familiar with the lesser known aspects of the metropolis, but they will also compel you to look at it from unusual angles—like witnessing a theatrical performance from backstage, awestruck. Very gradually, this network of "other" trails may come to replace that ready-made map we always start off with—and which we might be better off leaving at home sometimes.

Yet, ever since its beginnings, the New World has constantly demanded and presumed that real and metaphorical adjustments be made to its topography, and so New York maps are potentially unlimited. Unsurprisingly, they have become something of a collector's item: shop-windows are full of them, and they can be purchased from the antique prints stand in the local market. One tempting collection is titled *Twelve Historical New York City Street and Transit Maps from 1860 to 1967*. I also know of an artist, Joyce Kosloff, who reinvents and creatively alters Manhattan maps, and I remember one of Paul Auster's best novels, *City of Glass*, in which another disturbing texture of paths takes substance through the seemingly meaningless ramblings of a mysterious character.

At this point, you really *can* get lost in the city.

I would have liked to find out something about the Mr. (or Mrs.) Petrella who donated the "Point" to those whose curiosity is roused by such unusual objects in the city. Maybe even talk to him (or her) and establish the whys and wherefores of that amusing nuts-and-bolts map of the city, and discover exactly what it was about the city, street, or block that lay behind its preparation. Or the meaning of the Chinese handwriting, or how passersby reacted to it all at the beginning, when the newspaper kiosk was still in business.

I did have a go. There are only four or five Petrellas in Manhattan, and this morning I phoned them all up. Some of them were intrigued and responded politely, others were churlish and dismissed my questions with haste. I didn't get anywhere, and the Mr. or Mrs. Petrella remains a mystery. So, the newsstand had closed down and the Petrellas had disappeared into thin air, leaving that unique, enigmatic memento in their wake, right in the heart of old New York. I suppose I should start searching outside Manhattan—in Brooklyn, Queens, the Bronx, or maybe New Jersey. But then things might get a little overcomplicated.

I shall have to make do with the photographs I've taken. And hope that at least for a while the "Petrella Point" will avoid being swallowed up by the restless vortex of the "city which never ceases to change."

(A year or so after this book came out in Italy, an unknown reader called me, after trying several Maffis in the phone directory. He was just back from New York, where he had used my book as a guide to its streets and places. He had also been to see the "Petrella Point": and there, outside the stand, sat Mr. Petrella, a tall man in his seventies, with white hair and bright eyes, drawing in the open air. He had asked Mr. Petrella for his telephone number, which he now gave to me, and on my return to New York a few months later, I finally called him up. And we met—at the corner of Canal and the Bowery. We spent half an hour talking of many things, including the stand, of course, and how it all came to be. Meanwhile, an uninterrupted stream of people flowed by our side and, strangely attracted, several persons—old, young, Chinese, blacks, Latinos, tourists, New Yorkers—stopped to ask for directions. Mr. Petrella always answered with thorough explanations: a task he shared with his stand, an unappointed traffic director in the city maze.)

3

Underworlds

A couple of days ago I went to see Before Central Park: The Life and Death of Seneca Village at the New-York Historical Society, an exhibition that—albeit synthetically—took as its theme a little-known story and dealt with it masterfully. Between 1820 and 1850 the area currently occupied by the western section of the park, to the side of the "Great Lawn," was home to a settlement of African Americans and immigrants (mostly from Ireland). It was a real village (even if later it was described disparagingly as "a shantytown") made up of wooden houses, schools, churches, and cemeteries, and toward the middle of the nineteenth century it was savagely razed to the ground to make way for the famous park. Despite a wave of objections and protests, the village inhabitants were scattered to the four winds, and their whereabouts became something of a mystery: they had become invisible—that kind of invisibility (of people outside mainstream society) that is quite a common occurrence in American history. As Ralph Ellison wrote in his 1952 novel, Invisible Man, "I am invisible . . . simply because people refuse to see me."

While strolling about the exhibition rooms, looking at the documents, maps, objects, captions, reproductions of bills of sale, and the petitions sent by the inhabitants of Seneca Village, I thought of the "city underneath," which events of this kind bring so vividly to light. Above all, in the foyer, I was struck by the reproduction of an article from the New York Herald dated 11 August 1871. It read:

> Yesterday afternoon, while laborers were engaged in uprooting trees at the new entrance to the Central Park, corner of Eighty-fifth street and Eighth avenue, they discovered, fourteen inches beneath the surface, a black rosewood coffin, richly mounted and in a state of good preservation. On the lid was a plate with the engraving, "Margaret McIntay, died February, 1852, aged sixteen years, three months and fourteen days." Within the coffin was the body of a woman, decayed almost to a skeleton. At a short distance from the spot another coffin was found, enclos-

ing the body of a negro, decomposed beyond recognition. This land was
dug up five years ago, when the trees were planted there, and no such
coffins were there at that time.

*I was taken aback by the article not only because of the implications it had as to
what lies "beneath" the city (those sociogeological layers brought so laboriously
to the surface), but also because of its disturbing conclusion: those coffins that
vanish only to reappear, that invisibility (almost as if it were a threatening
memento) that suddenly becomes visible. And it was as if the objects on display
at the New-York Historical Society had become more eloquent.*

The obsession with what lies underneath the surface is peculiarly
American, on a par with the obsession with what lies outside. Yet while
the outside represents everything that is extraneous to the American way
of life (the "alien," the "foreigner," and the "menace from outer space," to
use the terminology of mass cultural products, often so effective in unveil-
ing the hidden dynamics of a society), the underneath is a far more disturbing dimension. This is because it acknowledges and openly declares
that the threat (or, putting it more mildly, the sense of unease) comes from
within—from something that is inside, buried in the labyrinthine tunnels
of the past or the compressed layers of the present. In particular, I remember an early-twentieth-century drawing by William Balfour Ker called *The
Hand of Fate:* an exclusive high-society party disrupted by a hand that,
from the underground depths of society, bursts through the floor and
reaches upward. And I also remember a 1960s cartoon by a famous car-
toonist (his name escapes me—could it be Richard Cobb?), which outlines
a profile of American civilization in the form of factories, skyscrapers,
highways, televisions, and computers—and, buried beneath the surface,
the remains of native civilization, skulls, skeletons, arrows . . .

The *underneath* of New York, the American metropolis par excellence,
is the most disconcerting of all. Much the same has already been said of
London and Paris, as the works of Dickens and Gissing, and Sue, Hugo,
and Zola testify—and Walter Benjamin considered the Parisian *passages*
and Métro stations as places providing access to the collective unconscious. But Europe, steeped in its past as it is, really holds no surprises, what
with its archaeological remains, its ruins, crypts, and vaults, its underground canals and sewers, the whole repertoire of gothic and romantic,
realist and surrealist. What *does* surprise is the singular and often unap-
preciated fact that the *underneath* of a city like New York is overwhelmingly present, too.

Perhaps the most famous image of this *underneath* (both on the screen and in real life) is that of the puffs of steam emanating from New York streets—candid will-o'-the-wisps wafting from the manhole covers, or solid columns emerging from the high, orange and white mobile tubes scattered here and there about the asphalt. The city as a living organism, an enormous dragon curled up inside the guts of the metropolis, a mysterious and powerful energy to be released in small doses, smoke signals of a people hidden away beneath the sidewalk: fantastic images come to mind . . .

It has nothing to do with any of this, of course. The fact is that New York, as Harry Granick explains in his classic little work of 1947 (*Underneath New York*), is a "city without chimneys." A steam-based heating system—with steam produced and distributed on a centralized basis—has replaced autonomous combustion or electric energy systems, and this means that vents have to be opened up around the city: hence those little puffs that are especially evocative in the surreal, nocturnal metropolis, among the yellow streetlights, the bouncing cars, the torment of piercing sirens.

However, as we noted earlier, the *underneath* is present in just about all of New York: in the huge block of shale (which alone allows for the building of skyscrapers) surfacing here and there in Central Park or Inwood Hill Park; in the web of *downtown* streets that retraces the tangle of Native American and Dutch trails and traditional cattle paths; in the valleys, hills, and waterways belonging to a none too distant past; and in the African American cemeteries, the immigrant villages, and the multifarious shantytowns that the city has covered up and removed—a whole world "underneath" to which Anne-Marie Cantwell and Diana diZerega Wall have devoted a fascinating book, *Unearthing Gotham: The Archaeology of New York City* (2001). Up until a few score years ago, one particularly desperate settlement extended as far as the site where the monstrous United Nations skyscraper now looms large (a metaphor not without its implications). Just south of it, sophisticated houses for well-heeled New Yorkers were built in the wealthy complex of Sutton Place, and immediately the dictates of invisibility made themselves heard: no windows facing north were to be allowed.

Both geographically and historically speaking, almost everywhere in the city an acute sense of continual overlapping—of an *after* driving underground a *before*—can be felt. For example, if you pop over to Lexington Avenue between East 25th and East 26th Streets, you will find yourself staring at the massive armory of the 69th New York Regiment. (Such armories can be found all over the city, and indeed, *in all American cities*. The decision to build them goes back to the 1870s when the outbreak of the first widespread working-class uprisings convinced even the most doubting of Thomases that social classes *did*, after all, exist in the United States, too.) Leaving aside its overall ugliness—the castlelike facade and the infelicitous choice of a rounded shape—it must be said that this, too, is a historical landmark, possessed of a dense past and an *underneath*. Indeed, in 1913 the barrack halls and armory housed an exhibition that entered the history books under the name of the "Armory Show." For the first time in the United States, European avant-garde masterpieces, from Cézanne to Duchamp, were exhibited alongside the works of aggressive American realists, with sensational and far-reaching consequences for the world of American art.

Yet—and here the *underneath* emerges to the surface in all its ramifications—this topographic place within Manhattan is significant for other reasons, too. In order to build the Armory, several blocks of brownstones (those distinctive reddish-brown sandstone buildings that are one of the defining aspects of "old New York") had to be demolished. And in two of these houses, back to back, at 104 East 26th and 111 East 25th, respectively, had lived Herman Melville and Henry James, the first for many years up until his death, the second just for six months in 1865. Neither knew anything of the presence of the other. Melville had already been forgotten by the public and publishers alike, as invisible to the one as to the others; James, never a great lover of his homeland, returned to America reluctantly, and his visits became increasingly rarer.

And it is to this "New York which is no longer," a city whose buildings carry few commemorative plaques (and when they do, they are often inaccurate!), that Nathan Silver has dedicated an absorbing book, a text of modern urban archaeology evocatively titled *Lost New York*. In contrast to all the stereotypes concerning American "youth" and "superficiality," the sense of loss is extremely acute and recurrent in American culture. Silver's whole book is held together by this nostalgia for a past (precisely how long ago is immaterial) made up of solemn buildings or, more simply, of edifices that impress with their indulgent nod in the direction of imagination, of places that have encapsulated (in an almost condensed and therefore more intense manner) the energy of the city at any given moment: the great theaters and public places of the nineteenth century, from Niblo's Garden and the German Winter Garden to the Thalia Theater and the Atlantic Garden; the old Pennsylvania Station with its solid and fascinating tangle of iron structures; the refined hotels of Coney Island, the Oriental and the Manhattan Beach.

But there is more than one *underneath* to Manhattan. Let's take two examples, one metaphorical, the other real, both rather unnerving. For the first, we have to go back to the photographer and sociologist Jacob Riis, one of late-nineteenth-century Manhattan's most famous witnesses and chroniclers. In an 1894 photograph Riis immortalized one of the most renowned delinquent gangs of the era, the "Short Tail Gang," a mixed bag of ten insolent-looking characters crouching beneath a landing stage at Corlears Hook, on the East River—a slice of authentic metropolitan *underworld*. Of course, like it or not, this *underworld* has always been a central element in the sociocultural geography of New York. The story of the city's delinquent gangs is a source of undeniable—albeit ambiguous—interest, and Herbert Asbury's classic 1927 account, *The Gangs of New York: An Informal History of the Underworld,* narrates this story with great perspicacity (and it is not by chance that Martin Scorsese used it as a basis for his movie of the same name).

Naturally, it is too long a story to be dealt with here. Suffice it to say that its origins go back to the need on the part of newly arrived immigrants to defend themselves against the maelstrom of urban life, exposed as they were to racist and chauvinist attacks, and crushed by the machinery of competition and profits. In the German, Irish, Jewish, Chinese, and Italian streets of New York, unofficial groups bent on defending themselves grew out of what were really little more than small handfuls of youngsters used to getting by as best they could on a day-to-day basis. It was simply a question of defending one's territory, the most rudimentary form of mutual assistance in the growing face of community disruption and the ever-present threat of violence. These picturesquely named gangs—Dock Rats, Swamp Angels, Dead Rabbits, The Gophers, Red Peppers, The Carpenters, Plug Uglies, Daybreak Boys, Bridge Twisters—did, however, maintain close ties with their communities of origin, their popular and working-class cultural backgrounds, the very fabric of the city itself, and, often evolving in an openly multiethnic direction, they made an important contribution to the wealth of myths and rites, legends and heroes.

One of the most popular nineteenth-century Lower East Side theaters, the Grand Duke's in Baxter Street, was also rooted in this history: featuring furnishings of somewhat dubious origin, and boasting an enviable program of adventurous melodramas, the theater was opened by one of the youth gangs most active in the neighborhood at the time, the Baxter Street Dudes. And then, of course, there was the Bowery, a complex and intriguing hotchpotch of popular shows and widespread illegality. The paths and the territories, the trespasses and the exploits of these latter-day gangs brand the physical body of New York like a tattoo, and even today you can catch a glimpse of all this in what remains of the city's past (the popular architecture, the tortuousness of certain downtown streets, the intensity of the street life, and the overwhelming poverty of certain neighborhoods) and appreciate anew the sense and reasons behind these experiences.

For a period, this "underworld" was a rich source of American culture, and could easily be drawn upon to supply types, situations, events, and linguistic and literary inventions. Then, at a time and in a city increasingly dominated by business, all this became a business, too: Prohibition. Formally introduced in the 1920s to regulate the morality of private and public lives, Prohibition soon became a crucial factor in the businesslike transformation of the underworld into a powerful parallel economic force. Yet the "mythical" sheen surrounding the origins of the underworld has proved difficult to remove and resurfaces continually: in certain films directed by Francis Ford Coppola and Scorsese, of course, not to mention that harrowing "narration of origins," Sergio Leone's *Once Upon a Time in America*.

Today, this "underworld" is a well-concealed cyst inside the financial and money-grubbing body of the city. But traces of it are still to be seen. In the heart of Chinatown, at 16 Pell Street, a small plaque openly confesses that this building once housed the headquarters of Hip Sang Tong, one of the two illegal associations (the other being On Leong Tong) whose main concern, at the turn of the last century, evolved from territorial and community defense to the management of most criminal activities within the area. Close by, among what (ambiguously) remains of Little Italy, Umberto's restaurant is also renowned as the place where the Italian American underworld boss, Joey Gallo, was killed in 1972. In his interesting book of sociocultural history, *Infamous Manhattan*, Andrew Roth has organized, neighborhood by neighborhood (more maps!), the various crime trails in New York over the last two hundred years. And, if I am not mistaken, the Museum of the City of New York includes among its guided tours a trip to local "scenes of the crime."

And yet this "underworld" comes in many guises and cannot be linked solely to the world of Murder Inc. It is also the world of youth gangs, a desperate and inescapable reality in any ghetto, complex in terms of its evolutions and involutions. At once a necessary instrument of social cohesion and a safety valve for social tensions, the youth gang is also a vulnerable structure and easy prey for organized crime adept at transforming it into an instrument of drug trafficking, and exploiting it as a means of penetrating the ghetto for its own ends. But situations can differ, and the differences may be very slight. So, for instance, a notorious 1950s gang like the Puerto Rican Assassins later developed into one of the most important social realities, not only on the Lower East Side but probably in the whole of Manhattan; and till a few years ago, before the huge building at 605 East 9th Street was forcefully and disgracefully vacated, you could visit the multipurpose Charas community center (with cinema, music, theater, all manner of social services, and an active role in fighting drugs and gentrification in the area), headed by Chino Garcia, one of the former leaders of the Assassins. At that time, Charas was actively campaigning to "politicize" the biggest youth gang in New York, the Latin Kings: and thus, it could well happen that while Chino was telling you about the history of the Assassins in one of the large rooms of the former school occupied some twenty years ago, younger members of the Latin Kings (hardened ghetto youths with all the gang gestures and rituals) came a few at a time in front of the steps for a meeting with the center's social workers. The story goes on . . .

This "underworld" also comprises the universe of social marginality, a nocturnal universe admirably documented by Damon Runyon and Weegee, in fiction and photographs, respectively, during the 1940s and 1950s. It is a universe that used to revolve around the admittedly ambiguous and disreputable area of Times Square before Disney anesthetized it and turned it into some kind of icon to glamour—a massive, tacky, cartoonish affair (New York really is a city of extreme opposites)—a universe whose inhabitants had elaborated languages, forms of behavior, stories, and mythologies, out of sheer desperation.

Up to now we've been dealing in metaphors: the "world below" stands for everything that, because it is not ascribable to the dominant moral and social canons of the present, is driven *underneath*. However, there is a more literal form of "underneath" that is painfully real. I'm not talking of films like *Ghostbusters*, effective comical reworkings of the perennial sense of unease that blends with a kind of unutterable sense of collective guilt: evil energy that periodically threatens to come to the surface. And I'm not talking about urban legends like that of the white alligators that are supposed to haunt New York sewers, mutant heirs to a fad that ended up being flushed down the toilet (an anxiety, this, bound up with genetic mutations in the bowels of the city, which crops up again and again, as in the movie *Mimic*). And neither am I speaking of the strange retrievals that occur from time to time: not only cemeteries and villages but also ancient ships. (Such has always been the lust for land in this long narrow island that two centuries ago they used to sink ships along the banks and cover them up with earth and gravel in order to gain an extra yard or two.) Nor am I alluding to the tunnel of the first experimental pneumatic subway, on which work was immediately halted at the end of the nineteenth century in the midst of political and economic string pulling, only to be forgotten until 1912 when, following its chance discovery, the huge waiting room complete with crystal chandelier and grand piano caused sensation and amazement.

Ah yes, the subway. A contradictory and dramatic compendium of urban experience—*that* is what I am talking about. "In the flying underbelly of the city. Steaming hot, and summer on top, outside. Underground. The subway heaped in modern myth," wrote the African American poet and dramatist LeRoi Jones (now Amiri Baraka) in his influential mid-1960s play set in the subway, *Dutchman*. And it is true: the New York subway has never ceased to be the stuff of myth and metaphor, at times in an obvious manner (the descent into the netherworld, the resurfacing to "see the stars"), at others in ways more disquieting and complex. Poets like Hart Crane, Allen Tate, and Muriel Rukeyser have written about it; it has been the subject of films like Larry Peerce's *The Incident* and Walter Hill's *The Warriors*; it repeatedly takes center stage in the works of Erik Drooker (undoubtedly the world's most important contemporary graphic artist), who transforms it into a mythical place of the subconscious and prehistory, the curved walls of stations covered with rock paintings that not everyone manages to see; in George Tucker's picture, *The Subway*, it is the choice place of supreme urban alienation; it is an endless source of urban folklore (on a stand at the Grand Central Terminal, I picked up an amusing booklet titled *I've Been Working on the Subway: The Folklore and Oral History of Transit*, written by Sally Charnow and Steven Zeitlin); it has formed the backdrop to notorious acts of violence whose social and emotional impact was considerable (those of Bernard Goetz, the white man who took the law into his own hands against a group of rowdy blacks). And precisely the idea of the subway as a metaphor for the city of New York is explored by Michael W. Brooks in his *Subway City: Riding the Trains, Reading New York*, a fascinating and densely packed book intermingling literature, art, architecture, costume, and urban, economic, and technological history.

The subway is the very *underneath* of New York, then, but also that *underneath* that each of us experiences on a more personal basis: the feverish sense of fatigue on emerging from subway steps and along chaotic streets after the frantic dash from the airport, the sense of disorientation when confronted with scenes so different from those we have left, the diabolical and at times unbearable noise, the sense of turmoil as trains approach, the unpleasant vibrating of the long platforms, the muggy heat and the chill of air-conditioning, the headlong rush along certain stretches of track, the rainbow variety of faces and behavior, the idiosyncrasies of individual passengers, the all-enshrouding graffiti, the Chinaman playing Bach and the a cappella choir singing *Carmina Burana*, the broken-bottled quarrel in a rapidly emptying carriage, the interminable hanging around and the never-ending journey to Coney Island or the northernmost tip of Manhattan . . .

It is, however, the people living underneath the city that I'd rather speak of—a tale that must be told with patience. Imagine you are walking along Riverside Park on the West Side: it is a beautiful day, with clear sunny skies, seagulls, boats sailing on the Hudson, a sense of peace and well-being, a benevolent metropolis that cradles you lovingly in its arms, brimming over with promises . . . Underneath you, beneath the pavement, sits the Tunnel: and the nightmare begins.

In the mid-nineteenth century, Riverside Park was an anonymous muddy riverbank. When the tracks of the Hudson River Railroad made their appearance, around them multiplied the shanties of a homeless community that by the early twentieth century already numbered more than a hundred. The Great Depression did the rest. Then, in the mid-1930s, it was decided that the area should be redeveloped to make way for a long promenade to be used by wealthy West Side residents. The homeless were evicted and two and a half miles of railroad tracks (from West 72nd Street to West 123rd Street) were embedded in a reinforced concrete structure covered in earth. The Tunnel was large enough to allow for the long diesel trains to be put together and to contain all kinds of objects and machines, and it remained in use until the mid-1970s when the transportation of goods by rail slumped. First it was abandoned, then closed. But in 1991, when a team of maintenance workers began work on the building of a new railway junction in the area, they came across a community of about fifty people who had been living there for several years— a mere handful out of the five-thousand-odd wretches who are thought to be living in the bowels of the city. They had actually been *living there*, in the sense that they had transformed those subterranean spaces into proper rooms and living areas, furnished with whatever could be picked up off the streets early in the metropolitan morning.

Margaret Morton, a photographer friend of mine who has passionately charted the existence of these invisible people over recent years (I got all this information from her *The Tunnel: The Underground Homeless of New York*, a book of photographs and oral statements), explained to me that the inhabitants of the Tunnel had chosen this particular place because it is located in a rich area of the city. Geographically and socially mobile yuppies are always on the move, and this means there are plenty of objects being thrown away or abandoned—stoves, fridges, ovens, sofas, and mattresses; and when they are not employing crooked methods to discourage "recycling" (who knows why?), the neighborhood's restaurants and food stores supply the Tunnel's inhabitants with pretty tasty tidbits. Not that that makes things any better.

It is a situation repeated elsewhere underneath Manhattan. For instance, in the subway tunnel of Second Avenue, which was built, opened, and then abandoned a few years ago; or in one of the disused stations, of which there are about ten in Manhattan alone; or even in fully operative stations like the one at Lafayette and Bleeker that, with its five levels descending into the entrails of the city and the haphazard mix of people living there, is considered one of the most dangerous; or in the tunnels beneath the railroads of Grand Central Terminal or Penn Station; or in those underlying Central Park, which have acquired urban legend status with some, and the disbelieving scorn of others; or, lastly, in any of those subterranean spaces that desperation manages to get its hands on (I've been told there is a grating on the Bowery that people enter at night and leave first thing in the morning; and the crime-thriller writer Patricia Cornwell has set one of her novels, *From Potter's Field*, among these inhabited tunnels)—"Life Below," as was titled a celebrated series of cartoons by Will Eisner during the 1940s.

The New York subway stretches out for 731 miles. It has twenty-three lines, 466 stations, and a hundred toilets (nothing compared to the nine hundred it once boasted). The network of tunnels underlying the Grand Central Terminal is staggering: with a full thirty-four miles of track compressed into a space totaling a square three-quarters of a mile, it is the biggest station in the world. So, there is a veritable wealth of spaces, intricate passages, and openings at the disposal of whoever is repulsed or marginalized from the city—for the most part, drug addicts and the mentally insane, but also people who, for whatever reason, have simply dropped out of society and are unable to adapt to the idea or reality of reintegration.

Jennifer Toth has dedicated a book to this invisible and elusive population (the figures are necessarily approximate: realistically speaking, they number between five and six thousand, but some insist on a figure closer to twenty-five thousand). It is not a wholly convincing work, marred as it is by the odd lapse into sensationalistic journalism, but the overall picture of a sprawling metropolis that spurns its swelling broods of undesirables and drives them underground is positively spine-chilling. *The Mole People: Life in the Tunnels Beneath New York* tells tales of extraordinary marginalization: of people who are no longer capable of living "on the surface," flimsy little saplings growing spontaneously where light filters down from above, lovingly looked-after cats and dogs, movingly furnished rooms, tunnel-born children who reach adulthood already at the age of five or six, groups that have organized themselves for survival and resistance to attacks, individuals who spend the whole day anxiously looking for and preparing food, a mysterious population living in the darkest depths of these labyrinthine tunnels that now communicates solely in cries and grunts, and a voluntary network of information and mutual assistance. This universe is also extremely violent, and a highly sensitive public matter: Toth's book has, for instance, been bitterly attacked as being vague and unreliable by Joseph Brennan, another scholar writing on the subject.

Up until a few years ago, the roads and parks of Manhattan provided shelter for the growing numbers of homeless. Tent towns and shantytowns sprang up like mushrooms here and there on the island, some of them genuine makeshift small towns, others just a few yards away from the wealth and bright lights of traditional tourist spots. I remember one in Tompkins Square Park, and another called "Bushville" between East 4th Street, East Houston Street, and Avenues C and D; and I also recall Morton's high-impact yet deeply humane photographs of the phenomenon—a world fighting tooth and claw for survival and dignity against terrible human odds. Later, this world of tent towns and shantytowns—utterly incompatible with New York's glossy image—was wiped out by the drastic and violent actions of the police and accompanying bulldozers. Descending beneath the city, their inhabitants probably joined the swelling ranks of invisible New Yorkers.

Someone told me that if I went to the 9th Precinct, the police station located on East 5th Street, I could request that someone accompany me "underground" to visit one or two of the mole people communities. I decided not to. To be honest, I find it impossible to equate all this misery and desperation with the idea of a show. Instead, Ralph Ellison's *Invisible Man* came back to my mind—and its main character who, after wading through the infernal wasteland of post–Second World War America, and all too aware of his own unavoidable invisibility, hides away in a building inhabited by whites only, in a basement walled in and then forgotten during the nineteenth century, where he recreates a precarious and temporary identity as the new Dostoyevskian man from *Notes from the Underground.*

Ellison certainly wasn't alone in providing a literary expression for the American obsession with what lies "underneath": Edgar Allan Poe and H. P. Lovecraft both employed the crypt as a metaphor for the *deep* (yes!) sense of unease associated with the "underneath" of society. But Ellison's "invisible man" is perhaps the nearest one can get to those hordes of invisible men and women who live (now you know it) under your feet, under the very pavements of Manhattan.

Some days after my visit to the New-York Historical Society exhibition, a strange thing happened while I was heading downtown. I was fairly close to the Flatiron Building (the splendid skyscraper that to me is a precious New York

symbol) when, on a side street, I spotted a confusion of police cars, with orange lights flashing and sirens blaring. As curious as a monkey, I went to see what was happening.

Policemen and firemen had already cordoned off a small area on the sidewalk with yards of yellow tape, and inside this area were four or five people. In the middle, one of those typical gratings dotted here and there about the New York sidewalks had been lifted, and a fireman kneeling on the edge of the rectangular trapdoor was gazing downward and poking about with an iron hook. I sidled up to one of the more trustworthy-looking bystanders and asked him what had happened, and he told me that someone had apparently fallen through the grating and down the trapdoor. I didn't bother asking how such a thing could have happened, and instead stood watching the movements of the four or five policemen and firemen standing in the cordoned-off area.

There really didn't seem to be much commotion. Probably, the unfortunate pedestrian had already been pulled out and taken away. But the gestures and to-ing and fro-ing of the firemen and policemen, their insistent poking about and looking down into the trapdoor, and the fact that they kept going back to the edge of the hole to peer down attentively, almost made me think that the victim was still down the trapdoor, and that the trapdoor was much larger and deeper than it looked.

Then a shiver ran down my spine. A policeman and fireman muttered something to one another. One shook his head and the other grabbed hold of the grating and with his iron hook placed it over the trapdoor, then stood on top of the grating to make sure it fitted flush with the edges. The show was over, everyone went home. But I almost had the impression that the pedestrian had disappeared, and that the policemen and firemen were resigned to the impossibility of ever getting him or her back.

In short, that someone else had become invisible, underneath New York.

4

Villages

*T*he Vejigante Café, at 155 East 106th Street in the middle of El Barrio (Spanish Harlem), is a tiny little place. I went there one October afternoon after wandering around the broad, crowded streets while Papoleto Melendez, the Nuyorican (as New York's Puerto Rican artists enjoy calling themselves) poet, told me about characters and episodes of life in the neighborhood, past events, his childhood in these blocks, how they had changed, what remained of the past. We visited "La Marqueta," the long covered market tucked beneath the Park Avenue Elevated (and Papoleto shook his head: "Gone flat . . . used to be much bigger, ya know . . . full of shops and lights, people, hubbub"). We stopped off for a few minutes at a Caribbean cultural center to chat about The Capeman, the musical by Paul Simon and Derek Walcott (it narrates the story of a youth gang battle—one of the many that also inspired West Side Story: but initially the other Nuyorican poet, Pedro Pietri, was to have written its lyrics). Again and again we passed by shops and stores lining East 116th Street (also called Luís Muñoz Marín Boulevard, after the 1940s politician and governor of Puerto Rico). Above all, in these wanderings of ours, while taking in the new perspectives and savoring the infinite variety of the city, we kept stopping in our tracks: to chat with people lolling about street corners, sitting on stoops, or leaning out of windows.

Then, while the sun was going down, we ended up in this place for a beer. The Vejigante really is a rather unusual café, because despite its small size it also functions as a meeting place, a reading room, and a showroom for Puerto Rican craft articles. Bizarre, colorful masks—timely reminders of Caribbean folklore—hang from the walls, and near the bar stand tiny showcases containing wooden sculptures, fanciful jewels, and works in soft terra-cotta; books and magazines are strewn about on the three small tables and crammed into the bookshelves next to the entrance.

An unpredictable kind of place, the Vejigante Café. When we entered, Mario (a moving spirit of the place and one of Papoleto's close friends) was rattling on in Spanish to a man dressed in white from top to bottom—hat, jacket, vest, and pants—who seemed interested in purchasing some masks, but after a few minutes he came and sat at the table next to ours and started talking to us in the most wonderful English, resonant and sonorous. He told me that after teaching art history in Puerto Rico for some years, he had become disillusioned with the academy and decided to opt for a more precarious but enthralling form of independence. Now he spent a good deal of his time at the café, reading, writing, and entertaining the customers—and talking. He's got the gift of gab, has Mario, and Papoleto and I give him free rein, we egg him on; meanwhile, the streets outside vibrate to the overlapping notes of salsa and merengue, the piercing voices of youngsters in colored jackets, the sharp cries from sidewalk to window and back again, and the musical singsong of the elderly basking in the fast-fading rays of the day and the season.

And so, in this tiny Spanish Harlem café—light-years away from Fifth Avenue and Times Square—a long yarn is spun: starting with the condition of artists in the ghetto, it ponders the question of huge federal government cuts to the funds for cultural projects, touches the Puritan fear of physicality in American culture, celebrates the triumph of the body in the art of Titian and Rubens, and culminates in the (shared) admiration for the small, controversial picture by Courbet, L'origine du monde.

When one of the café's other moving spirits, Maria (seems to be the name of the day today), appears at the door with a dish of pasteles, the subject moves on to food and touches upon material culture. And that sense of communal intimacy that I had become aware of on first entering the neighborhood—the feeling that I was inside a village in the metropolis—becomes more intense and all-pervading.

I ask Maria if she can give me the recipe for pasteles, a national Puerto Rican dish . . .

People will have told you that New York is a tentacular city, an alienating metropolis where anonymity and disintegration rule the roost. This is certainly true. Even in the most openly inviting (or dull) touristy areas, the sheer size of the city is enough to cow you into a sense of feeling lost, or even vulnerable. And you don't need to watch Martin Scorsese's *Taxi Driver* for confirmation of the city's ruthlessly high-strung urban-living style: venturing a few steps off the traditional tourist routes will more than suffice. *Pace* New York mayors!

Even at its very special heart—which goes by the name of Manhattan—New York is a tough city, a "metropolis-metropolis," at once fiercely individualistic (the rat race, the survival of the fittest) and, more importantly, *made up of individuals*. Consider for one moment the standard photographs and freeze-frames of journalistic reports: a sea of faces and bodies that emerge from anonymity only by carving out a completely separate and absolute individuality—almost as if nothing else existed between the two poles of faceless masses and individual monads. Maybe the ice-skating rink at Rockefeller Center, one of New York's many unavoidable icons, is the perfect metaphor for what I wish to say: beneath the looming skyscrapers, everyone cutting arabesque figures à la Jackson Pollock in the ice, swirling and swooping round and round to the hypnotic music, and taking great care not to bump into each other . . .

True, the great metropolis is alienating and the rat race begins anew every morning. But this is a piecemeal perception, and is even wide of the mark. New York is also, significantly, a metropolis *made up of groups,* and its inhabitants are more sociable than might at first be thought. You can feel this walking around the streets, hanging about the cafés, and even descending into the depths of the subway: you are *on your own*—at times acutely so—but in constant, mysterious association with others. And I believe that this contradiction is precisely part and parcel of the charm with which the city is imbued.

But there is more. This mammoth metropolis seems to ride roughshod over all things, seizing hold of them and redefining them in a vortex whose brutish capacity to shatter and transform impedes any kind of stability or settling. And yet it is also a *city of villages*—of neighborhoods where speed slows, the vortex relents, the puzzle becomes recognizable contour and design, and familiarity gets the better of anonymity. Now, it is not always easy to uncover this reality of villages, because the eye is too often dazzled by bright exteriors or befuddled by the dullness of commonplaces. And, unlike your traditional tourist paradise, these villages do not exactly welcome you with open arms: they are often dark, removed, dangerous, and forbidding places that are difficult to enter (assuming one wishes to in the first place) on the right foot and in the right frame of mind.

Indeed, there is always the risk that visitors to these metropolitan areas will succumb to the unhealthy and sensationalistic spirit of curiosity stoked up by the mass media. In the nineteenth century, people used to *go slumming* when the East End of London and the Lower East Side of New York, proletarian neighborhoods swarming with immigrants, became the "other side" of Victorian society (New York's Chinatown—complete with fake opium dens—was the number one attraction for tourists seeking their thrills). And there is also the risk of falling into the trap laid down by certain nineteenth-century anthropologists who superimposed upon these metropolitan areas ideological constructs elaborated to cope with the "primitive" people of Africa and Asia, thus equating them with a Black Continent inhabited by different and alien races.

In both cases, the idea that these areas are not really part of the city predominates—that they are either nonexistent places to be removed or abnormal growths that have formed on the body of the metropolis. And yet, these areas *are* the city and, in a certain sense, it is precisely *here* that the city actually was born. If we wish to uncover the city's roots, history, and identity, it is to these areas—in the midst of that restless vortex that is the rest of Manhattan—that we must look: in the intensity of its street life, in the intermingling of its cultures, and in the sense of solidarity that seeps through metropolitan anonymity and disintegration.

Take, for example, the Lower East Side, where ties with the past and the role of memory are strongest and most vital. On the map, it occupies the area between East 14th Street and the ramps to Brooklyn Bridge, between Lafayette Street and the East River—an irregular quadrilateral, more than half of which falls under the name of *downtown*. At the beginning of the nineteenth century, when the city was still a tiny plot of land, this area was dotted with water meadows, farms, orchards, and hills. Then, in its southern part, around Collect Pond (more or less the site of present-day Federal Plaza and Foley Square), building began: refined houses for the nascent middle-to-upper classes, theaters, and meeting places, but also factories and workshops of a metropolis in the making, and nearby a port in great ferment. The Collect Pond shortly became murky in appearance, an unwelcome stench arose, and the buildings on the banks worryingly started giving way. The rising middle class abandoned the area and moved northward. The pond was dried up by means of a canal (which is still thought to run beneath Canal Street), more factories were built, the popular amusements quarter at the entrance to the Bowery expanded, and the whole area sloughed off its original skin. The close proximity of the port, the commercial thoroughfare of Broadway, and the financial district of Wall Street determined the area's fate as the city frenetically and irresistibly expanded in width and length.

Then, from the middle of the nineteenth century onward, hundreds of thousands of immigrants from all over the world arrived to join those small communities of blacks who, first as slaves and later as free men, had lived in the area ever since the mid-1600s. After the immigrants had been put through the humiliating hoops of Castle Garden and, later, Ellis Island (where they were quarantined, scrutinized, examined, vetted, and, sometimes, given another name), a large number of those admitted ended up in different parts of the country. But another significant percentage settled in the narrow streets and overcrowded tenements of the Lower East Side: Germans who had left their native land following the revolutionary uprisings of 1848, Irishmen seeking refuge from the social calamities of famine and failed potato crops, and—after digging silver and gold mines, building embankments for the Intercontinental Railroad, and cooking and laundering in the West—significant numbers of Chinese in flight from what can only be called *pogroms*. Later in the nineteenth century, it was the turn of Eastern European Jews harried by tsarist repression, and Italians brought to the brink of starvation during the process of national formation. Not to mention much smaller numbers of Spaniards, Greeks, Turks, Cypriots, Moroccans, gypsies . . .

The Lower East Side became the immigrant quarter par excellence, the gateway to America in an era when "America" was most intensely syn-onymous with "mirage." Living and working conditions were horrific. About the time of the First World War, the neighborhood contained half a million immigrants, and in certain blocks the population density was double that of Bombay and three times that of London. And then there were the grueling hours of work in clothing industry workshops; the end-less and uncontrolled social plagues of child labor, domestic work, and prostitution; streets and houses deprived of ventilation and lighting; incessant exploitation; individuals, family units, and whole generations shattered and deformed under the relentless steamroller of the extraction of surplus labor. All in all, a bloodcurdling story that can be gleaned from the novels of Abraham Cahan and Anzia Yezierska, the autobiographies of Marcus Ravage and Rose Cohen, and the photographs of Jacob Riis and Lewis Hine.

However, the history of these metropolitan villages by no means con-sists purely of brutalization and physical and social degradation. When immigrants and America crossed paths, a whole series of bitter dynamics came to the fore. Perhaps most importantly, these dynamics made liars of those guileless, early-twentieth-century sociologists who upheld that the process of Americanization would have come about slowly, mechanically, and painlessly: the mythical "melting pot" that would finally transform immigrants into Americans. What actually happened in neighborhoods like the Lower East Side can more accurately be described as a meeting-cum-confrontation, a kind of tug-of-war situation that would change pro-tagonists on both sides: glorious strikes (like that of the shirtmakers, which, under the leadership of young, recently arrived immigrant women, lasted several months in 1909 before coming to a victorious end); the agi-tations of anarchists, socialists, and communists; a dialectic of German, Irish, Yiddish, Italian, and Cantonese cultures; a stubborn longing to resist and fight back in the workplace, at home, and in the streets; and an overturning of homegrown traditions and habits, which at the same time called into question the American gospel.

On that magnificent stage we call the street, everything came into reci-procal relation with everything else: languages, religions, cultures, and habits simmered, blended, and were finally transformed in a kind of ongoing subterranean alchemic process. This daily tug-of-war (thousands of immigrants from all over the world turning into American proletarians) transformed the neighborhood into an immense laboratory. Unsurprisingly, it is precisely in this laboratory that we find the beginnings of cinema (David W. Griffith) and popular shows (Eddie Cantor, Irving Berlin), the establishment of a Yiddish theater, the emergence of an exquisitely American realist tradition in painting (John Sloan, the Ash Can school, Jerome Myers, Ben Shahn), and, later, abstract expressionism (the New York school), the first significant examples of Jewish American and Italo-American novels and the literary experiments of modernism, a mature political and radical form of journalism and social photography, and the first stirrings of the Beat Generation and the avant-garde cultures of the 1960s and 1970s. All of this (and much else besides) erupted into being and matured in the Lower East Side laboratory, only to overflow its confines and redefine the city of New York again and again. More than that, it reinvented America itself and helped to shape the twentieth century.

This dialectic between exploitation and resistance, brutalization and creativity, is inherent in the *whole* of experience on the Lower East Side. Indeed, when the first phase of its history came to a halt around the 1920s, the "gateway" was by no means closed. Of course, there was a kind of diaspora in the direction of other neighborhoods, and things did simmer down somewhat, but its characteristic function as a laboratory never disappeared. The area remained very much itself even during the 1930s, 1940s, and 1950s, enduring all the violent counterblows that national and worldwide history had to offer, decline and standstill, stagnation and renewal. When, in the 1950s and 1960s, a new chapter began in the open story of immigration to the United States with the arrival of other Asians and, above all, Puerto Ricans, the laboratory function of the Lower East Side once again took center stage.

Little Italy was on the wane, and the Jewish ghetto had seen better days, but at the same time Chinatown was expanding and "Loisaida," an emblematic Spanglish deformation of "Lower East Side," was coming into being. Most importantly, the area's original village-inside-the-city character remained, as can be seen in Jerome Myers's painting entitled *Life on the East Side*: in the foreground, a street scene, with the road reduced to a narrow path, elderly bearded men, women with brightly colored handkerchiefs on their heads, children darting in and out the stalls of the marketplace, densely packed bodies, and a sense of communal living. In the background, tall and mysterious, impending yet detached, stand the grey profiles of the towers and skyscrapers of Manhattan. Or take Anzia Yezierska's tale of 1920, *The Fat of the Land:* after rejecting the tumultuous

Lower East Side for the ascetic comforts of Riverside Drive, the main character later returns to her original neighborhood to savor anew the animated streets, the pleasures of haggling over prices, and the sense of belonging to a community.

So perhaps one afternoon you should make a beeline for the haunts comprised (and compressed) within the irregular quadrilateral. When I made my first visit to this area more than twenty-five years ago, I departed hesitantly from the corner of Baxter Street, Worth Street, and Columbus Park: in the middle of the nineteenth century this was the site of infamous black and Irish slums, the so-called Five Points (Dickens, who knew a thing or two about slums, was horrified when he visited it during his trip through America). Then I cut across toward Mulberry Street and Bayard Street, once upon a time the most congested and disreputable area inside Little Italy. From there I got caught up in the chaos of Mott Street, Pell Street, and Doyers Street, a Chinatown district that can't have changed much over the last hundred years. I proceeded along a stretch of Elizabeth Street (the "Elisabetta Stretta" of Sicilian immigrants) where the atmosphere was far more genuine and less tacky than nearby Little Italy (it is suffering the pains of gentrification now, but some old haunts still remain, like the Albanese butcher shop). I felt as if I was moving inside a kaleidoscope of places, colors, faces, sounds, and images: towering above me were the century-old tenements whose russet-brown bricks had blackened with age, the rusty fire escapes, and, all around me in the streets, an incredible confusion of people, teeming about tranquilly, to-ing and fro-ing; and a host of small stores pouring their merchandise onto the sidewalks, a cobbler on the corner, a bulletin board covered in ideograms with local community information (deaths, births, job offers and requests), rows of elderly people seated in front of shops and local bars, and the reverberating sounds of different languages newly molded by life in the metropolis.

I remember crossing the Bowery, which once proudly hosted performances of riotously popular shows running the whole gamut of human experience (from Shakespeare, Tolstoy, and Wagner to Buffalo Bill, the Barnum Circus, and the Peking Opera), and which is now the busy domain of wholesale commerce and aimless existences. And I remember taking Grand Street, only to get lost in the maze of nineteenth-century streets of what used to be (and in part still is) the Jewish ghetto with its countless shops, commercial activities, and the daily ups and downs of living and survival in the new metropolitan *shtetl:* Orchard Street, where even today things are proffered, haggled over, and bought on a sidewalk reminiscent of a bazaar; Norfolk Street, with its stately synagogues, at once austere and fanciful in style; Rivington Street, with its *matzos* shops and kosher wines; Hester Street and Essex Street, where the past has less willingly relaxed its grip on the present, sprinkled with dusty shops displaying seven-branched candelabras and deluxe bound editions of the Talmud, and the piquant aroma of pickles stuffed inside the enormous barrels of local grocers; East Broadway, with a towering building that used to house the central offices of the *Jewish Daily Forward,* founded by Abraham Cahan (and now the site of a Buddhist temple); the signs of rabbis and congregations, the public bathrooms for women, the murals that narrate the social history of the quarter . . .

When I took Clinton Street and headed north beyond Delancey Street, I realized that the atmosphere was changing: from China, Italy, and the Jewish *shtetl* I was now moving beneath a Caribbean sunshine. Although I knew little about it at the time, I was entering Loisaida. Synagogues now battled it out with tropical gardens, yet despite the more glaring evidence of degradation, there was also a strong sense of community, of village. In front of Casa Adela, a small Puerto Rican restaurant along Avenue C (it serves excellent *mondongo,* or tripe, and refreshing vegetable juices), three old ladies take bets on the unlicensed lottery, a group of elderly people sit around a foldaway table playing dominos, the air is filled with the aroma of *cuchifritos* (fried foods) drifting in from the local kiosk, and Spanglish yells and counteryells chase one another along the street. And a few hundred yards away stands the building that houses the Nuyorican Poets' Café, the mythical downtown stage for poetic, musical, and theatrical creativity in multicultural New York.

While my yesterdays have been blending with your todays, we have ended up in the heart of Alphabet City, the Manhattan area guides usually warn you against entering, especially after dark. Walk northward along Avenue C—or Loisaida Avenue as it is now officially known—until you reach East 9th Street (Henry Roth's *Call It Sleep* is set exactly in this area). Pass in front of the Sixth Street Community Center, and immerse yourself in the park on Tompkins Square: here you will meet with other scenarios, intimate scenes, promptings, and tensions. This is perhaps the most complex and contradictory area in Manhattan, where the clash between exploitation and the will to resist gains in intensity with each passing day, and the century-old history of the Lower East Side continues. To me, it is also the most fascinating area in Manhattan: more real than other parts of the city, the place where most of my friends are on this side of the ocean, where I feel most "at home" in the metropolis.

Beyond Tompkins Square, along St. Mark's Place, East Village begins. A glamorous and ambiguous *punk-chic* zone, East Village spearheads the SoHo assault of wealth and snobbery on the whole of the Lower East Side, although fortunately its attacks have been in part repelled. At this point, how can one resist the peace and quiet of the Life Café or the Leshko Café or the Café Orlin? Or the Polish cuisine of Christine's, the Ukrainian dishes of Veselka, the Indian specialties of Panna II, the Italian cookery of Brunetta's? Or the attraction of bars and theaters like LaMama, the Theater for the New City, or the P.S. 122? And when you arrive at the far end of St. Mark's Place (whose multiethnic past is visible everywhere), you could always take a break in front of the immense Cooper Union, the celebrated school of applied arts where Abraham Lincoln, Mark Twain, and the striking shirtmakers once spoke, and decide what to do next.

Yet the Lower East Side is not the only village in New York. There is, of course, Greenwich Village, which, as its very name suggests, makes no bones about its own collocation inside the great metropolis (indeed, if it is true that "wich"—from the Latin *vicus* and its medieval High German descendant *wich*—already means "village," the name is a classic example of redundancy). Here, too, in the quadrilateral around Washington Square Park and the tangle of irregular streets between the park and the Hudson River, northward until West 14th and south almost down to Canal, history's heavy footsteps have left their mark, determining more of the area's contemporary appearance than first meets the eye. Henry James himself, in his 1880 novel *Washington Square* (set in the 1840s), had pitted the solidity of the Washington Square area—its having "something of a social history"—against the vagueness and abstractions of the city (its "theoretic air") stretching northward.

No doubt about that: Greenwich Village positively oozes with social history—maybe less so than the Lower East Side, but it is equally possessed of a powerful symbolic value. Indeed, its microhistory can even, in many ways, be said to be an aid to understanding the city's macrohistory, its contradictions and *chiaroscuro*, what is present and what is absent. We start with the Native Americans, who, at the time of Dutch domination, called the village that developed in this part of Manhattan "Sapponckanican" or "Sapohannikan" ("tobacco field"). We continue with the formerly enslaved blacks, who, for much of the seventeenth century, were actually owners of allotments in the area south of present-day Christopher Street and east of present-day Hudson Street: Paulo Dangola, Symon Congo, Anthony Van Angola—new names for new identities in a process that would become familiar for successive waves of immigrants. And then there were the African Americans who, as fugitive or manumitted slaves or, after the Civil War, as legally free men, settled mostly in the web of streets around Grove, Carmine, Thompson, and Sullivan, after drifting away from the southernmost area of Five Points.

Around 1840 there were approximately sixteen thousand African Americans in New York, out of a total population of three hundred thousand. And, beside an African Free School and a station on the Underground Railroad (the network of churches and private houses that hid slaves fleeing from the South during the pre–Civil War years), the African Americans also found time to inaugurate the African Grove Theater on the corner of Bleeker and Grove. Between 1821 and 1829 the theater repeatedly staged performances of *Othello* and *Richard III*: at the beginnings of a career that would lead to numerous European accolades, the young black actor Ira Aldridge usually interpreted the two Shakespearean characters. Black spectators paid no entrance fees, while the few whites who attended were invited to take their places in a segregated area because they were "unable to behave properly in a black establishment."

Then it was the turn of the Irish and the Italians. Seeping in from the confines of the nearby Lower East Side, the two communities (particularly the Italians, whose numbers increased year after year from the 1860s on) muscled in on African American territory and took up occupancy side by side. When the black community began its march toward the north of the city, the Irish and Italians took their places between Thompson and Sullivan and especially in the area between Bleeker and Carmine, where, for example, the Church of Our Lady of Pompeii rose on the site of what was previously a black church.

The Italian community in New York could count on a number of famous (or shortly to be famous) names, including Lorenzo Da Ponte (Mozart's librettist), opera singer Adelina Patti, Giuseppe Garibaldi, Antonio Meucci, and yet others besides. But for the most part, Italian inhabitants in the Village were made up of workers, bricklayers, street vendors, barbers, and a growing number of specialized craftsmen, shopkeepers, street musicians, and restaurateurs. The community was dominated by a number of loved/hated figures: the *padrone*, a middleman who allocated jobs in exchange for a percentage (or *bossatura*); the banker (often a grocer), who, for a certain sum of interest, would look after people's savings and send whatever was required back to their homeland; and, of course, the "Mano Nera" (Black Hand), the New York version of the *mafia, camorra,* and *'ndrangheta,* which, as time proceeded, came to replace all spontaneous forms of territorial defense in the metropolis. More than anything, however, it was the dreaded sweatshop that ruled the "colonia" (as it was often called): young Italian—and Jewish—immigrant women soon became familiar with the long hours of work and dangerously unhealthy environments that this infamous institution represented. This proletarian, popular character of the Italian settlement in Greenwich Village was to long outlast the legislative measures undertaken to reduce immigration to a trickle in the mid-1920s. Throughout the

1930s, 1940s, and 1950s, the area south of Washington Park remained an extension of Mulberry Street–style Little Italy, complete with meeting places, dives, family-run restaurants, the Caffé Roma, the Caffé Bertolotti, the Caffé San Remo, shops selling pasta and cheese (and a good red wine that cut out a very special niche for itself during the Prohibition years), and small-time theater—a familiar and intimate villagelike atmosphere that was further enhanced by a series of narrow, winding streets.

Despite Caroline Ware's groundbreaking volume (*Greenwich Village, 1920–1930*, published in 1935), the history of immigration and of its impact on life in Greenwich Village remains an extremely complex and relatively unfamiliar subject. And other historical blind spots remain, too. For many decades, an invisible boundary line running along the southern side of Washington Square Park effectively divided that Village from another Village whose wealth and refinement were symbolized by the solemn brownstone houses (which have in part survived to the present day) and, to the back, the mews, or roads lined with stables and carriage depots—the other side of Greenwich Village, itself with a long and symbolic history. When the city was still largely concentrated on the southern tip of the island, this area was an uninterrupted expanse of green. And it was here that well-heeled families would flee to escape the suffocating humidity; it was here that city businesses were transferred when epidemics struck the small urban settlement (cholera in 1798, yellow fever in 1820, smallpox in 1823, and cholera again in 1832 and 1849); and it was here that the first state penitentiary was located, giving rise to a limited albeit significant network of local services (hotels, staging posts, restaurants, and shops). All of these left their mark and helped determine the character of the village "outside the walls." And so, when the close-knit web of streets around the port and Wall Street started becoming too overcrowded, a highly significant phenomenon took place: for the first time, the rising middle class (traders, entrepreneurs, lawyers) drew a distinct line between the workplace and place of residence. The city ran upward along Broadway: to the east of this lively thoroughfare was an area that was still too closely bound up with the port, but the green expanse to the west was already well established among the rich as a place of refuge. There was no escaping this choice.

Further elements contributed to establish this other side of Greenwich Village. In origin, the area that is today occupied by Washington Square was used as a mass grave for the thousand-odd victims of cholera in 1798, the poor and nameless, and those who had been hanged (the gallows were set up in the northwest corner of the park). And so it remained until 1826, when work began on transforming the area into a parade ground.

For the next twenty-five years or so, parades and military exercises were held here, while in the meantime the wealthy Village to the north continued to expand and the Greek Revival buildings of New York University were built to the east. The fact that the area was successively subjected to these two developments effectively meant that the vertical growth of New York somehow "skipped" the heart of the Village. Indeed, the terrain gave way too readily (and, symbolically speaking, it was perhaps unsuitable: again, the "underneath" of the metropolis!) and was considered an inappropriate location for the high-rise constructions—offices, apartment blocks, and popular tenements—that had already begun their skyward-soaring journey elsewhere in the second half of the nineteenth century.

Also, the layout of streets in the area was the most enmeshed and disorderly in New York. The people responsible for the 1811 town planning scheme (which imposed the notorious grid system: streets and lots divided up into equal blocks) were unable—or unwilling—to meddle with the Greenwich Village maze; as a result, West 4th Street intersects with West 10th Street, West 11th Street, and West 12th Street! The sum result of all this was that commercial traffic within the area was severely hampered. The area to the north of the invisible boundary line thus remained the most sought-after on the part of the wealthy propertied class, and it was built in their image: Greek Revival, Gothic Revival, brownstones, gardens, mews, ailanthus trees (also called, significantly, "trees of heaven"), and so on—the "old New York," the rich and refined "urban village" handed down to us in the works of Henry James and Edith Wharton.

Poor immigrants and wealthy New Yorkers, then. And soon, a third element was to be active, in the strange alchemy of Greenwich Village. The very "separateness" of the neighborhood—its intimate and reserved character, the otherworldly nature of its tangled alleyways, its low rents, and the overwhelming presence of an immigrant population—all helped ensure that the area to the south and west of Washington Square became a center of attraction for growing numbers of artists and politicians from the mid-nineteenth century on. Edgar Allan Poe, Herman Melville, Walt Whitman, and Mark Twain all fell under its spell: they discovered the area, came back to it on a more or less regular basis, and even lived there (Pfaff's beer house at 653 Broadway became their main meeting place). Then, between the late 1800s and early 1900s especially, the phenomenon became more pronounced. The rebellion against the suffocating puritanism of "Main Street" (that Midwest that was the birthplace of so many American authors) combined with the call to arms of foreign avant-gardism, and explosive internal tensions (these are the years of the great strikes organized all over the country) combined with the traumas and enthusiasm sparked by immensely significant international events like the Russian Revolution of 1905, the First World War, and the Russian Revolution of 1917.

Writers, female poets, militants, dramatists, feminists, painters, critics, and intellectuals—many of them destined to leave their mark on the cultural milieu of the age—crowded into Greenwich Village during the years between 1890 and 1920: Stephen Crane, O. Henry, Hart Crane, Edna St. Vincent Millay, John Dos Passos, John Reed, Emma Goldman, Theodore Dreiser, Eugene O'Neill, John Sloan, Mabel Dodge Luhan, Edmund Wilson, and many, many more—a lengthy and highly impressive list, to be sure. Paradoxically, most of these artists or intellectuals were escaping from (or rebelling against) their native villages—and then they rediscovered familiar coordinates and new energies in this unique cosmopolitan village at the heart of the metropolis. As John Reed once wrote: "Within a block of my house was all the adventure in the world; within a mile was every foreign country."

So, in the difficult years bridging the nineteenth and twentieth centuries, the topography of the Village mushroomed to include the "new theater," the "new painting," the "new poetry," the "new woman," the anarchists and the Industrial Workers of the World, Freud, Ibsen, and Strindberg, postimpressionist painting, left-wing magazines like the *Masses* and the *Liberator,* working-class rallies and the extraordinary Paterson Strike Pageant (when silk factory workers from nearby New Jersey staged a version of their long dramatic struggle at the Madison Square Garden under the direction of John Reed), and cozy, smoky haunts like Polly's Restaurant, Christine's, Grace's Garret, and the Pepper Pot: an acutely contradictory story brimming over with romantic impulses and intense individualism, serious research and plain humbug, which Albert Parry described in his emblematically entitled book *Garrets and Pretenders* (1933).

This magmatic phase came to a close with the First World War and, more importantly, with the ferocious repression of the Left in 1919–20. The following decade, dominated by Prohibition and the often desperate anxieties of the Lost Generation, was more a contrived (and sometimes commercialized) repetition of the preceding phase, as Malcolm Cowley openly admits in his intense overview of the period, *Exile's Return* (1934). Partly as a result of the Village's overtures to the outside world in the form of a newly extended Sixth Avenue beyond Bleecker Street and the opening of a subway line beneath the neighborhood, the fruitful dialectic between immigrants and political and cultural radicalism gradually diminished, and the two worlds increasingly went their separate ways.

Something of that feverish energy was to linger on, however, in the streets of the Village. In the 1940s and 1950s, the neighborhood bore witness to other experiences: the Beat Generation, action painting, the Living Theater, and the folk revival. But something seemed to be lacking now, in the stock image of *that* Village as a place where everything was to be experienced in the tension of the moment: the sense of a profound historical background—of that "social history" of which James spoke and which, as we have seen, was no small thing. The rest is "today's history": a neighborhood largely dominated by real estate and tourism, by its proximity to the immense art market of SoHo, and by the turmoil of certain areas associated with sex and gender (like Christopher Street, the symbol of the gay movement)—yet also a neighborhood that, in certain parts, has managed to preserve a peaceful, timeless atmosphere, beautiful views, and several remnants of the past.

So, take my advice: if you happen to find yourself in Washington Square one sunny autumn morning or one balmy springtime evening, have just a look at the celebrated arch (it was designed by Stanford White, the artificer behind much of Manhattan before his untimely murder at the hands of a rival suitor; and one midwinter evening in 1916 a group of scallywags led by John Reed and the painter John Sloan climbed to its top and proclaimed the "Free Independent Republic of Washington Square"). And, a few steps away from the intense chess games on the stone chessboards, take just one moment to look at the statue of Garibaldi (I read somewhere that the position of the "Hero of the Two Worlds"—drawing his sword with his left leg forward—is erroneous, and that the sculptor died before being able to correct it: from that moment on, Garibaldi has risked lopping off his kneecap). Even venture farther on until the corner of Prince and Greene streets where the Caffè Fanelli is located, perhaps the last surviving symbol of an Italian past. . . . But then try to resist the temptation of the lights, animation, and attractions of the streets that lead down toward SoHo (Thompson, Sullivan, MacDougal), or of Bleecker Street and West 4th Street beyond Sixth Avenue. This is a tourist trap now—a Village that celebrates itself and the memories of itself, a shopwindow quarter. No, do as I do when I feel like opting out of the more frenetic side of New York: seek out the hidden recesses, the quieter settings—those little streets that, as O. Henry wrote in his story "The Last Leaf," "have run crazy and broken themselves into small strips called 'places.' These places make strange angles and curves. One street crosses itself a time or two." Here, on both sides of Seventh Avenue, Hudson Street, and Greenwich Street, in the direction of the Hudson, you will rediscover a city of the past that has, in certain respects, survived into the present: the low houses that so outraged Le Corbusier, the great theorist of skyscrapers and reinforced concrete; the small, densely packed gardens whose overhanging branches stretch down to caress the benches below;

the tranquil bars hidden away in the darkness; the small courtyards connected one to the other by gates and arches; the lanes, paths, and culs-de-
sac; the fleeting glimpses of houses retreating from the main streets; the
sidewalks nuzzled by slender trees; the tiny corner shops; the sound of
footsteps in the hazy silence; the warm stones of a bygone architecture;
and the unceasing machinations of a benevolent labyrinth that bewitch-
ingly leads you astray only then to bring you back ("The streets are always
disappearing around here," as a friend of mine living in the area once told
me).

Loiter for as long as you wish about the street corners, take in the rar-
ified peace of the St. Luke-in-the-Fields garden and mull over the sudden
slopes and slants of Abingdon Square, where the usual perspectives of
Manhattan seem to explode and implode: these are the places where New
York eases up (and eases you up), although it's still New York. At this
point, in these out-of-the-way recesses, in the midst of that crazy tangle
of streets, you can find the places where Edgar Allan Poe lived and first
read *The Raven* in public; where John Reed wrote *Ten Days That Shook the
World;* where John Sloan painted his great urban scenarios; and where the
militants of the Industrial Workers of the World and the journalists of the
Masses used to meet. You may come across the White Horse Tavern,
where the Welsh poet Dylan Thomas drank himself to death, and Patchin
Place, where e. e. cummings composed so many of his joyful and irreverent pieces, and the "narrowest house in Manhattan" at 751/2 Bedford
Street, where Edna St. Vincent Millay wrote (possibly): "My candle burns
at both ends." This, too, is New York, albeit *another* New York.

And lastly, Harlem. Yet another village in the metropolis, Harlem covers an area that stretches from East 110th Street and the northern edge of
Central Park to Riverside Drive in the west, the Harlem River in the east,
and 162nd Street in the north. Here, too, any attempt to tell the story of
the neighborhood necessarily implies telling the story of the city itself.
Peter Stuyvesant, the already mentioned choleric Dutch governor of
Nieuw Amsterdam, laid the foundations of the Nieuw Haarlem village in
1658 alongside the river that would later take its name, in the vicinity of
present-day East 125th Street: rolling hills, streams, hollows, woods and
green fields, farms, farmers, and a fair number of black slaves. At the
height of English domination, in 1666, the area was provided with a
southern boundary that ran obliquely from present-day West 129th Street
on the Hudson to present-day East 74th Street on the East River, and in
1683 it became an integral part of the city of New York.

Even as late as the early nineteenth century, Harlem's destiny seemed
to follow closely in the footsteps of that of Greenwich Village: it was to
be a place "outside the wall" where the rich could escape from the sum-

mer furnace and pestilential stenches of the city in the south. The area of
flat land in the center and to the east (Harlem Plain) and the hilly area
of land to the west (Harlem Heights) complemented one another perfectly, making for a restful panorama and a bracing climate. Slowly but
surely the farms disappeared, while the number of sprawling estates and
stately abodes multiplied. In 1837 the railroad arrived and the flatlands
lying to the east were subjected to increasingly intense building pro-
grams—a rural village and a residential area: but also, from the mid-1800s
on, a place of temporary settlements, out-and-out "shantytowns" populated by newly arrived Irish and German immigrants (as we have already seen
in the more or less contemporary case of Seneca Village, these were years
of extreme geographical-social mobility).

Following the Civil War, Harlem developed at an increasingly rapid
rate: the first lines of the Elevated opened their way northward along
Second, Third, and Eighth Avenues, a process that led to greater stability among immigrant settlements and an increase in the number of residential nuclei. Downtown, the city was becoming more convulsive by the
minute, and the tangle of commerce and business greedily gobbled up
entire neighborhoods and vast areas of land; but in the case of Harlem,
the bet was to transform the area in what would become the suburbs of
the 1940s and 1950s—a residential area for the middle and upper middle
classes. Hence, in the closing decades of the nineteenth century, Harlem
featured the building of a distinctive and refined architecture that, even
in the midst of the desolate ghetto of today, stands as a living reminder of
that shortsighted bet and angrily bespeaks the indelible contradiction of
a society: long rows of buildings in red stone and terra-cotta and yellow
sandstone of Ohio, in styles that vary from Romanesque revival and
Italian Renaissance to Gothic revival; arches, bow windows, entablatures,
columns and ashlar, high stoops, solemn-looking churches, majestic
Queen Anne–style mansions, five-, six-, or seven-story buildings featuring immense gables and lofty garrets, large apartments with many rooms,
spacious avenues, broad sidewalks . . .

Between 1880 and 1890, the transformation of Harlem was brought
about by a handful of aggressive developers, veritable *ante litteram* yuppies.
However, they stumbled into a fin de siècle marked by a wave of reces-
sions and social upheavals: the real-estate market nose-dived time and
time again, and the risky idea of turning the neighborhood into a sophisticated residential area was thwarted by the selfsame advance of the city,
by its march northward along expanding transport facilities, and by its projection beyond the confines of the island toward the Bronx and Queens.
The stately buildings increasingly came to resemble cathedrals in the
desert. Thus, while rich New Yorkers banded themselves together, as if

under siege, around the Heights and Mount Morris Park, the first German, Jewish, and Italian families "fleeing" from the Lower East Side started arriving, lured by a property market in urgent need of oxygen and keen to realize whatever profits could still be had: these were the flimsy layer of immigrants who could be said to have "made it." And their arrival served only to hasten the departure of those rich "one hundred percent Americans." But not even the advent of these upwardly mobile immigrant families could stave off the problems of a real-estate market that, over the previous twenty years, had gone about building those enormous apartment complexes and now saw them left empty—complete with all those large rooms originally destined to satisfy the needs and rituals of large middle- and upper-middle-class families (and their numerous servants). It is at this point that the African Americans made their appearance.

To follow the path that led African Americans to Harlem means once more retracing the history of the whole city: from the first settlement around Wall Street to that of Five Points and, from there, driven onward by successive waves of immigration, to Greenwich Village. Yet, following the arrival of the Italians and the Jews, the African Americans did not hang around for long in the Village, either. The next move, around the end of the nineteenth century, was to Tenderloin and San Juan Hill. Legend has it that on taking charge of the sinister and vaguely defined area between West 20th and West 55th Streets and 7th and 10th Avenues, an American police captain nicknamed it Tenderloin, in anticipation of the lavish kickbacks that could be expected ("From now on, it's only tenderloin for me!" he was heard to declare when he took office). As for San Juan Hill, the double cross-reference is to the bloody battle in which Teddy Roosevelt and his Rough Riders took part during the Spanish-American War of 1898, and to the violent racial tensions that exploded repeatedly in this architecturally and urbanistically unfortunate area located between 55th and 64th streets and 10th and 11th avenues: an abrupt surge in the topography of Manhattan.

When, for the above reasons, Harlem opened its doors to the African Americans, the umpteenth exodus began. But other factors were at work, too, in this beginning-of-the-twentieth-century scenario: the acute poverty of the southern states, combined with the disillusion experienced by many in the wake of unfulfilled post–Civil War promises and the fears generated by the widespread savagery of the Ku Klux Klan, served to swell the ranks of a new mass migration that would reach its height around the time of the First World War. The northern cities, and in particular New York (a cosmopolitan Mecca complete with a great port overlooking the Atlantic), were the chosen destinations, but it soon became clear that neither Tenderloin (then in the clutches of urban overhaul with the building of the new Pennsylvania Station) nor San Juan Hill (with its insufferable congestion) would have been able to contain this new, massive influx.

At this point, a young black entrepreneur, Philip A. Payton Jr., came into the reckoning. Payton convinced a number of real-estate owners to let him their properties, set up the Afro-American Realty Company and took to renting some of the apartments originally destined for the "one hundred percent American" white middle and upper middle classes to black families. Once set in motion, the mechanism went ahead of its own accord and the developers could heave a sigh of relief. The larger complexes were sold or hired out to local investors and intermediaries, the apartments were restructured in such a way as to boost their number (livability and practicality being of decidedly secondary importance), high rents were maintained in order to cover expenses, and the "new history" of Harlem was on its way. And when, at the end of the First World War, young black American soldiers (who had become familiar with a thoroughly different reality from that experienced in the southern states) made their return from the front, the area north of Central Park became loaded with different psychological and material implications. Shortly this influx from the South was joined by that of the Caribbean (with all the linguistic, cultural, and religious complexities that might be expected), a process that would give rise to the first, authentic "black city" of Manhattan. Or, perhaps we should say, another "village inside the city."

The "new" Harlem was at first a highly irregular triangle whose base stood along 131st Street between Eighth Avenue and the Harlem River, and whose vertex was located on Lenox Avenue at 142nd Street. During the 1920s it had become an equally irregular trapezoid, taking in the area between 130th and 144th streets, Eighth Avenue, and the Harlem River. And in the 1930s it went down as far as the park ("trickling down" even farther a good ten blocks on its western side) and up as far as 166th Street, widening out to include Amsterdam Avenue. The major roads were—and still are—Seventh Avenue, Lenox Avenue, and 125th Street, genuinely public places within the "village" where most of the commercial, social, cultural, and political activities are concentrated. Here, for many years, Lillian Harris (better known as Pig Foot Mary) wheeled her barrow of boiled pig's feet, skillfully investing the abundant proceeds in real estate within the neighborhood; here, the intersection between Lenox Avenue and 125th Street, the site of many rallies and gatherings, was known as "Street Corner University"; here, the Harlem photographers and chroniclers, James Van Der Zee and Austin Hansen, set up their studios; here lived the jazz singers Florence Mills and Alberta Hunter, the musicians W.

C. Handy, Fletcher Henderson, and Eubie Blake, and the writer James Weldon Johnson; here, establishments like Small's Paradise, the Renaissance Theater, and the Apollo Theater were set up; and here could be found the headquarters of the most important Harlem newspaper, *New Amsterdam News*, and of the fighting Brotherhood of Sleeping Car Porters . . .

Harlem's history is long and involved, and Gilbert Osofsky's *Harlem: The Making of a Ghetto* is required reading for anyone wishing to delve further into the matter. It includes, for example, the story of that remarkable blossoming of talent during the 1920s, when the neighborhood became a laboratory of literary, musical, and theatrical experiment: the Harlem Renaissance, ushered in by black intellectuals like W. E. B. DuBois and Alain Locke, saw the emergence of talents like the poets Langston Hughes, Countee Cullen, and Claude McKay, the narrator Jean Toomer, and the anthropologist and writer Zora Neale Thurston; the explosion of jazz, the great orchestras, and celebrated soloists; a frenetic nightlife in the streets, in establishments that soon became legendary and in salons like that owned by A'Lelia Walker at 108–110 West 136th Street. It also brought with it considerable ambiguity: this was the neurotic, anxiety-ridden Jazz Age, and many white downtown intellectuals, aesthetes, and artists turned to Harlem in search of new "stimuli," a diverse elation, and an equivocal "primitivism" after the exhausted commercialization of Greenwich Village. The *maître à penser* of this generation of seekers, and the contradictory promoter of a Harlem at once real yet overly aesthetic and existential, was the critic and writer Carl Van Vechten. And the Cotton Club, the new Mecca of Harlem nightlife, remained rigidly segregated: Duke Ellington played there, but the bouncer wouldn't allow W. C. Handy (the "father of the blues") to take a seat inside and listen to him.

The Wall Street crash of 1929 snuffed out the lights of the Harlem Renaissance, too. An even more desperate poverty took root in Harlem's broad streets and refined buildings; with unemployment levels going through the roof, rents rising, and general living conditions worsening by the minute, the rage and anxiety of the people found expression in the riots of 1935 and, later, in 1943. As Langston Hughes wrote:

> What happens to a dream deferred?
>
> Does it dry up
> like a raisin in the sun?
> Or fester like a sore—
> And then run?

Does it stink like rotten meat?
Or crust and sugar over—
Like a syrupy sweet?

Maybe it just sags
like a heavy load.

Or does it explode?

New generations of writers—from Richard Wright to Ralph Ellison and James Baldwin—now narrated the story of the neighborhood; new groups went about their organization; new personalities came to dominate the headlines, like Malcolm X, whose Organization of Afro-American Unity set up an office in the Hotel Theresa on the corner of 7th Avenue and 125th Street, and who was later murdered during a rally at the Audubon Ballroom on West 166th Street between Broadway and St. Nicholas Avenue. And new revolts flared up on its streets during the decades that followed. A friend of mine who now teaches in Washington once told me the events of an afternoon in 1968: he (a white youth) had gone for a stroll around the ghetto to savor anew its splendid architecture when, all of a sudden, he felt a hand around his arm—an old black man took him quietly but firmly to the nearest subway station and told him: "Now you better get on the first train back downtown." The news of Martin Luther King's assassination had just been announced on the radio, and the ghetto was about to explode.

One morning, take a walk to the top of Mount Morris Park (the rocky hill that now goes under the name of Marcus Garvey Park), where a cast-iron bell tower stands. It is an octagonal structure whose small Doric columns support a platform and a small, covered observation post: this is the last fire observation tower remaining in Manhattan, a city that has always been particularly prone to devastating fires as a result of its old wooden buildings. The hill also became famous thanks to Henry Roth when he started writing again after his long writer's block following the publication of *Call It Sleep*: the first volume of his strange autobiography, *Mercy of a Rude Stream*, is in fact titled *A Star Shines Over Mt. Morris Park*. The location plays a key part in the volume and is described during the period when the Jews started populating the area after abandoning the Lower East Side, just before the arrival of the African Americans.

From the hilltop you get a great all-around view of the neighborhood's low horizon and its animated topography—the ridges, the long spacious avenues, and stately buildings. And most importantly you can see the stoops, those entry steps that so thoroughly characterize "old New York," and which here take on an appearance all their own: they are so high and imposing that they seem to anchor the phantom-ship buildings, with their masts and decks, poops and figureheads, to the sidewalk.

While descending the hill of Mount Morris Park in the direction of Lenox Avenue (aka Malcolm X Boulevard), the words of Claude McKay in his classic 1928 volume, *Home to Harlem*, may well come to mind: "Harlem! How terribly Ray could hate it sometimes. Its brutality, gang rowdyism, promiscuous thickness. Its hot desires. But, oh, the rich blood-red color of it! The warm accent of its composite voice, the fruitiness of its laughter, the trailing rhythm of its 'blues' and the improvised surprises of its jazz." A veritable riot of emotions difficult to resist when walking the streets of this historic ghetto, in the shadow of such extraordinary architecture, up and down hills where the island seems to rear up, spin upon itself, and then plunge back downward among the crowds of people walking at your side, standing on corners, or loafing about on entry steps.

All around, the past is never far away from the present. That church down there on the northwestern corner of West 131st Street and Lenox Avenue is called Ebenezer Gospel Tabernacle, but it was originally built in 1889 as a Unitarian church. And so did it remain until 1919, when it became the Congregation and Chebra Ukadisha B'nai Israel Mikalwarie, a place of worship for a tiny community of Orthodox Jews coming from Eastern Europe. Then, in 1942, it was sold to an African American congregation. Going northward, the broad sidewalks of the Boulevard are a constant reminder of the fact that Harlem was originally intended to be a city and a residential area, avoiding all the congestion that had marked the beginnings of downtown. Yet one cannot help but notice the heart-breaking degradation that afflicts so many of the blocks in the area: the blinded, boarded-up windows of the buildings, the patchy grass of dusty, brick-laden lots, the depressing sense of abandonment in the alleys and side streets. This is a Harlem whose history has been written in scratches and scars onto its streets and houses: the hardships and the tragic struggles to survive are there to be seen in the faces, gestures, attitudes, and words of its people. And that is what often makes taking a look around the area, almost out of curiosity, so difficult and unpleasant.

That Harlem, too, is a place of contrasts is undeniable: they can even be read in the place-names. For example, just a few blocks off from the corner of Malcolm X Boulevard and West 125th (one of the main streets of the neighborhood, the center for shops and offices, the heart of business and the ghetto economy), you will find Strivers' Row and Sugar Hill—both telling names.

Strivers' Row is a complex of residential buildings erected in 1890 by David H. King Jr., who entrusted the project to some of the most important architects of the time, including the ubiquitous Stanford White: refined-looking houses of a sophisticated design arranged in small blocks with (an unusual occurrence in Manhattan) alleys at the back. Originally built for the white Protestant middle classes, the houses were offered first to upwardly mobile middle-class immigrants and then to the black middle classes. They were inhabited by famous musicians, lawyers, architects, doctors, and professional people of all kinds (and also by Harry Wills, the boxer whose ambition to fight for the world heavyweight title in the 1920s was thwarted by the resistance of organizers fearing the advent of another Jack Johnson, the black fighter who held the title uninterruptedly from 1908 to 1925).

Sugar Hill, conversely, is the glorified ideal of well-heeled Harlem. At the beginning of the 1800s the grand estates of Alexander Hamilton ("The Grange") and Samuel Bradhurst ("Pinehurst"), names of lasting importance in the history of the city and the nation, were located here. Although the area then fell in line with the overall transformation in the neighborhood, it nonetheless retained an air of sophistication and class. The houses and churches are ample evidence of this. Take the incredibly kitsch Our Lady of Lourdes on West 142nd Street, which incorporates elements belonging to three different nineteenth-century buildings: the facade and eastern wing come from the National Academy of Design; the stone pedestals flanking the main staircase are from the "Marble Palace," the immense department store designed by A. T. Stewart; and the apse was taken from the eastern side of St. Patrick's Cathedral. In the area you will also find the City College of New York (the university for less well-off students), the castle of James A. Bailey (the celebrated entrepreneur who, together with James A. Barnum, redefined the role of the circus as a specific form of mass entertainment in the nineteenth century), and Hamilton Terrace (widely considered one of the most beautiful streets in New York: a riotous orgy of stone and brick in the most glorious range of shapes and colors, carvings and sculptures, and myriad forms of disparate ornamentation).

Hordes of people bustle all about you, and once again it feels like you are back in a village in the metropolis. Perhaps you are stuck on the corner, unsure of where to go next. You might pop along to the legendary Apollo Theater where staff invite you to step inside the foyer and take a look at photographs, program bills, and posters to get an idea of the immense contribution made to the black performing arts of both yesteryear and today. Or you could head for the Schomburg Center for Research in Black Culture, on Malcolm X Boulevard and West 135th Street, to look for material related to the history of the ghetto and the Harlem Renaissance. Or walk down toward the Studio Museum on West 125th

Street and Malcolm X Boulevard to see an exhibition by an African American artist. There again, you might want to seek out Minton's Playhouse on the ground floor of the Cecil Hotel, on West 118th Street, where Charlie Parker and Thelonious Monk used to play. Or even go along to the neo-Gothic Abyssinian Baptist Church at 136–142 West 138th Street, and listen to some excellent gospel music on a Sunday morning. But, if the truth were known, you'd give your right arm at this present moment to see Pig Foot Mary still alive, wheeling her barrow of steaming pig's feet along the street . . .

So, there you have it: the Lower East Side, Greenwich Village, Harlem, Spanish Harlem. If you now pick up a map and draw a circle around these areas, you will feel that it is *they*—and not, arguably, Fifth Avenue or Times Square or even Central Park—that make Manhattan what it is: the metropolis par excellence and the symbol of modernity, vertical and horizontal gigantism, chaos and anonymity, frenzy and change. Places whose startling contradictions—be they locked away neatly in the past or achingly alive in the present—live side by side with this peculiarly intimate dimension, with this astonishing community feeling.

. . . the pasteles, tortelloni made from potatoes, green bananas, plantains, and yautía roots (all peeled and grated finely), milk, oil and salt, and stuffed with diced pork meat, smoked ham, currants, alcaparrado, and peas, and wrapped in plantain leaves and left to simmer in a covered saucepan for three quarters of an hour, turning from time to time.

This recipe for pasteles sneaks its way into my notebook beside a recipe I had copied down for cholent—*a traditional Jewish dish that resembles a kind of stew with peas, potatoes, barley, and onions, all thickened up with a sprinkling of flour, seasoned with pepper and paprika, and left in a heated place for a whole night. (In the immigrant Lower East Side, women used to prepare* cholent *in a saucepan, then take it along to the baker's, who would keep it in his oven overnight for ten cents, each saucepan carefully distinguished one from the other by the addition of colored ribbon. A few days ago, Hasia Diner, a professor at New York University, told me of her research into the culinary habits of immigrants and how these, too, are traversed by the processes of Americanization.)*

Anyway, the pasteles are proving to be a hit, and from the moment Maria puts the dish on the table it's been nonstop coming and going in the Vejigante Café. Friends, acquaintances, friends of friends, and people I'd met on the street an hour or so ago with Papoleto all appear as if by magic. They taste the pasteles and then hang around. Mario and Maria take a couple of small folding tables from the back and set them up in the street in front of the café, near the old men playing dominoes, a group of youngsters listening to a Jimmy Cliff cassette on the stereo, and the women leaning out of windows. Papoleto and I buy a few cans of beer, line them up on the small tables, and place what remains of the pasteles in front of them. As we do so, an improvised local street party thunders into life between outbursts of laughter, the singing of songs, and yells and calls from one side of the street to the other. The crazy colored masks hanging in the window of the Vejigante gaze down on us benevolently, and Spanish Harlem, El Barrio, smiles all about us on an evening that is now a red lake.

I'll hang on for a while here with Papoleto and the others, shaking hands and chatting, drinking beer and tasting the pasteles and other sweetmeats that people dropping in have brought over. Then, a little later on, when perhaps they'll be playing the sweet-sad notes of the calypso (that melancholy entwined with happiness), Papoleto will accompany me down to the bus stop where I'll wait for the number 1, direction downtown. And then I'll gallop off down the slender, winding body of Manhattan, up and down her hills, toward East 4th Street and Loisaida Avenue, toward what here is mi casa.

From one village to another.

5

Museums

*T*he storm never quite seems to break, and it's unsettling. I fiddle about with the papers and books on my desk, try to get some reading done while sitting on the couch, and peer down into the street from my fifth-floor window: "a New York state of mind," as Billy Joel would say. I finally decide to go up onto the roof and watch the battle being waged between the wind and a mass of black clouds (how fascinating, these New York roofs, early in the morning or late in the evening or, quite simply, at moments like this, when the city skyline takes on the semblance of a storm-tossed sailing ship!).

But even a visit to the roof on an afternoon like this leaves me disgruntled, and after ten minutes of stiff winds and the odd raindrop I decide to take to the street and head uptown. Maybe I'll take a look to see how the trees in Central Park are coping with all these violent gusts . . . I walk along Avenue C and East 6th Street toward Astor Place, and from here, with the black storm clouds gathering overhead, I take Line 6 of the subway and get off at 59th Street. Resisting the temptation to get lost for an hour or two in the enormous F.A.O. Schwartz toy store, I head off toward the park.

By now the wind is furious, bending the trees backward and sending whirlwinds of leaves into the air. A sight to behold. I stroll along the broad sidewalk, uncertain if I should go straight or enter the park, when suddenly, all around me, as if by magic, the solemn pachyderms of culture set off on their solemn parade: I am walking along Museum Mile, a sequence of museums that has turned this stretch of road into one of the jewels of New York. Under a darkening sky, I watch them trudge along down or just behind Fifth Avenue: the Frick Collection, the Metropolitan Museum of Art, the Whitney Museum, the Guggenheim Museum, the National Academy of Design, the Cooper-Hewitt Museum, the Jewish Museum, the International Center of Photography . . . Well aware of their personal magnificence, of their role in the life and public image of the city, the museums seem to possess a sternness bordering on the haughty. For, it is well known, New York is a city of museums: together with the banks, they are its real cathedrals, its true places of worship.

At long last the much-coveted storm breaks. Forced to seek shelter, I run to the low grey building with a rectangular garden on Fifth Avenue, on the corner with East 70th Street: the Frick Collection. I must say right away that I have no particular liking for Mr. Frick, regardless of the number of masterpieces he managed to cram his house with. Henry Clay Frick lived from 1849 to 1919, and his name languishes in my memory as the manager who, acting on behalf of the steel magnate Andrew Carnegie, unleashed all manner of repression against the workers in Homestead, Pennsylvania, in 1892. The end result was seven people dead, a union in ruins, and a 20 percent drop in salary. Carnegie, who was traveling in Europe at the time, sent a telegram: "Congratulate all around. Life worth living again. Beautiful Italy . . ." Feel free, of course, to make up your own mind on the matter.

Frick undoubtedly had no cash flow problems when it came to buying up the masterpieces of world art. Among his purchases: Sir Thomas More by Holbein the Younger, The Harbour of Dieppe by Turner, Lady Meux by Whistler, then works by Titian, Constable, Hals, Rembrandt, Vermeer, Hogarth, Bellini, Gainsborough, Boucher, El Greco, and Fragonard; not to mention enamels from Limoges, antique furniture, Oriental carpets, bookcases, vases, porcelain, crystal . . . all distributed higgledy-piggledy about the house. A house that you will, of course, visit: the dining room, the library, the West Gallery, the Oval Room, the East Gallery, the music room, the fireplaces, writing desks, and divans, glass windows facing the south garden and another overlooking Fifth Avenue and Central Park, and then the "Colonnade Garden Court" . . . Which brings me to the small central cloister: a columned rectangle featuring dense clusters of plants, a huge skylight, pure white statues by Rodin lent by the Thyssen-Bornemisza Collection in Madrid (one in particular struck me with its calm sensuality—The Dream), and, on descending a few steps, an oblong pool whose central jet of water cascades onto two concentric, concave dishes, and smaller jets of water at opposite ends that gush from the yawning mouths of two bronze frogs. A delightful gurgling sound to listen to while sitting on one of the stone seats, with Mr. Frick's favorite organ music echoing about the cloister: Irish airs, Fauré, Saint-Saëns, Handel, Wagner . . .

I imagine you have seen (or will see) the museums of New York.

You will have wondered at (or will wonder at) the Museum of Modern Art, the much celebrated MoMa of Monet's *Nymphs*, Van Gogh's *Starry Night*, Andy Warhol's *Marilyn*, Georgia O'Keefe's drawings, and the photographs of Dorothea Lange and Alfred Stieglitz, and perhaps you will have had (or will have) your photograph taken in the sculpture garden, between a Giacometti and a Brancusi. And you will have ascended (or will ascend) the long spiral staircase designed by Frank Lloyd Wright for the Guggenheim Museum, savoring Chagall's *Paris Through the Window*, a *Nude* by Modigliani, and Manet's *Before the Mirror*. You will have gotten lost (or will get lost) in the bewildering labyrinth of rooms in the Metropolitan Museum, perhaps while tracking down the splendid works of Cézanne, Picasso's *Gertrude Stein*, Rembrandt's *Self-Portrait*, and Vermeer's *Young Woman with a Water Pitcher*; or while marveling at the limpid linearity of the Temple of Dendur, commissioned by Caesar Augustus; or while pausing for thought in the newly erected Ming garden in Astor Court. And, inside the inverted grey pyramid structure of the Whitney Museum of American Art, you will have seen (or will see) the charming *Circus* by Alexander Calder, the luminous solitudes of Edward Hopper, the American flags by Jasper Johns, the urban panoramas of Louis Lozowick, the glowing vitality of *Brooklyn Bridge* of Joseph Stella . . .

You will also have been (or will also go) to the Morgan Library, the Frick Collection, the Cooper-Hewitt Museum, the International Center of Photography, the Museum of the American Indian, and the American Museum of Natural History. And in your walking to and fro, you will have negotiated (or will do so) another of New York's inevitable maps.

I have done it, too, and will continue to do so, albeit in a haphazard fashion characterized by long absences and periods of indifference. It is a question of priorities, really: I think the first things we should look for in a city are the places it contains, the feel of it, the different views, the streets, and the people, and since these things are subject to continual change, they must be appreciated anew again and again. Museums are (almost) invariably there, rather like the masterpieces they house, and— as Walter Benjamin taught us—by now we know those masterpieces almost by heart due to an endless series of reproductions (and anyway, hasn't it all become so difficult to observe them with the necessary calm when coping with throngs of people to the left, right, and center?).

Yes, call me irreverent. But the problem here really is that of those "mythical" places in a metropolis, from which you "can't stay away," because they are endowed with a "must-see" status—they are so deeply identified with the metropolis that the act of *not seeing them* is tantamount to confessing that you *haven't actually been there*. And so a visit to the MoMa is rather like sending a postcard back home: tangible proof. Nothing wrong in that, of course. But New York also possesses a host of smaller jewels that are no less symbolic than the MoMa or the Met. They are well worth an attentive visit, also because, in contrast to those "pachyderms of culture" with all their masterpieces hanging on the walls or hidden away in glass cabinets, these other jewels are often organized in such a way as to truly engage the visitor, and turn him or her into the beneficiary of what is not only *exhibited* but literally *staged*.

So if late one morning you find yourself in front of the Plaza Hotel and cross Central Park in a diagonal line until you come to Strawberry Fields (opposite the Dakota Houses where John Lennon was gunned down), it would pay you to exit the park right here and walk four blocks north. Just before you reach the majestic American Museum of Natural History, you will come across a squat parallelepiped with the usual Doric columns and capital above the entrance. Here is situated the New-York Historical Society, with access at number 2 West 77th Street (I have already mentioned it in relation to Seneca Village, but the time has come to say more).

The society was set up in 1804. Its archives contain a magnificent photo taken from the roof of the Dakota Houses in a northward direction in 1881, showing a wide expanse of uncultivated lands, huts, excavations, and paths; on the left, an iron support belonging to one of the Elevated lines; on the right, the western boundary of the park; and in the middle, the lofty tenement of the American Museum of Natural History, which, over the years, would grow until it reached the size of a real castle. The building that would eventually house the society did not yet exist in 1881, but the society was already active. Today it is the oldest museum in the city and contains some of America's most valuable archives.

The society makes available to the public a wealth of material that includes something on the order of 650,000 volumes and pamphlets, 500,000 photographs from the mid-1800s to the present day, 10,000 different newspaper titles, 15,000 maps, innumerable musical scores, 750,000 advertising announcements from different periods, thousands of restaurant menus, an enviable archive of documents relating to slavery and the abolition movement, collections of paintings, drawings, and sculptures ranging from colonial times to the present day, the original watercolors of John James Audubon, an exhaustive collection of Tiffany lamps, the sketches and projects of New York's most famous architects, precious naval and military collections, letters written by Abraham Lincoln and other American presidents, and the documents, diaries, and correspondence of anonymous citizens, fugitive slaves, frontline Civil War soldiers, nurses, housewives . . .

I remember working long hours in the society rooms years ago, cautiously flicking through the pages of old magazines and watching the mosaic of a city gradually assemble before my very eyes. Because it is New York itself, of course, that stands at the center of the archives and the collections, the guidebooks and the "Hudson River Weekends," the expositions of paintings or the performances of the Actors Company Theater, and in particular the exhibitions. Among the subjects are Seneca Village (precisely), the evolution of Times Square (Signs and Wonders: The Spectacular Lights of Times Square), and the centenary celebration of the birth of Greater New York in 1898, when the city spread its wings beyond its original Manhattan island confines to encompass other boroughs.

Now, on leaving the New-York Historical Society, walk back diagonally across the park and exit on Fifth Avenue, near the area where Manhattan opulence and refinement crosses swords with Harlem and Spanish Harlem (further metropolitan contradictions). Almost in front of you, between 103rd Street and 104th Street, is an enormous white building with a staircase that houses the Museum of the City of New York, founded in 1923. This, too, is a must. Or at the very least, it is heartily recommended.

The society and the museum dialogue with one another from opposite sides of the park. In some ways they may even be thought to overlap (some years ago a merger was hinted at, but nothing came of it), or, rather, slot perfectly one into the other: the society with its research center, and the museum with its more didactic-cum-spectacular approach. Years ago I also worked for a long time in the museum, marveling over the photographs of Jacob Riis, and I remember that whenever I arrived in the morning, there were always hordes of schoolchildren milling about the rooms, gazing starry-eyed at the expertly displayed objects and pondering over the questions and exercises that had been prepared especially for a public of children and adolescents: the city's history was being brought home with an uncharacteristic verve and relevance.

Again, the statistics speak volumes: more than a million and a half objects consisting of paintings, prints, photographs, theatrical costumes, garments from the 1700s and 1800s, toys, manuscripts, rare books, works of art, sculptures, dolls' houses, and other things besides. Or, to be more precise: paintings by American artists like Ralph Blakelock, Asher Durand, Reginald Marsh, and Franz Kline; photographs by Riis, Berenice Abbott, and Carl Van Vechten; lithographs by Currier and Ives; portraits of famous Americans from the last three hundred years; an incredible collection of theatrical materials (scores, bills, stage directions, caricatures, scene designs, and reviews); furniture, musical instruments, silverware, clocks, ceramics, copper and pewter vases, and porcelain; fire engines; naval and military collections. And there are some rare treats, too, like the first canvas painting to make its appearance in Nieuw Amsterdam (the *Portrait of Katrina van Cortlandt* by van Mierevelt, circa 1630), the first terra-cotta model of the Statue of Liberty prepared by Frédéric-Auguste Bartholdi, the studies for the *murales* of Ben Shahn and Reginald Marsh, or the Stettheimer Doll House, a 1920s piece that comes complete with a miniature art gallery featuring the paintings and sculptures of the main avant-garde artists working in New York at the time . . .

Here, too, however, it is the exhibitions that take pride of place. Subjects have included the World's Fair of 1939, the city's homeless, Greenwich Village between 1830 and 1930, the ethnic community centers, Duke Ellington, African Americans in Manhattan, the social photography of Jacob Riis and five other contemporary photographers (among them Margaret Morton, mentioned earlier in connection with the tunnel people), and the Irish in New York. Talks have been organized on subjects like the relationship between skyscraper construction and land rent, or the circus tradition in New York, not to mention the guided visits to Hispanic East Harlem and Chelsea. The museum's program is more a kind of brightly colored kaleidoscope of projects that are all centered on the need to offer a dynamic approach to the metropolis, and it contrasts markedly with the notions of spectator passivity that seem to underlie the ruling ethos in museums. I greatly regret missing out on one particular evening called "Tellabration: New York's Night of Storytelling," when artists and writers came along to "tell" their very own New York: an intriguing blend of writing, words, and urban folklore that must surely have succeeded in communicating a different, three-dimensional vision of Manhattan, all too often flattened in static images.

I did not, however, miss out on Taíno: Pre-Columbian Art and Culture from the Caribbean, an exhibition organized by the Museo del Barrio in the grand neoclassical building (originally an orphanage, if I am not mistaken) that stands to the side of the Museum of the City of New York at 1230 Fifth Avenue—a highly stimulating exhibition that I think was the first to document the Caribbean roots of a large section of the metropolis in such a thorough and winning manner. ("Taíno" was the name of the original inhabitants of "Borinquen," or Puerto Rico; and Barrio, "city," is now the name given to that area of Harlem inhabited by people mostly of Caribbean origins.)

I was assisted in my visit by two exceptional companions: the painter and muralist Maria Dominguez (who at the time was a member of the museum staff) and the performing poet Jésus Papoleto Melendez, two friends who (together with Pedro Pietri and other Nuyorican poets) have been indispensable to my understanding many things about Puerto Rican New York over the years. They took me around the exhibition rooms dedicated to the clothes, ornaments, and appurtenances (like the exquisite *duhos*, wooden thrones carved—usually by women—in the shape of animals) of the *caciques*, or Caribbean tribe chiefs; or the room dedicated to the sacred ceremony of the *cohoba*, a hallucinogenic substance that played a central role in religious rituals whose participants imagined they could get into contact with an "other" universe, parallel and upside down (this was one of the effects of taking *cohoba*). I was then taken to the rooms dedicated to Taíno cosmology, with its mysterious *trigonolitos*, or three pointed objects in worked stone that continue to puzzle experts even today: are they mountains, volcanoes, breasts, phalluses, or cassava shoots? The Taínos called them *zemi*, spirits and otherworldly presences possessed of supernatural powers. Among the exhibits is a magnificent example, a colorful riot of small pearls mounted in stone, on loan from the Museo Preistorico ed Etnografico Pigorini in Rome. At the end of my visit I was accompanied to the rooms dealing with the ordinary daily life of the Taínos: their houses, their fabrics, their food (with the omnipresent cassava), the game of football played in the *batey* (a paved courtyard surrounded by statues representing divinities) often during the course of the *areytos* (huge family or tribal gatherings consisting of dances, songs, and celebrations and, once again, the reciprocal telling of stories and experiences).

It is an exhibition of extremely rare objects (some displayed for the very first time), splendid photographs and videos recounting the stories of the Puerto Rican elderly, topped off by a kind of laboratory room built expressly for children. In this room (Maria entertained me at length on this) a number of museum items had been reproduced as a pretext for a series of manual and intellectual activities, as a cue for the overturning of customary perspectives, the stimulation of curiosity, and the asking and answering of questions; judging from the appearance of the room at the end of the day, I would say that the children reacted with great enthusiasm to this new way of experiencing museums and their objects!

I understand that this exhibition is a point of arrival and departure for the Museo del Barrio. It was founded by some parents, artists, and teachers of Spanish Harlem in 1969, and for some time was housed in a school, then in a series of other smaller spaces and shops along different streets, and finally, in 1977, it ended up in this magnificent building—a kind of outpost (within the glimmer and glitz of wealthy Manhattan) of the *barrio latino* that stretches out feverishly behind, just beyond the murky tunnel beneath the Park Avenue Elevated. And, in its present location, it became one of the founding members of the Museum Mile Association, featuring a collection of eight thousand objects of Caribbean origin and courses of professional formation for teachers and cultural operators—and a very special attention to the world of adolescents.

So, there you are, right in front of the Museo, uncertain as to your next step. Well, you could always head south for a couple hundred yards and make a visit to the Jewish Museum at 1109 Fifth Avenue; alternatively, you could set off northward in the direction of nearby Harlem to seek out another cornerstone of multiethnic Manhattan—the Schomburg Center for Research in Black Culture at 515 Malcolm X Boulevard. But if you have the time, and don't mind the idea of cutting across the city overland from north to south, might I suggest you take the number 1 bus and get off on Broome Street: from there, walk eastward until you get to Orchard Street.

What we have here is a totally different ball game. The majestic pomp of Fifth Avenue and the greenery of Central Park are just a distant memory among these narrow streets and hoary dilapidated buildings; the crowds milling around have nothing of the museum-visiting tourists about them; poverty and degradation are there to be seen and touched. Walking about, you can hear or read the myriad languages of America. You are bang in the middle of the Lower East Side, the historical heartland of multiethnic Manhattan. In a certain sense, you have traced your way back to the very roots of the city. Near here are the two oldest synagogues in Manhattan—the Congregation Chasam Sopher on Clinton Street and the Congregation Anshei Slonim on Norfolk Street (which has been renovated after years of complete neglect and is now the multipurpose Angelo Orensanz Foundation cultural center). And there is also a small museum whose express intent is to safeguard the city's origins: the Lower East Side Tenement Museum.

When you reach 90 Orchard Street, on the corner with Broome Street, stop off at the bookshop (which also houses the museum) and take a peek at the various objects and volumes, or pick up one of the catalogs and choose from among the many weekend activities that have been organized, or sign up for one of the guided visits to the old tenement that is currently being restored just a few yards to the north on the opposite side of the road at number 97. It was right here, in this five-story house, that the adventure of the Tenement Museum began: in the mid-1980s Ruth Abrams, an experienced social worker who was already working on the idea of opening up a museum about immigration, came across this building (which had been boarded up and left to its own derelict devices since 1935). She rented one of the shops on the raised level, and it was here that the seeds of the future museum were sown: materials were collected, social workers and historians were invited to lend a hand, and work was begun on the renovation of the first apartments.

As more was learned about the history of the building, so the museum housed within its confines developed. Slowly yet surely, everyday objects were uncovered and more things came to light concerning successive waves of immigrant families and names from the distant past. Between 1865, when the tenement was actually built (typical of the area, a three-room apartment featuring one room in the front, one in the middle, dark

and stuffy, and one overlooking the small closed courtyard at the back—
a *railroad apartment*, as this kind of architectural solution used to be
called), and 1935, when lodgers were evicted and entrances to the building were boarded up, something in the order of ten thousand immigrants
from twenty different countries spent some time in it. The building at 97
Orchard Street is a metaphor for the United States: or, rather, for
America.

Time passed, and three apartments were renovated and named after
the Gumpertz, Baldizzi, and Rogashevsky families (a fourth would later be
"assigned" to the Confino family). Crossing the threshold of these apartments is an experience akin to passing through the looking glass: you are
taken back in time, you move within a past dating back more than a century, and you bring back to the present something of its history and stories. I remember working here, too, on some beautiful October mornings
almost fifteen years ago: all around me plumbers, carpenters, bricklayers,
and architects set to work while the neighborhood rose from its slumber
and paraded in front of the large windows of the small office. I visited the
rooms on the top floors, which had remained virtually unchanged since
the building had been boarded up in 1935, and I can still recall the overpowering impression it made on me: the sense of stupor and mystery—of
anxiety even—I experienced on treading the creaking floorboards and
brushing against the old peeling wallpapers, on seeing the washtub in the
darkness of the middle room and on looking down through opaque windows onto the streets below . . . all experiences I had read in novels or seen
in the yellowing photographs of the past, but which now became real and
tangible, all around me.

And now it is your turn. Although work on the building proceeds slowly, 97 Orchard Street has achieved National Historical Landmark status
and is today more lively and meaningful than the Museum of Immigration
on Ellis Island (the tiny island adjacent to New York where immigrants
were detained in quarantine). Yet the Tenement Museum is more than just
a museum, bookshop, and renovated building: it organizes conferences
and slide projections, guided visits to the neighborhood, theatrical shows
staging family stories, and photographic exhibitions (particularly memorable was the exhibition dealing with the works of the 1930s photographer Arnold Eagle). And then there is the *Tenement Times*, an excellent
newsletter whose collection of memories, stories, recipes, photographs,
and glimpses of private lives and experiences does much to restore the
atmosphere of the immigrants' Lower East Side—yet another way of
approaching history.

Once you leave the Tenement Museum, you need only to go down
Orchard Street until you come to Canal Street. Walk the length of it

beyond the Bowery, then take a left down Mulberry Street where you will find another precious little museum (once a school) housed inside a stately building on the corner of Mulberry and Bayard Streets. The scenario has changed again: a hundred years ago this was the heart of Little Italy and one of the most run-down—albeit vital—areas of the city, and now it has become part of a Chinatown whose territorial expansion shows no sign of slowing down. Between the 1970s and 1980s, relations between Little Italy and Chinatown became more strained, and the flow of capital from Hong Kong and Taiwan (thought to be on the verge of being returned to China) in the decade that followed led to a sharp rise in crime in the area. With its narrow, cluttered streets, its sidewalks dotted with the odd-looking vegetables and wriggling fish of local stores, the comings and goings of the locals and their rapid-fire chitchat, the Chinese ice-cream seller, the shop selling tea and fortune cookies, and one of my favorite restaurants (the Bo-Ky), Chinatown lays a special claim on my Manhattan heart. It is one of the first places I go to on arriving in New York, and one of the first places I take people to when they come and visit me in the city. And I feel at home when I ascend the staircase of the immense building located at 70 Mulberry Street and push open the glass door that opens out onto the few rooms of the Museum of Chinese in the Americas.

The museum took its present name just a few years ago. Earlier on it went by the name of the Chinatown History Museum, and before that, at the time of its creation in the early 1980s, the New York Chinatown History Project. The two men behind the original project, Charlie Lai and John Kuo Wei Tchen, knew the streets of Chinatown like the backs of their hands: they rummaged around the basements and lofts and sifted through the back rooms of shops and the memories of the elderly in order to compose anew the identity of a group that had survived decades of total isolation. Indeed, in 1882, the Chinese Exclusion Act (renewed again and again during the years that followed, and made even more restrictive) had effectively put an end to the further importation of Chinese workers. Immigrants who had already been living in the country for years could no longer be joined by their wives and fiancées, which originated the so-called bachelor society, lonely men whose virtual status as hostages on American soil only ended in 1943, when the vicious Exclusion Act was repealed to allow American soldiers of Chinese origin to bring the wives or fiancées they had married or met on the battlefield into the country. The psychological, social, and cultural mess resulting from this long period of isolation is something of a festering wound in the Chinatown of today, and the New York Chinatown History Project was precisely the means whereby the silence and oblivion of those years was broken.

Today, the archives of the museum (two small rooms with a skeleton staff that worryingly risks further streamlining as a result of cuts on the part of a scroogelike city administration) contain a precious range of materials which have often been put together in decidedly adventurous fashion: papers, letters, documents, the daily knickknacks of the elderly "bachelors," an entire collection of material pertaining to a Cantonese opera company (costumes, stage directions, scripts, musical instruments, and scene designs), the only existing copies of Sino-American newspapers published in the eighteenth and nineteenth centuries, guides and manuals prepared expressly for those immigrants who sought to get around the Chinese Exclusion Act . . . And there is more: 3,500 photographs, three hundred hours of recorded interviews, twelve hours of documentary material on video and film, a library of more than two thousand volumes, essays, articles, pamphlets, an astonishing collection of materials and artifacts, and a delightful newsletter, the *Bu Gao Ban*, which provides up-to-date information on museum activities. A genuine gold mine for scholars and, more importantly (this has been the real scope of the museum since its beginnings), for a community in search of itself and its history.

The Museum of Chinese in the Americas has developed its research largely by means of exhibitions, which are its main strength (and, simultaneously, the area most susceptible to budget cuts). Hence Eight Pound Livelihood told the story of Chinese washermen in America, Chinese Women of America rescued the virtually unknown role of women before and after the Chinese Exclusion Act from the silence of history, and Salvaging New York Chinatown: Preserving a Heritage was dedicated to reconstructing life in the neighborhood more than fifty years ago; Both Sides of the Clothes blew the lid off the largely feminine world of the clothing industry laboratories after the Second World War, Remembering New York Chinatown summarized the first ten years of the museum's existence, and Sites of Chinatown explored the map of Chinatown locations as seen through the eyes of creative local artists. The Where Is Home? Chinese in the Americas exhibition featured two hundred daily objects (not the usual porcelain stereotypes but, for example, the eight-pound irons traditionally used in laundries) in an effort to answer the question that for all immigrants remains the most crucial, and the most cruel.

The charm of the museum (its daily bid to survive in the face of so many obstacles) lies precisely in this close tie with the community of which it is an expression, in the constant attention it pays to the reactions (criticisms, requests for changes, suggestions) of a public that first and foremost (but not only) consists of Chinatown inhabitants themselves, and in this profoundly fascinating "dialogic" way of running a museum and organizing exhibitions. In other words, it is a continual work in progress that comes into being, develops, "breathes" and is transformed, poses questions and asks questions of itself, all while managing to avoid the presumption or paternalism that at times characterizes the behavior of researchers and collectors.

The notion of a "dialogic museum" informs the most interesting activities of many of these "other" museums and of several local historians in New York. Take, for example, Arthur Tobier, a freelance writer who has worked on several projects connected to the Museo del Barrio. For about the last twenty-five years he has devoted his efforts to the recording of "oral histories," which he then uses to prepare his own exhibitions, valuable pieces in an "ongoing history of New York City." And this idea of a "shared authority" (from the title of a book by historian Michael Frisch, which has contributed so much to the elaboration of this notion) transforms the museum's exhibitions into small and intense masterpieces that are of considerable interest even to those who are not members of the Chinatown community, but wish to understand its complex and largely ignored history. In other words, it is an authority shared by the community and researchers, founded on the passion for a dialectical relationship with all those (individuals, groups, and classes) who, day after day, have anonymously contributed and continue to contribute to their own history and, by default, to the history of the city itself.

By now, having left the Museum of Chinese in the Americas, and standing on the corner of Mulberry Street and Bayard Street, while the sun sets on the arabesques of fire escapes patterned on the house facades, you are probably quite worn out. A whole day spent traipsing up and down the island from one "alternative" museum to another takes its toll. It is time to head back home for a jasmine or mint tea, or whatever takes your fancy. Although you might consider stopping off along the way and, together with your tea, savoring a slice of cheesecake or carrot cake. Seeing as you are downtown, you could take a stab at the Café Orlin, overlooking St. Mark's Place and almost on the corner of Second Avenue: situated a few steps down from the street, the lovely atmosphere of this century-old café is an invitation in itself to sit down, have a chat or a read, and do some people watching. After all, even a place like this is a museum sui generis: a place where you can breathe in Manhattan and absorb the history and life of New York.

The light is fading now beneath a curtain of rain and cloud. I walk about the rooms of Frick's house seething with almost timorous visitors; I admire the splendid pictures of the collection and stand a long time in front of Rodin's

Dream. *Then I lapse into a state of befuddlement as nearly always happens to me after being bombarded by museum works, and walk down the steps of the rectangular cloister in search of respite. I find a seat and listen to the burbling of water in the fountain, the thunder clapping its way across the skylight, the organ music.*

Just as Wagner's march from Tannhäuser *gets under way, right there in the muffled quiet of Mr. Frick's cloister, with all its absorbed visitors and stock-still custodians, an amusing thing happens. With a wheeze, one of the bronze frogs blowing lovely soft jets of water suddenly starts spitting out a fierce gush in the direction of the central fountain where, up to now, the water had been dripping so lightly from one dish to the other. At a stroke, the delicate equilibrium is broken. The fountain dishes rudely overflow, and the jet of water ricochets to splash those who had been sitting around in contemplative silence. Exclamations, bursts of laughter, a general springing to feet follow, and any feelings of awe or stupor that Mr. Frick's masterpieces and lavishly furnished rooms may have helped to foster are dispersed. Something must have happened to the mechanism regulating the emission of water, and for a couple of minutes the custodians—now deprived of their uniformed aplomb—are at a loss as to what to do. At first embarrassed, then amused, they squint this way and that from behind the cloister columns: the atmosphere of healthy irreverence turns the scene into something right out of Mark Twain or Charlie Chaplin.*

In the meantime, the storm is letting up. I take one last look at the seditious frog, unruffled as he splashes the water about, and head toward the exit tittering. Outside, the pachyderms of culture seem to have lost their air of solemnity and arrogance, and now resemble something akin to a row of drenched little chicks.

6

Words

I wonder what will become of 114 Liberty Street. The building is deeply scarred and all boarded up, and as you pass in front of it along a narrow footwalk, you can see the ghastly expanse of Ground Zero on the other side. I wonder what will become of the whole area. I know of the many projects being prepared (and of the many polemics already accompanying them). And I have just bought a most interesting book, edited by Michael Sorkin and Sharon Zukin, by the title of After the World Trade Center: Rethinking New York City (2002), which offers very stimulating insights. But I don't want to go into all this—I feel that, after 9/11, too many words have accompanied too many images, and perhaps the best way of saying something (in a city where so much is spoken and said and written and shown) is by being silent.

Instead, I try to recall what the building was like the last time I came here to look for it. An early-twentieth-century building, squeezed in between a coffee shop and a "Pronto Pizza—We Deliver," with large semicircular windows on the second and third floors, and rows of square windows on the floors above (very likely it started off as a clothing industry factory). I remember that, in the lobby, the superintendent watched me suspiciously as I hurriedly glimpsed at the panel listing the names of some companies, a couple of medical studios, the odd foreign name . . .

Yet, some sixty years before this building was constructed (and this is the reason behind my interest in the site, even today after its tragic transformation), 114 Liberty Street was the address of Mary Cecilia Rogers, the unwitting protagonist of one of the most famous and disturbing acts of violence of the period (another version has Mary Cecilia living not far from here, at 126 Nassau Street, and this confounds still further one's attempts to make headway through the labyrinth of New York places: I leave you to make up your own mind on that). In the "small town" of the time, Mary Cecilia was also known as the "Beautiful Seegar Seller," because she used to work in John Anderson's tobacco shop at 319 Broadway, a gathering place for New York's finest, and patronized (whether for the excellence of its cigars or the beauty of the girl is a moot

73

point) by hordes of latter-day yuppies and by celebrities like Washington Irving.

On 25 July 1841, the girl walked out of the house and, in the best metropolitan mystery tradition, never came back. A few days later, her bloated corpse was found floating on the water at the entrance to a cavern on Hoboken Beach, on the banks of the Hudson and close to the leisure and picnic spot known as the Elysian Fields. This was a popular weekend attraction for many New Yorkers, including well-known personages such as the politician Martin Van Buren, the poet William Cullen Bryant, and the man himself—Washington Irving. (Just a few yards away was the summer residence of the famed fur merchant and Manhattan property owner, John Jacob Astor: a square in his name and beaver drawings on the subway station walls below are a continuing reminder of his presence today.)

The mystery surrounding the death of Mary Cecilia Rogers was to remain unsolved. Her name was, however, linked to that of another key figure of the "small town": Madame Restell, the "scandalous abortionist" who had already been attracting the flak of the self-righteous for her activities at the time (as well as arousing their envy for the stately house she had had built on Fifth Avenue). An interesting chapter, indeed, in the annals of midcentury social history, and even if rumors that the girl had died at the hands of Restell following an operation were never confirmed, alternative hypotheses fell on barren ground. After a few months, the case was reassessed in singularly unusual fashion in the pages of Snowden's Ladies' Companion: "The Mystery of Marie Roget," by Edgar Allan Poe. Although the episode, scenes, and protagonists had been transferred from New York to Paris, Poe's text contained an explicit subtext that made reference to the "Beautiful Seegar Seller," complete with quotations from American newspaper articles that had reported the case.

I leave 114 Liberty Street and the open wound of Ground Zero and walk along Broadway in the direction of the Bobst Library on Washington Square South. Poe's tale lingers in my mind. His decision to carry out a kind of "geographical dislocation" has always fascinated me: his sticking to literary conventions that imposed European scenarios while talking about New York and, at the same time, his decision to disseminate the text with anything that might prove helpful for the American reader to understand that de te fabula narratur—"the story is about you." In "The Mystery of Marie Roget," the trick is openly declared from the beginning, more so than in Poe's other two great metropolitan tales, "The Man of the Crowd" (1840, set in London) and "The Murders in the Rue Morgue" (1841, set in Paris). Yet traces are to be found in these tales, too, especially in the latter, where the babel of languages (which plays such a decisive role in the plot) leads the reader back to a reality that is more New York than Paris.

I then turn into a Washington Square animated by Saturday afternoon crowds (students, secondhand book dealers, left-wing newsies, joggers increas-

ingly on the verge of collapse, musicians, well-camouflaged pushers, truncheon-
wielding policemen, busybodies, tourists, and passersby), and continue to pon-
der over Poe's tale and his implicit warning as to what the "small town on the
island" was becoming, and would become: a metropolis steeped in contradictions
and mysteries, complexities and wonders, and almost more disquieting than its
infamous Old World counterparts. I tell myself that seeing as I am there at the
Bobst Library, it would be worth my while looking for something about Mary
Cecilia Rogers and Poe's tale—just to understand these texts and subtexts that
narrate the city on the island a little better.

How is New York to be narrated? Henry James wrote somewhere that the
city was *unspeakable*. And, in the opening scene of *Manhattan*, Woody
Allen shows us an author enthusiastically trying to come to grips with
chapter 1 of his own book, striving to define the city and commit his
thoughts to paper about his relationship with it: idolized and mytholo-
gized? Romantic and packed with beautiful women and smart guys? A
metaphor for the decadence of contemporary culture? A place made cal-
lous through drugs, violence, and television? A city coiling with the sex-
ual power of a great cat? . . . All false openings, unsatisfactory. And so?
Well, the writer opts for "New York was his town, and it always would be,"
which sums up pretty well everything contained in all those openings. It
also brings to mind what John Steinbeck wrote in an article for the *New
York Times Magazine* on 1 February 1953:

> New York is an ugly city, a dirty city. Its climate is a scandal, its poli-
> tics are used to frighten children, its traffic is madness, its competition is
> murderous. But there is one thing about it—once you have lived in New
> York and it has become your home, no place else is good enough. All of
> everything is concentrated here, population, theater, art, writing, pub-
> lishing, importing, business, murder, mugging, luxury, poverty. It is all of
> everything. It goes all night. It is tireless and its air is charged with ener-
> gy. I can work longer and harder without weariness in New York than any
> place else.

In fact, a deep-seated and privileged relationship does exist between
New York and the literature of the United States, although it is also
highly complex and contradictory. Of course, the cultural geography of
the country allows for the existence of other cities: Boston, to begin
with, and then Chicago, New Orleans, and San Francisco. Then there
are wider areas that cannot be ascribed to a city as such (or to one city

in particular): New England, the Midwest, the Mississippi Valley, the South, the Southwest, California . . . All of these cities and areas have, in different historical periods and with different characteristics, contributed something to the literature of the United States. Although these places *are* important, they can be more successfully likened to crossroads that are more particular and circumscribed in nature; New York, in contrast, is a permanent presence on the literary map of the country, and it cannot be circumvented.

On the other hand, one often hears people say that "New York is not America" or "New York is the least American of American cities." True, but also wrong. Yes: the European influence, the city's extraterritorial nature, its characteristic "on-the-threshold" status, that particular way of glancing over its shoulder across the Atlantic, and forward beyond the Appalachians . . . all this makes New York very much a city sui generis, in a class by itself. But then you realize that America also collapses inside New York, and that here you can grasp the rest of the country (hidden, refracted, and broken up, like the design of a puzzle scattered about on the table in so many pieces), sprawled out before us on its streets and in its history, and etched into the faces and the words of the city. The two extremes, the two poles, the two systems (New York and America) dialogue with one another much more than at first appears or is admitted. Perhaps the most fitting description of this relationship was actually made by a nineteenth-century author, William Dean Howells. An intellectual devoid of avant-garde pretensions and immune to any kind of snobbery, Howells wrote in A *Hazard of New Fortunes* (1890), one of the novels that has most successfully tried to describe the metropolitan experience: "There's only one city that belongs to the whole country, and that's New York."

Now, it may well be that the central position occupied by New York on the geographical and literary map of the United States depends on its cosmopolitan character—all those different tongues, cultures, denominations, and traditions that (as we have seen) have proved decisive in the *making* of this metropolis. Or maybe it depends on its position as an unavoidable point of arrival and passage (more so than Boston or Philadelphia, New Orleans or San Francisco): at once a port from (and on) the Old World and the gateway to the New World. Or on the contributions (from within and without, and on the part of different social classes and cultural traditions) that have never ceased to redraw the map of social and intellectual geography, as cultural historian Thomas Bender has demonstrated in an excellent book of 1987, *New York Intellect*. Or perhaps it depends on the mythopoeic values implicit in its being an island, with everything that the island (as we have seen) evokes—I am referring to that "myth-creating process" that F. Scott Fitzgerald summed up in the closing pages of *The Great Gatsby*:

> Most of the big shore places were closed now and there were hardly any lights except the shadowy, moving glow of a ferryboat across the Sound. And as the moon rose higher the inessential houses began to melt away until gradually I became aware of the old island here that flowered once for Dutch sailors' eyes—a fresh, green breast of the new world. Its vanished trees, the trees that had made way for Gatsby's house, had once pandered in whispers to the last and greatest of all human dreams; for a transitory enchanted moment man must have held his breath in the presence of this continent, compelled into an aesthetic contemplation he neither understood nor desired, face to face for the last time in history with something commensurate to his capacity for wonder.

Fitzgerald evokes a "myth of origins" that drastically cold-shoulders a whole section of *American* culture (that of the natives, the Caribbean and Mexican American populations, the immigrants and social classes), but which also possesses a pivotal role in the birth of a national literature. And which, perceived as such (i.e., with all its limits and implications), helps us to understand exactly the deep-seated and privileged role that links the metropolis to the literature of the United States.

Other elements also serve to animate what is undoubtedly a complex matter. Take, for example, the dialectic that has always existed between the metropolitan dimension (the cosmopolitan port, the garment industry, the tangle of rivers, canals, and railroads, the commercial network, the differentiated world of work, the universe of great daily newspapers, and a publishing world that has become more international than specifically American) and the mosaic of villages (the many islands within the city-island). In a certain sense, this dialectic has allowed for the containment (in accordance with the finest New York tradition, in the most convulsed, turbulent, and contradictory way) of diverse extremes, both loved and hated by successive generations of artists on the run from the interior (or the exterior) of the American continent. It is a dialectic that fascinates even the most casual of visitors. Someone, somewhere (was it Dan Wakefield in *New York in the Fifties?*) wrote that writers always end up in New York and even when they leave it they come back.

But then there is also another fact to consider: out of necessity, under the pressure of the iron laws of real estate, space on the island (the "place of origins") was inevitably a limited commodity, which resulted in a series of architectonic and urban solutions remarkable for their boldness and imagination, as well as their violence and arrogance. Consider New York's

broken profile, always on the move, upping and downing: a genuine symbol of urban—and American—living. Then consider the kind of contradictory impact it most probably had on different writers and artists, and
the challenge it must have represented to writers intent on its literary representation. And another thing: the map of the city (the tangle of trails
and courses and, consequently, of stories—which lies at the heart of the
modern novel, at least from Dickens onward) is projected and dilated
onto a gigantic screen. The effects are various, the impact powerful. The
sheer quantity and size of the buildings that wrap themselves about you
and observe you through millions of window-eyes reinforce the eloquence
of Henry James's metaphor in the "Preface" to his *Portrait of a Lady*
(1881): "The house of fiction has in short not one window, but a million"—from which writers with different eyes and from different perspectives look out onto the human scene.

All these things help make New York a vital, constant, and complex
presence in the literature of the United States. And it is for this reason
that in this literature, ever since the early nineteenth century (exactly at
the time the country and its people were beginning to detach themselves
from the Old World), a never-ending interrogation resounds—about New
York, fulcrum and magnet, dream and promise, delusion and destruction,
enigma and threat. An interrogation that, over the course of time, has
assumed a tone of irony and self-irony, idyll and nostalgia, refusal and disenchantment.

So I invite you to make an experiment, which could also turn out to
be fun. Try (ideally) grouping together on your living room table all those
novels, tales, and poems that, over the last two hundred years, have had
something to do with New York, and divide them up according to their
approach to the city. At a certain point you will see how difficult it is:
indeed, a real challenge. But also an interesting way of passing the time.

You will probably start off with Washington Irving and *Diedrich
Knickerbocker's History of New York* (1809), a humorous, debunking reap-
praisal of the city's past and present, its inhabitants and its collective
modus vivendi. In different ways and forms, a similar spirit rubbed off on
the texts of twentieth-century intellectuals like Edmund Wilson, H. L.
Mencken, and, perhaps most importantly, Dorothy Parker, who, during
the 1920s, used to meet up with her friends of the Round Table (that
group of irreverent gossips) in a specially reserved room at the Algonquin
Hotel: another urban myth. Washington's influence may also be felt in the
works of narrators like Damon Runyon, whose improbable big- and small-
time delinquents populate the colorful universe centered around Times
Square; or James Thurber, whose stories are an intriguing mix of the comical, the grotesque, and the surreal, a kind of O. Henry figure without the

sentimentalism. And it is present also in the sophisticated and, at times, rather snobbish and rarefied tone of the *New Yorker* (or perhaps it would be more accurate to say it *used* to be present: the magazine has unquestionably changed its spots since its earliest days), a publication renowned for its ruthless bird's-eye views of local idiosyncrasies, manias, and presumptions, as well as the realities and tragedies of the "pulsating city." It would seem that such a tone is an ideal means of staving off the temptation to mythologize (even if, on closer inspection, it actually creates a myth all of its own: that of the artistic and intellectual metropolis, a separate and self-sufficient territory that Woody Allen's movies amply illustrate).

At this point you might want to start off another imaginary pile of books, this time characterized by the *enthusiastic* construction of the myth. Inevitably, Walt Whitman springs first to mind: the poet-bard, the body-voice that encompasses the multitudes of the city and the country, that races along the streets of Brooklyn and Manhattan assimilating and synthesizing all that lives and pulses within their reach and transforming it into poetry. Mentally browsing through his poems and prose, you realize that you could quote any number of texts (or would his 1860 work, "Crossing Brooklyn Ferry," suffice?), but you will probably end up choosing *Specimen Days* (1882): "And rising out of the midst [of schooner and sloops], tall-topt, ship-hemm'd modern, American, yet strangely oriental, V-shaped Manhattan, with its compact mass, its spires, its cloud-touching edifices group'd at the centre—the green of the trees, and all the white, brown and gray of the architecture well-blended, as I have seen it, under a miracle of limpid sky, delicious light of heaven above, and June haze on the surface below." This is Whitman's Manhattan, the "hilly island": a new and sunnier version of the "city upon a hill" that provided the driving force behind Puritan dreams of rebirth along the coasts of the New World (what does it matter if doubts and reservations were to afflict the bard toward the end of his life?). And such is the character of the myth for a whole series of writers after Whitman, albeit not always in so intense and unambiguous a manner. For example, in his lengthy poem *The Bridge* (1930), Hart Crane celebrates New York as a cultural, historical, and geographical crossroads and sees in the Brooklyn Bridge precisely the symbol and synthesis of what has been and what will be, of east and west, of old and new. And the African American writer James Weldon Johnson turned the city into a new promised land, thus helping to foster the idea of a "myth inside the myth" (that of Harlem on the verge of its "Renaissance"). At his moment of dying, Johnson says, the idea of not seeing meadows, woods, or valleys would not be a source of pain or embitterment ("My City," 1928):

> But, ah! Manhattan's sights and sounds, her smells,
> Her crowds, her throbbing force, the thrill that comes
> From being of her a part, her subtle spells.
> Her shining towers, her avenues, her slums—
> O God! The stark, unutterable pity,
> To be dead, and never again behold my city!

In Johnson's verse there is unquestionably an echo of Whitman but, more than anything, a refraction from Fitzgerald, especially in the final melancholic touch, which seems to be on a similar wavelength to many of the latter's finest pages. For there can be no disputing that the singer of the Jazz Age has bequeathed us some of the most intense images of New York. His is a splendid, scintillating city overflowing with promise, but at the same time the cracks are showing: cruel disappointments run through it, and with them a sense of alienation that would come to the fore as soon as the euphoria of the 1920s had dried up.

As in the case of Whitman, it is difficult to select any one of these Fitzgeraldian images: there are so many (even taking *The Great Gatsby* on its own), and all of them as limpid and delicate as a work of blown crystal. Arrange them carefully on top of your pile and then choose a passage from "My Lost City" (1932), a work in which that sense of delusion is particularly acute:

> It was three years before we saw New York again. As the ship glided up the river, the city burst thunderously upon us in the early dusk—the white glacier of lower New York swooping down like a strand of a bridge to rise into uptown New York, a miracle of foamy light suspended by the stars. A band started to play on deck, but the majesty of the city made the march trivial and tinkling. From that moment I knew that New York, however often I might leave it, was home. . . . In the dark autumn of two years later we saw New York again. We passed through curiously polite customs agents, and then with bowed head and hat in hand I walked reverently through the echoing tomb. . . . Then I understood—everything was explained: I had discovered the crowning error of the city, its Pandora's box. Full of vaunting pride the New Yorker had climbed here [on top of the Empire State Building] and seen with dismay what he had never suspected, that the city was not the endless succession of canyons that he had supposed but that *it had limits*—from the tallest structure he saw for the first time that it faded out into the country on all sides, into an expanse of green and blue that alone was limitless. And with the awful realization that New York was a city after all and not a universe, the

whole shining edifice that he had reared in his imagination came crashing to the ground.

But the "resplendent city of New York" remains a firmly established fea-
ture of American literature. It is the New York that lives and smiles—
brimming over with the everyday and that sense of wonder that comes
from simply walking its streets and glancing all around you—inside the
poetry of Frank O'Hara: "It's my lunch hour, so I go / for a walk among
the hum-colored / cabs . . ." ("A Step Away from Them," 1956). It is the
city that Joseph Mitchell undoubtedly loved and explored in his superb
tales-cum-*réportage* for the *New Yorker* between the mid-1940s and mid-
1960s (and now available in *Up in the Old Hotel*, 1993): steeped in wonder for the city and its inhabitants, and in the real delight in telling of
stories at once strange and common, "stories of fish-eating, whiskey,
death, and rebirth." And it is the city that informs so much of Allen
Ginsberg's verse: a cruel city capable of inflicting pain and suffering, but
also a place where one lives and loves and creates in direct osmotic contact with its peoples, streets, houses, and smells.

The myth, then—the myth that swoops down on us from near and far,
and from which one must escape in order to come to terms with the city
as it is. This pile of books is getting pretty high—a Manhattan skyscraper.
Another pile of books will have to be made, almost as a contrast, beginning—naturally enough—with Edgar Allan Poe and Herman Melville,
nineteenth-century writers ruled by a gloomy, negative, and pessimistic
vision. Here, Manhattan almost becomes an ambiguous text that "does
not permit itself to be read," as the opening of Poe's "The Man of the
Crowd" (1840) states. Or else, in Melville, it becomes a city whose sidewalks have been built upon the hearts of those who have disappeared, as
in the novel *Pierre; or, the Ambiguities* (1852), and whose walls, "black by
age and everlasting shade," close in upon the innocent, as in "Bartleby the
Scrivener" (1853).

This literary mode—of disenchantment and betrayal (the dark lens
through which the metropolis is observed)—is also an integral part of the
literature about New York. It is there in the yearning of Henry James
(*Washington Square*, 1880; *The American Scene*, 1907) and Edith Wharton
(*The Age of Innocence*, 1920) for an "old New York" that is no longer and
maybe never even was, for the village-city of childhood days, a well-defined
and familiar place that has now been swallowed by frenzy and chaos, by the
sheer enormity of lines and the stridency of contours, by the hypocritical
norms of a senseless way of living, reduced to a pure, incomprehensible
hieroglyphic. And it is there in the browbeaten daze of William Dean
Howells: the curiosity for new urban scenes, the sense of awe on beholding

the new forces and fractures of the city-metropolis, the perception that America will be ever more New York and not Boston, and that while that may perhaps signify the modern age, it also signifies the failure of the past (*A Hazard of New Fortunes*, 1890). It is the embittered visionary register of Stephen Crane who delves deep into the Bowery slums and captures the sense of individual and collective defeat, the sufferings of life on the edge, without hope and—what is worse—inside an illusion that refuses to die and actually results in death (*Maggie, Girl of the Streets*, 1894). It is the voice of Theodore Dreiser who, on the map of the city, follows the rise of the protagonist and the defeat and suicide of her companion (*Sister Carrie*, 1900). It is the voice of John Dos Passos in *Manhattan Transfer* (1922), the first great attempt to narrate the city by means of modernist techniques, an American response to the European urban novel of James Joyce, Andrej Belyj, and Alfred Döblin: a thousand lives meet in the streets only to be crushed finally by a metropolis that looms fantastically and gigantically overhead and all around, and which those who survive have no choice but to abandon, even if that means heading off into nothingness.

And it will also be the voice of Harlem, once the initial enthusiasm of James Weldon Johnson and others has waned: a path leading, from the promises of a new life, to a disillusionment full of nostalgia and yearning, and even anger, for what did not happen (or perhaps never could have happened). As in some of Langston Hughes's poems, or in Ann Petry (*The Street*, 1946) and James Baldwin (*Notes of a Native Son*, 1954). Or, lastly, as in Ralph Ellison, whose Harlem, "in the very bowels of the city . . . is a ruin" (*Shadow and Act*, 1964).

You go on with your book piles, perhaps with the help of books like *Literary New York* (1976) by Susan Edmiston and Linda D. Cirino, or *Remarkable, Unspeakable New York* (1995) by Shaun O'Connell: and then you will notice that a sort of miniature version of literary New York is gradually taking form on your living room table. Or perhaps, even better, one of those board games in which the map has a decisive role to play (I've just bought one of them from a store on West 57th Street, The Compleat Strategist: it is called *Ellery Queen's Game*, and players are expected to solve some of the cases with the help of clues scattered here and there about the metropolitan labyrinth).

From promise to disillusionment—a path that was also followed by literature in the 1930s, when the city increasingly became a social context, rather than simply the sum of individual affairs, the articulation of geometric lines. The narratives of Michael Gold (*Jews Without Money*, 1930), Albert Halper (*Union Square*, 1933), Thomas Wolfe (*Of Time and the River*, 1935), or the theatrical works of Elmer Rice (*Street Scene*, 1929) and Clifford Odets (*Waiting for Lefty*, 1935), all picture a metropolis that is all promise, and then becomes a challenge and, in the end, a harsh territory of conflict and, often, defeat. This is the direction followed especially by the literature of immigrants during the period—those upon whom the unbending materiality of economic laws imposed (as W. E. B. DuBois wrote in the case of African Americans) a *double vision*. Even at the risk of a dramatic existential and cultural schizophrenia, this double vision allowed people to see—from within and without, from all angles—exactly what the great American metropolis really was. And, metaphorically speaking, what America was too.

It is hardly a coincidence that the last chapter of Abraham Cahan's *Yekl* (1896), the first Jewish American narrative and the first novel to treat the immigrant city in an unsensationalistic way, is entitled "A Defeated Victor," while his last novel, *The Rise of David Levinsky* (1917), turns the resistant myth of the self-made man, complete with inevitable happy ending, on its head: Levinsky has conquered the city, but the city gets its own back by leaving him in a condition of devastating solitude. And in the tales and novels of Anzia Yezierska (*Hungry Hearts*, 1920, and *Bread Givers*, 1925), New York becomes the theater of a desperate fight for survival between the past (traditions, culture, language, and customs) and the present (work, new cravings and loves, daily necessities). Finally, in Henry Roth's *Call It Sleep* (1934), the key novel of Jewish American fiction (the novel that snatches it from the clutches of a marginalized genre and plants it firmly within the literary canon of the United States), the city truly maps an adolescent-like rite of passage in which Hebraism and Americanness, and the languages and traditions of the Old World and the New, meet and clash—a labyrinth that undermines the precarious equilibrium of young David, and almost leads him to his death, on one of the city's streets. A vision of the city surfaces again, more recently, in Hugh Nissenson's *My Own Ground* (1976).

It cannot, therefore, be suggested that from this imaginary pile of books (whose height now rivals at close hand that of the "celebrated city") New York always emerges unscathed, nor that it is always presented in a positive light: it is a ruthless, indifferent, and intolerant city that shatters, destroys, and grinds you down. And if we take a look at the 1950s, it is not as though things get any better. Consider the New York of J. D. Salinger in *The Catcher in the Rye*, and those three days of wandering around that represent a (negative) realization of the adult world, and that question destined to remain unanswered: where do the ducks of Central Park go in the wintertime? Or take the black-and-white nightmare of Ralph Ellison's *Invisible Man* (1952), the urban inferno of *Last Exit to Brooklyn* (1957) or *Song of the Silent Snow* (1989) by Hubert Selby Jr. Or, lastly, consider the nocturnal metropolis of so many police stories—Ellery

Queen, Rex Stout's Nero Wolfe, the 87th Precinct of Ed McBain—and, above all, the drained, defeated characters of that desperate (yet so tender) New York meistersinger Cornell Woolrich.

And yet . . . there is always something that strikes us about these novels, too, and that's when things start getting difficult with your orderly piles of books. Because while it cannot be denied that the metropolis looms large and monstrous over individuals and groups, it is also true to say that this labyrinthine map also contains air pockets, time warps, no-man's-lands that become all-men's- (women's-) lands, unexpected oases, where it is possible to become reconciled with self and the city. It might be the carousel in Central Park, a basement on the edge of Harlem, an all-night cafeteria, a subway car whizzing its way past, or just a street corner where you pause to exchange a few words with a passerby . . . Such is the ambivalence of writers when embracing the great metropolis—their perception of its multifaceted nature, the sheer variety of faces, and the dogged determination of individuals and masses in their dealings with a context of which they are aware and also, deep down, partially responsible for. Hence the difficulty in deciding which pile this or that particular book belongs to. It will be your dilemma when you pick up one of the most soul-stirring novels about New York, *Enemies: A Love Story* (1972) by Isaac Bashevis Singer; or when you browse through the short stories of Grace Paley (*The Little Disturbances of Man*, 1959; *Enormous Changes at the Last Minute*, 1974); or Jay McInerney's novel, *Bright Lights, Big City* (1984), where the alienating frenzy of 1980s Manhattan is eventually alleviated by the sense of a caring community, encapsulated in the soft smell of freshly baked bread in the early morning streets.

The same may also be said with regard to more recent "immigrant" literature. Take, for example, the highly animated, self-mocking pages of the Sino-American writer Louis Chu in *Eat a Bowl of Tea* (1961): no longer the stereotype beloved of tourists and sensationalists, Chinatown is presented as it really is for the first time. Or take the Puerto Rican writers of New York (the so-called Nuyoricans), whose dramatic narrations are always illuminated by a strong and warm desire to escape from the sense of alienation and isolation: Jesus Colon (*A Puerto Rican in New York*, 1961), Piri Thomas (*Down These Mean Streets*, 1967), Pedro Juan Soto (*Spiks*, 1970). Especially the theatrical and poetic works of Nuyorican writers like Miguel Algarín, Miguel Piñero, Sandra María Esteves, and Pedro Pietri explore a bleak metropolitan universe that is at once surreal and grotesque, haunted by memories and nostalgia for their island of origin, and yet also capable of opening up to reveal new roots beneath the asphalt and granite. Where, then, are these books to be placed? On which pile?

And another thing. New York is much more than an all-reflecting and glistening surface, like the many windows of its skyscrapers. It is a city with a history, it harbors a million stories. All of this is hidden away among its streets, its buildings, and its individual and collective pathways. So, in the novels of E. L. Doctorow (*Ragtime*, 1975; *World's Fair*, 1985) and Jerome Charyn (*The Isaac Quartet*, 1984; *Panna Maria*, 1982; *War Cries Over Avenue C*, 1985), the metropolis is once again text and context, meaty and rich in detail, drawn and explored with a strong physical sense of place, a deep understanding of that past which alone is able to bring the present to life. Chief among those contemporary writers who have been able to synthesize this host of contradictory approaches is perhaps Paul Auster: from the gloomy and alienating vision of *The New York Trilogy* (1985–86) to the vibrancy and compassion underlying the scripts of *Smoke* and, especially, *Blue in the Face* (1995).

By now your table (not to mention your head) must be in complete disarray: you could—nay, you *must*—add further books and start making other piles. But at this stage of the game perhaps you should leave the books stacked up on the table and go out for a stroll, and reflect on the sense of the metropolis (physical, material, tangible) that these books contain. They are novels, short stories and poems, but they are also authentic literary topographies. And I think that together with the love of narrating stories (that *storytelling* which is one of the specific features of American literature), the most conspicuous characteristic of "New York literature" is the close relationship that exists between the places of the city and the written word, between the real map of the city and that garland of words threaded together one after the other that make up a text. Such is the closeness and steadfastness of this relationship that these works (and many more besides) continue to be readable, read, and effective in their telling us about such a particular experience: a genuine synthesis of almost two hundred years of "living the metropolis."

In book called *The Bicycle Rider in Beverly Hills*, William Saroyan wrote (and it matters little that he was not speaking about New York): "In the end their walking stopped, but the streets remained, and remain, and so the books."

I emerge from the Bobst Library, the ruddy-colored cube on Washington Square that hosts the magnificent New York University library, and I feel somewhat befuddled. I have always been fond of this place: it is easy to move between floors and bookshelves, and in the maze of books on display you even find what you were not looking for. But at the end you feel somewhat overwhelmed: the immense windows that look out onto the confusion of Washington Square

become an irresistible temptation and you need to get out, in the streets outside, where everything you have read, discovered, and noted down can be left to settle for a while. That is how it is for me, anyway.

I have found something on Poe and Mary Cecilia Rogers: a colorful and amusing note in Meyer Berger's New York (1954), a lengthy extract from B. A. Botkin's anthology, New York City Folklore (1956), and an entire chapter on Madame Restell in Eric Homberger's beautiful Scenes from the Life of a City (1994). At this stage I should start looking for the newspapers and magazines that Poe refers to in his notes: the Mercury, the Brother Jonathan, the Journal of Commerce, the Saturday Evening Post, the Commercial Advertiser, the Express, the Herald, the Courier and Inquirer, and the Standard. But to be quite honest, I don't feel up to it. Next time.

As I head along University Place, the extension of Washington Square that leads straight to Union Square, a freezing wind descends upon the city from the north. A change in the weather. Maybe even snow. I realize that it has gotten late and start walking faster. I have an appointment with some friends in front of the Barnes & Noble bookstore—a genuine sitting room spread out over several floors where you can flick through books at your leisure and have a more detailed browse before deciding to buy them. Many Manhattan bookstores offer similar facilities, and this only confirms what can be seen on the subway or in cafés where swarms of people sit around absorbed in some book or other: that people really do enjoy reading.

I do not want to miss out on the "meeting the author," with Don DeLillo, who has just published another hefty novel dealing with the New York (and America) of the 1950s: Underworld, more than eight hundred captivating pages, fifty years of life scrutinized from an observatory up there in the Bronx. But after turning up punctually outside the Barnes & Noble bookshop in Union Square to meet my friends, we proceed to the upper floor only to discover that the conference room is packed and people are being turned away. Disappointed, we wander around the vast book-filled spaces of the bookstore and then make for the exit. The north wind blows its way along the streets and the odd snowflake drifts groundward: the evening is beginning to take on a spectral note. Over the next few days the city will change face. It will be bathed in a new light, in new tonalities, sounds, and scenarios. It will be bewitching and cruel. The whiteness of the snow and ice will make outlines and volumes stand out, and it will cover and erase. But in the freeze it will also expose men and things. . . .

To keep to the subject of books and narration, maybe we could go and see the new movie inspired by one of Henry James's works, Washington Square. It has become quite a fad lately to take James's works to the silver screen, what with The Bostonians, Portrait of a Lady, and The Wings of the Dove. I wonder what James would have made of it all, given the high dudgeon he had always felt (and expressed) on observing manifestations of mass culture. Especially in his New York.

7

Images

I was looking for a place on the outside from where I could observe Manhattan, and so today I took the orange ferry from Battery Park to Staten Island, the massive island that stretches out in front of Manhattan and protects it from the open sea (and which, in the company of Brooklyn, Queens, and the Bronx, became part of New York in 1898). There is not much to be seen on Staten Island: the archives kept in honor of Alice Austen (one of the pioneers of social photography in the United States) at the Historical Society, the Garibaldi-Meucci Memorial Museum (Meucci gave hospitality to Garibaldi for a period between 1850 and 1851) . . . not much else.

Indeed, if you do not actually live there (and are not overly interested in the above), the only reason for going to Staten Island is for the half-hour journey by sea and the marvelous views that are to be had of the metropolis. This ferry is an out-and-out New York icon. It is a time-honored symbol, at least as mythical as its tariff: 10 cents up until 1974, 25 cents until 1989 and then—much to the perplexity of the public at large—half a dollar. (The service has been free for some time now, although maintenance costs have suffered and just recently there have been numerous unpleasant accidents.)

The idea for the ferry came from railway magnate and go-getting entrepreneur Cornelius Vanderbilt (one of the so-called robber barons) in the 1830s. And, apart from serving commuters between the two islands since its inception, the daily round-the-clock ferry has also become a tourist attraction and a source of no little romance. A necessary and integral part of metropolitan folklore, the half-hour ferry ride is a miniature journey that takes you away from the island of Manhattan and momentarily suspends any direct involvement with it. The return trip resuscitates something of the original emotions experienced upon "arriving in New York," something that is very much part of American culture (and New York's culture in particular).

The ferry is intrinsic to the culture of the "hilly island." The ferry that connected the island to Hoboken, New Jersey, is, for instance, at the center of one of the decisive scenes in Edith Wharton's The Age of Innocence. *And it appears—a powerful metropolitan symbol—at the beginning and end of John Dos Passos's Manhattan Transfer. More than anyone else, however, it was Walt Whitman who celebrated this key element of New York's geotechnology: "Crowds of men and women attired in the usual costumes! how curious you are to me! / On the ferry-boats, the hundreds and hundreds that cross, returning home, are more curious to me than you suppose; / And you that shall cross from shore to shore years hence, are more to me, and more in my meditations, than you might suppose" ("Crossing Brooklyn Ferry," 1860). Or, as he wrote in Specimen Days (1882): "Indeed, I have always had a passion for ferries; to me they afford inimitable, streaming, never-failing, living poems."*

The city you see from the Staten Island Ferry is a city rising from the sea. It is half past five in the afternoon. I lean on the parapet and feast my eyes on the light that dances about the island contours. The sun warms the sky and caresses the skyscrapers in what is truly an impressive panorama: the former Standard Oil building in the shape of a paraffin lamp, the rounded steel-blue building at 17 State Street, the Morgan Bank topped off with a cream-colored pyramid, the ugly squat rectangle of the Citibank Building, the reflecting surfaces of the National Westminster Bank USA, the cathedral-like spires and columns of the Woolworth Building, the arches, the rosettes, the triple lancet windows . . . And there is more: the dirty grey-greenness of the Statue of Liberty, the vibrant blotch of structures making up the South Street Seaport, the soft-hued brickwork and the sweet-brave dance of steel cables of the Brooklyn Bridge. From the orange ferry the parading shapes, volumes, and colors of a wealthy, powerful, and symbolically potent Manhattan come across in all their completeness.

Yet it is also rewarding (depending on where you are) to observe and try to identify the dark, narrow streets that creep along beneath the massive buildings, the shadow zones suddenly bathed in light, the perspectives that open out before you every time the boat changes position, the small ancient buildings dwarfed by looming towers, the gleaming of the windows here and there, the distant rumbling of the traffic, and maybe even the teeming hordes of passersby. . . .

This half-hour trip on the Staten Island Ferry is a real feast for the eyes. And I start thinking about all those images of New York that have been superimposed on my retina over the years.

It is impossible not *to see* New York. That might seem obvious, but think about all the pictures, the photographs, the films, and the ads. Visually speaking, New York is all around us. Long before being a history of a city or places on a map, written words or sounds heard, New York is essentially an *image:* the image of a metropolis. The moving skyline of the skyscrapers, the evening-time garland of lights that is the Brooklyn Bridge, the art deco arabesques of the Chrysler Building shining in the night, the airy pink prow of the Flatiron Building pointing northward, the gallery of intent faces in the subway car, the steep flight of steps of the Public Library, the opulence of store windows along Fifth Avenue, street scenes from Harlem or Greenwich Village, Little Italy festooned for the feast of San Gennaro, joggers in Central Park with the elaborate building tops peeping out from behind the trees, children around a hydrant spattering water in the midsummer sun, a policeman with arms folded and paunch spilling over his belt, visitors standing in front of pictures at the MoMa, a blaze of lights in snowbound Times Square . . . Carry on at your leisure with the silent imaginary slides that you have as yet to inflict on unsuspecting friends: slides that are already inside you and already make up part of your very own New York.

Of course, all this complicates things tremendously. Expectations and anticipations are created—a sort of arbitrary preconsciousness—and our true vision risks being blurred. It is hard to see New York as if for the first time, with that "capacity for wonder" that F. Scott Fitzgerald spoke of (as we have just seen). And yet, if the city is to be seen beneath and beyond the surfaces of *those* images, one must try. It can be done, by training the eye to the vision again. Once more, the fact that New York requires some kind of mental gymnastics is food for thought: we must go beyond the everyday ephemeral that the city itself seems (or, according to some, *is*) ultimately responsible for.

In Howells's *A Hazard of New Fortunes* (the fact that I'm mentioning it again should not be overlooked) there is a famous scene in which Basil and Mabel March observe the city from the Elevated. From that particular observation point, the spectacle is almost better than the theater: "a family party of work-folk at a late tea, some of the men in their shirt sleeves; a woman sewing by a lamp; a mother laying her child in its cradle; a man with his head fallen on his hands upon a table; a girl and her lover leaning over the window-sill together. What suggestion! what drama! what infinite interest!" At the station of 42nd Street the two of them stand on the bridge spanning the tracks in direction of the Central Depot and look at the long stretch of the Elevated north and south:

> the track that found and lost itself a thousand times in the flare and tremor of the innumerable lights; the moony sheen of the electrics mixing with the reddish points and blots of gas far and near; the architectural shapes of houses and churches and towers, rescued by the obscurity from all that was ignoble in them, and the coming and going of trains marking the stations with vivider or fainter plumes of flame-hot steam— formed an incomparable perspective. They often talked of the superb

spectacle, which in a city full of painters nightly works its unrecorded miracles. . . .

Today it is not easy for us to get inside the skin of Howells's stunned spectators and experience the metropolitan spectacle on similar terms of almost primeval wonder. Maybe, however, it is possible to do it by suspending our direct relationship with the city for a moment and by seeking to submerge ourselves for a time in the host of images that the city has evoked: by visiting the labyrinthine depths of an exhibition, leafing through the world of dreams contained in a book of photographs, or entering the dark cavern of a cinema. And, at last, on emerging from this regenerative dip into a world of images, you are ready to look around and embark on a new journey of discovery. Then can the act of seeing in New York (the act of seeing New York)—on the streets, beneath the towers, inside the houses, in the tunnels, on the bridges, inside the kaleidoscope—once again become a deeply emotional experience.

A city full of painters, wrote Howells in 1890. And indeed he was right. From that time on the city gradually filled with painters, and this is another story of New York, and of great interest because in one way or another it has much to do with the birth of a genuinely American art. Not that an American art did not exist beforehand: about the middle of the nineteenth century (the era when the continent was "opened" and "colonized"), painting followed the westerly route, providing itself with subjects, dimensions, colors, brushstrokes, and views of a very particular nature. Of course, the influx of European landscape painting continued to make its presence felt, and the sublimity of the Great Plains and Rocky Mountains led to familiar reactions of romantic stupor. Yet the painters of the Hudson River school, for example, still managed to find their own individual voice (and an exquisitely American voice it was, too) in the warmth and all encompassing nature of the boundless landscape.

However, genuine changes only really occurred following contact with the metropolis—and with all the positive and negative urgings nourished therein—at the end of the century. The philosopher Ralph Waldo Emerson had written in 1837, "I embrace the common, I explore and sit at the feet of the familiar, the low" ("The American Scholar"), and for budding American painters and writers alike, the phrase became a kind of manifesto of independence. In the second half of the nineteenth century, almost in concomitance with the poet Walt Whitman, painters like Winslow Homer and Thomas Eakins made it their creed, to the point of even risking expulsion from the academic and institutional establishment. And it was Eakins himself, whose huge canvases were dominated by the presence of a powerfully realistic human figure, who set a chain reaction in motion.

Indeed, one of his pupils, Robert Henri, gathered around himself a very promising group of young artists, first in Philadelphia, and later in New York. Fascinated by the French Impressionists, and intolerant of society and the arts scene in their native land, these artists promptly went about painting different subjects in different ways. Their names were John Sloan, George Luks, Everett Shinn, William Glackens, Maurice Prendergast, Ernest Lawson, Arthur Davies and George Bellows, more popularly known as The Eight. One of the most interesting things about this group was the fact that they worked as artist-reporters on the main daily newspapers of the period: on being sent to the scene of some urban event or other, they made a quick sketch of it (often employing a kind of "artistic shorthand") and from this they would later prepare a proper illustration for the newspaper. Shortly afterward, the reproduction of photographs in newspapers and magazines was made possible by advances in technology, and the artist-reporter became a redundant figure, but during their relatively brief period of activity, The Eight were part of an experience that was unique both in artistic-technical and sociocultural terms. And when the group moved to New York under the guiding hand of Henri, their single and collective potentials positively blossomed.

Exposure to the *New York panorama* (a much-used expression that summed up nicely the endless variety of types, faces, views, and situations of the metropolis) seemed to enhance the curiosity and keenness of eye of the young painters. Their social and artistic commitment intensified and their skill in capturing the essential nature of certain street scenes was honed still further. And indeed, it was the street—and not interiors or portraits—that became the dominant theme of the group: local markets, corner scenes, the great building works and excavations, demonstrations and protest marches, the traffic, sunny parks, young workers trudging home at the end of the day, evening lights, the massive scaffolding of the Elevated, store windows and theater foyers, the towers and the alleyways, snow-covered sidewalks, views from the roofs, places of entertainment, boxing matches, cheap restaurants and small backyards: a varied, sorrowful humanity observed and depicted with warmth and affection, and completely devoid of the journalistic sensationalism that made its way to newsstands of the time. Taken as a whole, it represented a thorough breakdown of metropolitan life in all its constituent parts, something akin to a gigantic Balzacian sociological inquiry poured out onto canvas.

And how it was poured! The Eight stood static and overly regular perspectives on their head. They went straight to the street, choosing unusual or slantwise points of observation, picking out scenes that had been ignored or neglected up to that moment, painting moving bodies distorted by labor or writhing in yearnings. Their brushwork differed greatly from that of the academy: it had aggressive colors and encrusted surfaces, and a grimy touch far removed from the composed sheen and smooth brilliance to which the American public was accustomed. They were nicknamed the Ash Can school, a name that despite its originally sarcastic intentions was accepted by its members with pride. The metropolis had found its pictorial representatives, its novelists of the image.

And so here you are, standing in front of *Cliff Dwellers* (1913) by George Bellows or *The City from Greenwich Village* (1922) by John Sloan. The first, an evening-time street scene from the Lower East Side (people looking out of their windows and onto the fire escapes, crowding about office fronts and beneath the street lamps, clotheslines everywhere and the city rising mountainlike in the distance), features subdued colors ranging from yellow to brown, broad and rapidly applied brushstrokes, and a vividness of bodies and movement. The second, depicted from above, is a portrayal of the city by night with people leaving the streets and offices, the Elevated on West 3rd Street with a few cars and the odd passerby beneath and, in the distance, the almost surreal vision of Wall Street gleaming in the night: here we have dark volumes battling it out with sudden streaks of light, smears of color that rescue corners and particulars from the obscurity, and slanted—at times even unnatural—perspectives.

Canvases and sketches, engravings and charcoal drawings, vignettes for radical newspapers and magazines like the *Masses:* even today the wealth of works produced by The Eight remains the most vivid and moving documentation in our possession of the period between the end of the nineteenth century and the First World War. Because it really was something of a fleeting moment. Indeed, in 1913, on the initiative of some of The Eight and Jerome Myers—an excellent realist painter given to aloofness (rather like Jacob Epstein who, before leaving for Europe, provided the superb illustrations for Hutchins Hapgood's 1902 work, *The Spirit of the Ghetto*)—the great Armory Show of Lexington Avenue (which we have already spoken of in chapter 3) was inaugurated. Its aim was to provide a public platform for the first collective exhibition of American realism and, more importantly, to give the public a taste of what was going on in the arts in Europe—a world apart that only a few American collectors and travelers knew anything about.

But the Armory Show marked the beginning of the end for The Eight: the outcry and disconcertment roused by the aggressive and disturbing works of the European avant-garde (Marcel Duchamp's *Nude Descending a Staircase*) stifled the milder voice of the New York realists. Then came the war, the social and political unrest of the postwar era, and the contradictory upheaval of the 1920s: painting New York in the same way as before seemed an impossible task. Separate roads were taken. One realist school obstinately pursued its activities throughout the Jazz Age and especially during the 1930s, with Sloan and company being joined by artists of great worth like Art Young, the brothers Raphael and Isaac Soyer, Ben Shahn, Glenn Coleman, Edward Hopper, Reginald Marsh, and Isabel Bishop, all of whom were especially interested in portraying the bodies and faces in the metropolis, the million lives and million stories of its inhabitants, the hidden corners of an urban context that never ceased to change its skin.

But above all, New York became the "abstract city," the vortex of lines and energy and the explosion of colors and perspectives that belonged to Abraham Walkowitz, Stuart Davis, John Martin, Max Weber, Joseph Stella, and Georgia O'Keeffe. In tacit agreement with the syncopated rhythm of the city, with ragtime and with jazz, their canvases sought to bring to life on a flat surface the complex three-dimensional quality of an urban experience made up of skyscrapers under construction, the excavation of new subway lines, bridges and scaffolding, nocturnal neon lights, frenzy and speed, pummeling pneumatic drills, bus rides, water tank silhouettes on the roofs, cranes and chimney stacks, bright white windows in the dark, a constant prismatic capsizing of perspectives, a convergence/divergence of lines and force fields, a sense of overcrowding and proximity along the narrow perimeter of the island, and uninterrupted vortexes of cars and bodies (in his 1930 novel, *Jews Without Money*, Michael Gold wrote that his street "was an immense excitement. It never slept. It roared like a sea. It exploded like fireworks").

Take, for instance, Georgia O'Keeffe's *Radiator Building—Night, New York* (1925), a canvas livid with blacks, blues, and violets: in the middle, imposing, the skyscraper of the title, whose only sign of life is the series of illuminated windows—almost an electric circuit of whites, yellows, and blues—and an Oriental templelike summit sculpted by saber thrusts of light rays against the black sky, a lateral red stripe, and a puff of white steam. In *The Brooklyn Bridge: Variation on an Old Theme* (1939), by Joseph Stella, the world's most famous bridge becomes a musical nave in blues and greys, a cathedral whose two Gothic arches contain and compress the rest of the city. At the bottom, a first layer encapsulates the metropolitan symbols, the outline of the bridge, and the skyscrapers and, underneath, a second layer multiplies the motif of the yellowish eyes of the train in the darkness of the underground tunnels.

The city also becomes a "geometric city" in the works of artists like Charles Sheeler, Louis Lozowick, and Hugh Ferriss, who preferred the vision of a New York (real or imaginary) made up of shapes and volumes, rarefied geographies, and clean-cut, sharp, square outlines: the possibility of harmony, but also the spine-chilling prospect of sameness. In these two

modernist visions of the metropolitan sublime, ecstasy and unease, mar-
vel and anxiety shared the canvas cheek by jowl. These two approaches
were deeply bound together, supported—if not actually inspired—by
another visual means of communication triumphant in those years: photography.

When examined close-up, photography followed a similar path. In
fact, at the end of the nineteenth century, the need to find new ways to
express the city experience was bound up with the profound unease felt
by wide sectors of society when faced with a risk- and contradiction-rid-
den reality. Immigration from faraway lands, the urbanization of black
masses coming from the southern states and the explosion of working-
class protest all over the country exacerbated the fears of both the WASP
ruling class and a middle class that persisted in its foolish beliefs that frontier individualism, equal opportunities for everyone, the self-made man,
and the American "way of life" were genuine lasting alternatives to the
social adversities of the Old World. Certain areas of the larger American
cities were becoming severely congested, and this was thought to be the
most obvious threat: it was high time these living conditions—in the
blandly reformist conception of sociologists, journalists, and social workers—were *brought to light* in order that they might be neutralized.

This is precisely what happens with Jacob Riis, the Danish immigrant
we have already come across in chapter 1: using rough-and-ready photographic equipment (on more than one occasion he accidentally set fire to
apartments and basements with his magnesium lamps), Riis casts a light
over obscure and hidden existences and records what was often a shocking *modus vivendi et laborandi* in the tenements, the sweatshops, and the
poorly lit, stuffy apartments. As in "'Knee-Pants' at Forty-five Cents a
Dozen—a Ludlow Street Sweater's Shop" (1889), where male and female
workers are intent on cutting, tacking, and sewing trousers in the midst of
an untidy room: the surprised look of workers caught turning toward the
lens, the childlike smile of a laborer whose mouth is half-hidden behind
an enormous pair of scissors, the frenzied working atmosphere suggested
by the movement of bodies, a dog hunkered down patiently beneath a
chair heaped up with fabrics, the dirty windows . . . And it is precisely with
the help of photographs like this (which you can still see at the Museum
of the City of New York, and harrowing they are, too) that Riis manages
to put together *How the Other Half Lives* (1890). Annoying at times for its
banality and the odd racist stereotype, this famous volume is a damning
indictment of an urban context positively shocking in its squalor.

So there it is, the birth of social photography in the United States.
After Riis came Lewis Hine, also a reformer but above all a great artist who
turned to drawing up a veritable catalog of the new "American types."

With almost anthropological precision, Hine photographed a single, gigantic sequence of immigrant faces, laborers, women, children, and old people, arriving at Ellis Island, hanging about street corners, surrounded by the bags and suitcases of those who would probably never make it back home, busy in the ever-alike gestures of mass production. This is the case in "Madonna of Ellis Island" (1905) or "Immigrants at Ellis Island" (1908), two photographs that tear individuals and groups away from the sheer anonymity of their condition to capture their cultural and existential complexity.

When the city spirals upward all around him, with skyscrapers (from the Chrysler to the Empire State) laying down their respective gauntlets between the end of the 1920s and the beginning of the 1930s, Hine is there to witness their dramatic rise (albeit with a hint of nationalistic—Whitmanesque?—pride, it must be said). Above all, he is there to document what lies behind the soaring Manhattan skyline—construction tasks at dizzier than dizzy heights and the endless acrobatics between profit and wages, of anonymous laborers from all over the world.

Now, in Hine's photographs of the Empire State Building under construction and the men at work (Men at Work is, in fact, the title of one of his best collections, from 1932), there is already an irresistible sense of wonder at the volumes and designs involved, the contrasting and intermingling of lines, the arabesques of the girders and steel cables, the drills and turbines, of a city engaged in a continual process of expansion and transformation. And again, exactly as occurred in the world of painting, the realistic representation of the metropolis gradually shifted toward the abstract and the geometric. Indeed, alongside "social" photographers like Riis and Hine, other photographer-painters like Alfred Stieglitz and Edward Steichen were already at work, driven on toward a different use of the camera by the new urban landscape.

As in the paintings of Stella, O'Keeffe, Demuth, and Sheeler, their city representations became uninterrupted sequences of strong lines, reflecting surfaces and geometric volumes. It was an abstract and visionary world, coolly silent or magically iridescent depending on the time of day, the weather, or the point of view. Skyscrapers provided the main attraction for these photographers-painters, and in particular the Flatiron Building—so slender, ethereal, and light—a genuine architectural wonder that is photographed at all hours of the day and night, in the fog and rain, in the snow and sunshine, until it becomes an icon, in pure form.

Silence is what strikes us most in the images of photographers like Stieglitz and Steichen, Berenice Abbott (whose Changing New York, from 1939, is a splendid document), Walker Evans (with his photographs of the Brooklyn Bridge), William Klein (in his famous and recently rediscovered

New York), and Rudy Burckhardt, all of whom continued experimenting with the camera in close contact with the urban environment, its places, and its inhabitants. The metropolis speaks to us with eloquence, and often violently so, but there is a dreamy or nightmarish quality to all this: it does so *without words*. It is almost as if the city were showing us the other side, tacit and mute, of an experience that is nonetheless steeped in personal and collective experiences: something to place alongside the written word of literature and the merry-go-round world of spoken languages.

And it is hardly a coincidence that, from the 1930s on, a new instrument comes to take its rightful place in the world of painting as well, occupying a halfway-house territory with an intriguing power all its own: the "novels without words." The engravings of John Sloan and the paintings of Reginald Marsh already closely resembled novels without words—stages crammed with streets, places of entertainment, beaches and cinema and theater foyers. But the time was ripe for the establishment of a real genre. Reviving the great tradition of the early-twentieth-century Belgian avant-garde artist Frans Masereel, engravers like Giacomo Patri and Lynd Ward welded realism to abstractionism by projecting stirring black-and-white image-stories of life and survival in the city onto the page.

Photography and painting were never to abandon the New York arts scene throughout the twentieth century, as Peter Conrad has ably demonstrated in his fascinating book on the subject, *The Art of the City* (1984). While the realism of Joseph Levine, William Johnson, and Jacob Lawrence continued to explore the heart of the city, exposing it with irony and affection, the abstraction of artists like Jackson Pollock or Willem de Kooning (the so-called New York school) continued pouring pure energy onto the canvas and turning the city into a sign. But their paths would cross again—in certain pop art works of Robert Rauschenberg and Red Grooms, for example; or in the *trompe l'oeil* works of Richard Haas. The social photography of Riis and Hine, meanwhile, is taken up by Abbott and Evans, later evolving into the hallucinated recording of the metropolitan nocturne of Weegee (with his fires, street accidents, local homicides, and crowds of eager onlookers) and Diane Arbus (whose freaks are disconcertingly normal in appearance).

Just recently I've had the good fortune to see some interesting exhibitions at the Whitney Museum and the Museum of the City of New York. One was given over entirely to Joseph Stella, the great Italian-born artist who arrived in the United States at the beginning of the twentieth century. His early years in the country were characterized by works of fierce social critique, mostly in charcoal, while working for magazines like the *Survey*: the faces and bodies of immigrants, scenes from mines and laboring towns and the railroads and chimney stacks—an important documen-

tary account of what the "other America" was, and what it would continue to be. Then came the explosion of the 1920s and 1930s: aggressive colors, the visionary quality of the images, the vortexes of lines, and the
Brooklyn Bridge adopted as a symbol of an era, a culture, and a context.

The other exhibition, City of Ambition: Artists and New York,
1900–1960, provided a splendid overview of the relationship between the
arts and the metropolis through a striking range of images comprising the
works of realist and abstract artists, social photographers and photographer-painters, and engravers and photo-reporters. There was also a tell-
tale map of Manhattan that revealed how there was not one single place
in the long narrow island that had not been visited by an image, in black
and white or color, brushstroke or pencil, or frozen by a shutter release.
The third and last exhibition, Shared Perspectives, dealt with that perpetual dialogue in motion between painting and photography—almost a
challenge or a pursuit from which emerges the real sense of a "city of
painters."

The history of New York and its image is a "never-ending story"—
maybe because the city is so full of stories that it is impossible to capture
them all through the written word alone. I'm thinking about the contemporary work of Marlis Momber, whose photographs have been telling
the life of the Lower East Side neighborhood for the last twenty-five
years, and whose characters you can meet every day on the street corner,
in front of Jardin de la Esperanza or at Casa Adela; I'm thinking about
Margaret Morton's photographs of the homeless, the inhabitants of those
impromptu *casitas* erected in the midst of urban desolation, and of the
New York tunnel people; I'm thinking about the black-and-white or color
plates of Eric Drooker, the gifted artist whose visionary continuation of the
"novel without words" tradition has resulted in some of the most staggering and pointed of metropolitan scenes. And I'm thinking of Seth
Tobocman, whose cartoons continue the well-established tradition of the
urban cartoon *à la* Will Eisner.

Clearly, as Marilyn Cohen has written apropos the canvases and drawings of Reginald Marsh, the dominant element in all this is "the cinematic
vision of the city." So the time has come to return to the quotation from
Howells's novel that more or less set this chapter rolling, because in that
description of the city as seen by the two characters (every window containing a different scene) I think we already have a surprising foretaste of
what cinema would bring. In Howells's novel it is still a question of the
characters moving in front of the stills, but just a few years later it would
be the stills moving in front of seated spectators.

In fact, speaking of images in a New York context necessarily implies
that we also speak of American cinema, not only because the movies

practically started off here (the first public showing took place at the Bials & Koster Music Hall on Broadway and West 34th Street in 1896); not only because the origins of cinema are so closely tied up to the city's very own dynamics: the first movie producers were the sons of Lower East Side immigrants who worked in the clothing industry (cut and stitch together!), although by the time cinema had clearly become a serious business prospect they were flocking in droves to make their fortunes in Hollywood, where longer daylight hours allowed for an optimization of practices; and not only because cinema started off as a popular spectacle aimed at an ethnically and linguistically heterogeneous public (as an early-twentieth-century manual written for those interested in this new art/industry declared: the "ideal location is a densely populated working-men's residence section, with a frontage on a much-traveled business street"). Not for these reasons alone, but because right from the start it was precisely the landscape of New York that helped model the cinema and was indeed its first great inspiration: the street as a stage, the urban labyrinth, the continual movement, the incessant transformations, the sheer variety of its inhabitants, the overwhelming multitude of stories and events . . . These were all fundamental aspects of cinema—its DNA no less—as Siegfried Kracauer has demonstrated in *Theory of Film* (1960) and (at least as far as American cinema is concerned) as Robert Sklar has reminded us in *Movie-Made America* (1975).

It may safely be said that the first stories projected onto a white tarpaulin took their origins from the street (*The Life of a Bootblack*, 1907; *The Black Hand*, 1908; *The Story of Rosa in Little Italy*, 1908; *The Little Match Girl*, 1908; *The Rag-Picker's Christmas*, 1908; *The Child of the Ghetto. Rivington Street: The Strugglers*, 1910), as did the 450 brief films shot by David W. Griffith for Biograph between 1908 and 1912, prior to his famed yet controversial *The Birth of a Nation* (1915). They are stories of immigrants living between Little Italy and the Jewish ghetto, barbershops, tenement interiors, characters "endowed with a humanity that set them apart from stock caricatures" (in the words of Sklar), right up until the minor 1912 masterpiece starring a young and delectable Lillian Gish, *The Musketeers of Pig Alley*. The street formed an all-important backdrop in the films of Charlie Chaplin and Buster Keaton, too: all those astonishing chases, the sudden reversals, the surprises just around the corner, beneath the staircase, in the basement, and, well, did *you* see that manhole cover? A limitless theater of fortuitous incidents and accidents. So, once more that physical bond with the street and city locations, which, as we have seen, proved so important in New York literature, makes its reappearance at the dawning of the movies, and, indeed, there it will remain as the most eloquent and honored of guests. It is hardly a coincidence that the taste for *that* original theater—and for that street where everything starts and finishes, only to start back from the beginning again—and the pleasures to be derived from it, resurfaces anew in films like Susan Seidelman's *Desperately Seeking Susan*, Jonathan Demme's *Married to the Mob*, or Martin Scorsese's *After Hours*.

How, then, are we to get a grip on all those millions of moving cinematic stills dedicated to New York in these pages? All those documentaries and fictions? *Manhatta* by Charles Sheeler and Paul Strand and *Manhattan* by Woody Allen? *What Did Mozart See on Mulberry Street* by Rudy Burckhardt, and *In the Street* by James Agee, Halen Levitt, and Janice Loeb, and *On the Bowery* by Lionel Rogosin? James Cagney, Edward G. Robinson, and Humphrey Bogart fleeing from dead-end streets only to go back again? The days and Sundays singing in the rain together with Gene Kelly? Breakfasts at Tiffany's and apartments at the Plaza? The Broadway of Woody Allen and the Bronx of Robert De Niro? Central Park with its nighttime warriors, its fisher king, and its marathon man? Hannah and her sisters and Harry meeting Sally? The crowd of King Vidor, the lost weekend of Billy Wilder, the heiress of William Wyler, the faces and shadows of John Cassavetes, the ragtime of Milos Foreman? The Empire State Building of King Kong and Andy Warhol? The Manhattan murder mystery and doing the right thing in Brooklyn? The godfathers, the princes of the city, the king of New York, the goodfellas, and the seven-year itch? The ghostbusters and Rosemary's children? The taxi drivers and the pawnbrokers? The noirs of the 1940s and 1950s, then Serpico, the death wishes, and the French connection? Wall Street, 42nd Street, and the West Side? On the waterfront, the mean streets of Little Italy, the dragons of Chinatown, and the smoke in Auggie's cigar store in Brooklyn? SoHo, Central Park, Harlem, Washington Square, the Brooklyn Bridge, Grand Central, and the Chrysler Building? . . . Oh, and you will forgive me if I left something out.

Cinema is to New York what Dickens is to London and Zola to Paris: there is a whole city in there—a whole world. And, vice versa, only one city produces the millions and millions of moving images that go to make up story after story (Richard Alleman's *The Movie Lover's Guide to New York* is an exhaustive guide to cinematic places in New York). I think one of the most significant films to illustrate this relationship between cinema and the metropolis (and it is one of the films my students have to put up with on a fairly regular basis) is Jules Dassin's 1948 work, *The Naked City*, whose opening shots are decidedly Dickensian in character. There are no titles to interfere with what we are seeing: an aerial view of Manhattan accompanied by a background narration that talks about the film and the city; then, while being treated to some nighttime scenes, the metropolis is disassembled into its constituent parts: the river, Wall Street, the illuminated buildings, the deserted streets, the still offices, the never-ceasing pulse of the factories, the trucks carrying forth their goods for the next day, the woman cleaning the floor of what looks suspiciously like Grand Central Station, the host of a radio show announcing the next song, the glitter of rich, fashionable places, and the fitful shadows of a homicide in a dark apartment.

The background narration accompanies us throughout the film. The long, complex investigation takes place for the most part in the streets of New York, powerfully presented in visual and physical terms, and finishes with a thrilling chase through the Lower East Side, along to the Williamsburg Bridge and then up, up to the top of one of its steel towers, from where the island-universe appears for the last time. And the morbid background narration of producer Mark Hellinger accompanies us for the last time: "There are eight million stories in the naked city, and this is one of them . . ."

I wonder if after this deep-sea dive into the images inspired by New York (or, rather, which make New York: a complex matter this . . .) it will be easier to come back and watch, or see, the city. Care will have to be taken anyway because, as Alan Trachtenberg has argued convincingly in *The Incorporation of America* (1982), ever since New York became *the* great capitalist metropolis at the end of the 1800s, it has always done its utmost to conceal its true nature and reality, offering itself as pure enigma. It has hidden the public places abuzz with the mechanisms of power behind masked facades. It has turned the banks into Gothic cathedrals, the stations into Doric temples, the dwellings of businessmen into medieval castles, the offices into minarets, and the big department stores into neoclassical buildings. And it has locked away the mystery of profits, land rents, and real-estate speculation in soaring skyscrapers resembling ancient Assyrian-Babylonian ziggurats.

Thus, a dwarflike presence in the streets, dazed and confused by the image and the form, we risk not seeing the substance at all. Unless we can accept the invitation and the challenge implicit in all these reflecting surfaces, which are forever sending each other images of themselves: an invitation and a challenge, that is, to go through the looking glass—to solve the puzzle and unravel the mystery.

I was looking for a place on the inside from where I could observe New York, and so today I've been up and down Central Park, letting its eight hundred acres of greenery dance all about me: as if the covered carousel with its huge wooden

*horses close by 65th Street Transverse Road had suddenly spread out to encom-
pass the whole park.*

*It is no easy task to find a "place on the inside" in the metropolis. Everything
considered, it could have been any place on the Lower East Side or in Harlem,
along Broadway or down 14th Street; it could have been . . . But what I really needed was a kind of eye-in-the-storm location from which I could look out
onto the city as if I were standing in the wings at the theater. Or, reversing the
relationship between spectacle and spectator, as when you separate the two
drapes of the main curtain mysteriously before the show begins, to peep out and
see what's going on among the public in the stalls: you have to get used to this
kind of reversal in a city like New York—seeing and being seen.*

*At last I found my hidden corner, my own special observation post: along the
West Drive of the park and near the Strawberry Fields dedicated to John
Lennon, on the lake. It was a small wooden jetty with a sloping roof that gives
it the appearance of a gazebo, two L-shaped seats with parapets to the sides of
the central opening. I sat down with my back to the Drive, popped my legs
through the boards of the parapet, and let my feet dangle just above the surface
of the water. And there I remained for a good hour, watching the gentle rippling
of the lake, the inquisitive bustling about of the ducks, the slow movement of the
boats, and, just in front of me, the slender cast-iron bridge that links Cherry Hill
to the Ramble.*

*The peace and quiet of that place was exactly like being inside the eye of the
storm. The metropolis was spinning all around me. I could see tall peaks stretching above the treetops along Fifth Avenue and Central Park South; I knew they
were there behind me, along Central Park West (the turrets and bow windows
of the Dakota Houses, the spires and small columns of the San Remo
Apartments); I could feel them to my left and, going north, toward Harlem—
the cement, the steel, the cast iron, the granite, stone, and brick of New York
that wrapped their way about the intense green, the hills, the tiny valleys and
the expanses of water in the park. A "momentary stay against confusion," as
Robert Frost put it, writing about poetry.*

*From my own special observation post, from this tiny window opening out
onto a momentary sereneness in the midst of metropolitan turmoil, I observed
at length the amazing spectacle of contradictions, the continual refraction of the
peaks, and the artificial summits in the shuddering water. In the meantime, on
the opposite bank of the lake, a girl was placing a canvas on her easel and was
mixing the colors in her palette. Every now and then, she looked up.*

8

Sounds

Yesterday I got a phone call that aroused my curiosity to no end. It was the voice of an Italian who had been in the United States a few years (rhythm, pauses, accents, vocality, the hunting down of words). And his name was Federico. "I hear you're interested in New York gardens," he told me, and then he proceeded to sing the merits of one situated between Delancey and Broom Streets, Forsyth and Chrystie Streets, in the heart of the old Lower East Side. "Early on Saturday and Sunday mornings you'll find the Chinese there. . . . Chinatown, you know, is just a few yards away. . . . Some of them don't even speak English. They take their birds—the "Emperor's Birds"—to sing there. . . ."

And so this morning, at eight o'clock on the dot, there I was in front of the small half-moon–shaped area of green at the northern limit of Sara Delano Roosevelt Park: the Wah Mei Bird Garden. I spoke at length with Federico Savini and Anna Magenta, two Italians who had been living for some time in New York. Both were active members of the Forsyth Street Garden Conservancy, one of the many groups set up to create and protect gardens within the city. They told me of the herculean efforts required to save just a few square yards of earth, to lay out this garden with its multitude of different plants (some of them grow berries that certain rare species of birds go mad about, thus encouraging their return to the city), and to defend it from hordes of developers intent on squeezing the area for all its worth and transforming it for their nouveau riche clientele (some time ago the area really had its work cut out trying to defend itself from the forays of yuppies from nearby SoHo: their huge dogs wasted no time in messing up the gardens).

Then they told me about the Wah Mei, the "Emperor's Birds," and the deal struck with the elderly in Chinatown. They explained that many of the men living in the neighborhood hurry to order one of these birds (which come from the Yang Tze area in China and, more generally, from Southeast Asia) as soon as they've managed to put by a few hundred dollars. A wee bit bigger than our thrushes, the birds have a reddish-yellow plumage dotted with grey and olive

102

green—and a white outline around the eye: hence wah mei, *"painted eyelids," like the eyes of the beautiful* Xi Shi *who, as legend has it, lived centuries ago. The birds are very well looked after: the cages are kept spotless, special birdseeds are used, and, most importantly, the birds are taken to sing in the open air at least twice a week. It seems that this activity keeps the men of Chinatown busy in what little spare time they have left, and the demons of gambling (forever the scourge of the community) are kept at arm's length.*

As I spoke with Anna and Federico, a host of silver-haired, middle-aged men started turning up a few at a time. They were carrying wicker or wooden cages covered with cloths. The cages were laid out in rows, one beside the other, arranged among the garden plants or latched onto the fantastical architecture of gas and water pipes, which had been collected and laid out here and there. Only these men went into the garden. (Federico warned me not to go too near, a sort of unwritten pact: what had literally become a ritual had been disrupted by too many inquisitive people with cameras.) They waited a few moments to give the birds time to adjust themselves to the light of day, and then the cloths were removed.

In that instant, a unique concert of solos, fugues, canons, songs, melodies, and countermelodies burst upon the metropolis, silencing the din of traffic just a few yards away, transforming the whole scene before me into a kind of Oriental garden, and accompanying the measured gestures of the old people playing tai chi in the garden close by.

I wonder if a history of metropolitan sound has ever been written. It would be interesting to study all the different elements involved, the transformations that take place with each passing epoch, the effects on the life *of* the city and *in* the city, and the way in which culture recorded and incorporated it. As far as New York is concerned, a fine book by Robert Snyder titled *The Voice of the City* (1989) takes as its subject the birth and development of vaudeville, and reminds readers that one of the possible etymologies of the term used to denote this form of popular entertainment is, unsurprisingly, *voix de ville*, "voice of the city."

But what is the voice of New York? Has this voice changed now that the Elevated no longer cuts across *all* Manhattan with its vibrating steel structures, and the agonizing siren songs of massive ocean liners docked along East River and the Hudson are no more? Someone, perhaps Walt Whitman in 1842, wondered what had New York—noisy, trembling, bustling, stormy, turbulent New York—to do with silence.

True, there are (though they do exist) very few pockets of silence in this city, where sound is a kind of continual comment on everyday life, a genuine leitmotiv that sums up the thousand contradictions of the city—strident, aggressive, and violent, or sweet, soothing, and amicable. In certain subway stations, the thunder can be frightening in the extreme, a rolling rumble that almost induces feelings of panic as the train draws near. In others, however, as soon as you walk through the turnstile you may well be greeted by a group of middle-aged people, splendidly striking up, a cappella, the notes of Carl Orff's *Carmina Burana,* and collecting money in a cardboard box marked "Music Below the Pavement." J. D. Salinger was right when he wrote in *The Catcher in the Rye:* "New York's terrible when somebody laughs on the street very late at night. You can hear it for miles. It makes you feel so lonesome and depressed." And then you pause for long minutes in the chaos of Astor Place to listen to a street musician who teases fascinating melodies from his portable keyboards. Sure, with its honkings, sirens, skiddings, and brakings, the traffic is a constantly grating presence. But the streets of New York reverberate with an incessant variety of sounds and noises: the voices—full, high-pitched, and rhythmic—of those who live the streets, the witty remark of a young black leaning against the wall, the rustling of squirrels in the grass or among the branches above, the hurried scurrying along the massive sidewalk stones, the wooden thud of skateboards leaping up steps, the intermittent whirring of helicopter blades, the metallic frizzle of police car radios, the full-throated singing of a passerby . . . a succession of sounds that demands our attention, that creates a tension all of its own.

Once removed from their fortuitous and fleeting condition—their fluctuating consistency—they are sounds that, like the images we have of New York, tell us a great deal about the history and culture of the city. For example, someone whose name escapes me for the moment once said that the sound of the jackhammer typifies New York in the same way the chiming of Big Ben typifies London: and its resounding centrality—its sheer physical everyday reality—cannot but remind us (yet again) of the mainsprings hidden away in the depths of the metropolitan mechanism.

But the experience of sound in New York is extremely various in nature. I remember the first night I spent in Queens, many years ago. I was awoken by a peculiar hissing sound continually wailing away and changing pitch; sleepless from jet lag, I simply had to satisfy my curiosity. Unable to resist the temptation of discovering where the noise came from, I got up from the sofa bed in the sitting room where I was temporarily being lodged, afraid of turning on the light for fear of waking my hosts. Hands stretched out in front of me, I started fumbling about the house in search of where the sound was coming from, and on reaching the kitchen I let out an almighty yell: I had grabbed hold of the massive, boiling-hot pipe of the steam heating system. The sound had given me a sharp—and decidedly palpable!—lesson in the history of the city.

Since that time I have learned to recognize (and live with) the variety of sounds that fill the apartments with an almost physical density and bulk: the vibration of the air as it sneaks its way about the stairways of the high-rises, crying out in the corridors and shaking the doors; the howling of the wind that whistles through cracks in the guillotine windows; the deep droning of the air-conditioning system of the supermarket below the house; the sound of a phrase muttered in the narrow streets that echoes all the way up to the top floor . . . It is difficult not to be reminded of something that Fitzgerald wrote in "My Lost City": "The gentle playing of an oboe mingled with city noises from the street outside, which penetrated into the room with difficulty through great barricades of books . . ." But this sparks off memories of another night in New York (again, after I had just flown in), when a typically frenzied block party, or *jarana nuyoricana*, lulled me off to sleep at five in the morning with an extremely limited and aggressive mix of salsa and merengue being played at a nearby corner turned into a square and dancing hall.

All this music making in the city's public places . . . Of course, it is not an exclusively New York experience, but I do not think it is an entirely casual phenomenon, either. It has much to do with a very direct relationship with the metropolis, its spaces and its rhythms. True, ragtime did not start off in New York, but it did establish itself between New York and Chicago and become a defining musical characteristic of the city with its jumpy, syncopated rhythm, its constant repetition and unraveling of a dominant theme, almost a "three-voice canon with ground bass" (maybe it is for this reason that I love Pachelbel's Canon so much, and continue to associate it with cities like New York and New Orleans). Besides, when ragtime transformed itself into jazz there is no doubt that the sound of the Tenderloin, San Juan Hill, and Harlem poured back into it, providing it with life and body, with its incessant variation upon themes and the improvisations taken from life and survival in the streets. And then, I wonder in my ignorance if the presence of the piano hasn't been a determining factor in all this, what with its unique timbre and its own very special way of playing. And the metallic rhythms of the banjo? The almost human voices of the clarinet and the trumpet, and the constant roll of the drums? And the bands that reproduced all this urban polyphony: from Louis Armstrong to Duke Ellington, from the cool jazz of Lennie Tristano to the bebop of Charlie "Bird" Parker? This is a relationship between music and the city that is perhaps best defined by Duke Ellington's *Take the A Train*.

George Gershwin understood it all to perfection. A Jewish lad, he grew up in immigrant neighborhoods, taking on board the voice and the music of the streets, hanging out on street corners and patronizing saloons with little theaters in the back room rather than going to school. His *Rhapsody in Blue* is a splendid synthesis of this complex metropolitan score. And all the major figures in American popular music understood it: the popular music that was born and developed in New York—the so-called Tin Pan Alley (a great musical pun, this one: the name stood to indicate the area of the city where that kind of music was written, published, and played, but it is also a deliberate echo of "tympanum," or the eardrum), with Irving Berlin (that Izzy Baline who, following his arrival as an immigrant in America, worked for many years as a waiter-singer—another exquisitely urban voice!—in a Chinese restaurant, before changing his name and occupation), Cole Porter, and, of course, the Leonard Bernstein of *West Side Story* fame. And the Marx Brothers understood it, too: their whole language was an astonishing musical score whose utterance required an exacting sense of rhythm, timing, and pauses.

It can hardly come as a surprise that one of today's most successful shows is *Stomp*, which dominated the bill for so long at the Orpheum on Second Avenue, one of the legendary theaters dotted about the East Village—an extraordinary adventure in metropolitan music, recreated on stage by exploiting to the fullest the dancing body and all those objects directly related to the street: sticks, tins, garbage cans and lids. And neither is it by chance that recent years have witnessed the rebirth of Yiddish and klezmer music in the heart of the Lower East Side (at the Knitting Factory, when it was still located in the dilapidated old building on East Houston Street): yet another synthesis of voices and experiences that take on a unique dimension and tonality in an urban context.

Then there is the whole history of black music, from the melancholy and desperation of the urban blues to the aggressive rhythms of hip-hop and rap. I must admit that the latter fails to fire me with enthusiasm (much to the disappointment of my students), but there is no doubt that it encapsulates something of the sharp blades, the jagged corners, the rough fabric, and the tense edginess of day-to-day life in the metropolitan ghettoes. The history of rock in New York has been no less important, with names ranging from the Velvet Underground to David Byrne and the Talking Heads, from Patti Smith and Laurie Anderson to Billy Joel and Willie De Ville. And, towering above them all, Lou Reed, the rock singer of the city, with his crude ballads like "Walk on the Wild Side" and the splendid *New York* album, right up to his surreal and self-mocking participation—very "metropolitan"—in *Smoke* and *Blue in the Face*, two films that saw the light of day thanks to the united efforts of the director Wayne Wang and the writer Paul Auster (a genuine star cluster into which the many voices of New York plunge headlong: words, images, sounds . . .).

Music and the spoken word meet, intermingle, and blend as one here, and the dialogue between the two is continual. From the end of the nineteenth century on, literature recorded this voice of the city (in its usage of slang, and in the tight weaving together of English and immigrant languages) and transferred it to the page. And the same thing was accomplished by the musical comedy, a new genre that could boast celebrated operettas like *The Black Crook, The Mulligan Guard Ball, The Belle of New York, A Trip to Chinatown,* and genuine hits like *Give My Regards to Broadway, After the Ball, The Sidewalks of New York, Ta-Ra-Ra Boom-De-Ay!* and *The Bowery.* Literary modernism certainly did not sit back and watch. Indeed, it positively endorsed this dialectical relationship, especially in poetry (but how can one forget the sheer musicality of novels like John Dos Passos's *Manhattan Transfer* or Henry Roth's *Call It Sleep,* described as "the noisiest novel in American literature"?). And the Beat Generation, whose direct bond with the multilingual polyphony of New York is infinitely stronger and more representative than all subsequent flights into the Orient, did everything in their power to glorify this relationship between words, music, and the voice of the city, as can be seen in the ongoing prose of Jack Kerouac, the Whitman-like bardish song of Allen Ginsberg, the street epiphanies of Gregory Corso, the asphalt-concrete compositions of Diane Di Prima and LeRoi Jones, the visionary verses of Bob Dylan, and the debunking songs-cum-poems of Ed Sanders's and Tuli Kupferberg's Fugs.

This tradition survives today in the poetry of Harlem, the Bronx, and the Lower East Side, and especially in the works of Nuyorican poets like Pedro Pietri. Take, for example, his *Telephone Booth* poems:

> I will tell you
> how to get there:
> walk 3 blocks down
> & 8 blocks across
> & 4 blocks backwards
> & 7 blocks around
> & 6 blocks up
> & 9 blocks down
> & 5 blocks across
> & 1 block backwards
> & 2 blocks sideways
> & 3 blocks wherever
> & you will get there
> sooner or later

Or, as an another example, his *Prologue for Ode to Road Runner,* where words become music—music shaped in words—and the poet's rhythmic singing accelerates apace:

A downtown train
A downtown train
A downtown train
A downtown train
A down
down
down
town train down train town
A train downtown
A train downtown
A train downtown. . .

Over the last few pages the sounds of the metropolis have first become music and then, increasingly, words. In 1894 Stephen Crane wrote in his jewel of an urban narrative, *An Experiment in Misery:* "The roar of the city in his ear was to him the confusion of strange tongues, babbling heedlessly." In Crane's time several linguistic processes were under way. On the one hand, the American language was gradually distancing itself from its English counterpart. As wrote Finley Peter Dunne, the creator of Mr. Dooley, the scathing Irish figure blessed with a parlance all of his own: "When we Americans get through with the English language, it will look like it had been run over by a musical comedy" (*Mr. Dooley Remembers: The Informal Memoirs of F. P. Dunne*, 1963). On the other hand, a specifically New York jargon was developing as a result of the fusion of different languages held together by a particular connective tissue. According to A. J. Liebling (*Back Where I Came From*, 1990), "Basically, New Yorkese is the common speech of early nineteenth century Cork, transplanted during the mass immigration of the South Irish a hundred years ago." Certain terms and expressions originating from this neck of the woods have now become an integral part of the city's language, like *smithereens, shillelagh,* or *speakeasy.* With regard to these matters, H. L. Mencken's *The American Language* (1919) is a fascinating work, casting a precious light over the plurilingualism that lies at the heart of the American language and, in particular, of the New Yorkese.

Most important was the emergence of a genuine metropolitan slang consisting of linguistic forms and constructs, lexical deformations, syntactic structures, jargonish images, and new words coined to fit in with new metropolitan phenomena. Any attempt to trace the contorted path along which New York slang developed necessarily implies that we undertake another fascinating journey through the social and cultural history of the city. And this is precisely what Irving Lewis Allen has done in his *The*

City in Slang (1993), helping us to understand that even from this point of view the metropolis is always a living organism, pulsating and constantly in motion.

On reading Allen's book one feels that the sounds of the city echo all around us in the shape of words and meanings. We learn, for example, that Broadway has many nicknames: Fraudway, Mazda Lane (from the name of the famous lightbulb company, and with reference to the luminous spectacle to be seen along the street at night), Beer Gulch, Via Lobsteria Dolorosa (inspired by the restaurants serving up lobster specialties, starting off with those located around Times Square), Orange Juice Gulch (taking its origins from the 1920s and 1930s, when costermongers sold their fruit from barrows), Neon Boulevard, Tungsten Territory, and the Great White Way (invented one morning at the end of the nineteenth century after exceptional snowfalls). Allen also explains the meaning of certain expressions like *don't get ritzy with me* (from the Ritz Hotel), *red mike wit a bunch o' violets* (meat cooked in salt with cabbage: from the jargon expression for saltcellar, or *Mike*), *smart aleck* (from the name of a famous mid-nineteenth-century New York thief, Aleck Hoag), *shyster* (an unscrupulous lawyer, from the American-German *Scheisser*), *slaughter in the pan* (a raw steak), and *to lay someone out in lavender* (to send someone to jail, an expression whose origins are extremely complex: it goes back to the ancient custom of pawnbrokers—known in England as Lombards or, in its twisted form, lumbers—of tucking lavender bags into the linen underwear deposited with them; in English slang, however, *to lumber* also meant "putting someone in prison," and in the end the two meanings overlapped and blended together).

We hear once again the jargon of waiters and cooks, or the shouts of bouncers and hucksters, both past and present, and real tongue twisters like *Rosebeefrosegooserosemuttonantaters*. And then we are led into the more mysterious and dialect-ridden territories of specific sectors, like those bound up with precisely defined areas of the city. Take Times Square, for example, whose lingo was codified (or, better, was recreated, or even invented, before being released into the realms of urban folklore) by the writer Damon Runyon in the 1930s and 1940s: sports jargon rubs shoulders with those of the Mafia and the world of entertainment, words and expressions are whipped off the street only to be deformed or interpreted anew, and linguistic borrowings taking their origins from the provinces and small towns are remolded on (and for) the metropolitan experience (and William R. Taylor has some fascinating things to say about this in a lengthy chapter on the subject, in his *In Pursuit of Gotham*, 1992).

In everyday speech, dominated as it is by rhythm and speed, this *slanguage*—this "language of the city"—often becomes pure sound, continually remodeled and modified by pronunciation, accent, and forever-changing outside influences. It is a source of much amusement to deconstruct and reconstruct it, maybe with the help of the precious (and previously mentioned) anthology by Botkin, *New York City Folklore*, or the little book by Judy Levine and Nancy Jackson, *How to Speak New Yorkese* (1988), whose gentle comical blending together of distorted pronunciations, unlikely etymologies, and city culture is a treat: *assawayigoze* (that's the way it goes), *duhshuh-ul* (the shuttle that connects Times Square with Grand Central Terminal), *Statnylant* (Staten Island), *whyntchalookeryagoyn?* (why don't you look where you're going?), *eggzawsted* (exhausted), *lieberry* (library), *mash patadas* (mashed potatoes), *shuddup* (shut up), *dreckshuns* (directions), et al. . . .

But the sound of the city is made up of many different voices, and not just those of ever-mutating slang. When immigrants arrived in their masses around the turn of the nineteenth century, New York must really have been something to see, but the soundtrack must have been great to listen to as well, what with Irish, German, Italian, and Yiddish battling it out with Cantonese, Arabic, Spanish, and a host of local and dialectical variations. The Germans provided New Yorkese with *delicatessen* (or *deli*, an absolutely crucial addition to the city's topography) and apparently made a decisive contribution to the invention of the term *hot dog* by jokingly referring to the sausages sold in New York as *hündchen*, or "puppy dogs"; the Chinese made a present of *chop suey* to the United States, a cheap dish deliberately invented to satisfy the needs of an unsophisticated clientele (it seems that it derives from *shap sui*, a Cantonese term meaning "a little bit of everything"); Italians living in Brooklyn and Little Italy remodeled language and dialect in their continual reworking of American English, coming up with *sciaddappa* (shut up), *goraelli* (go to hell!), *Forte Gelato* (Fourth of July), *toidàvenne* (Third Avenue), *vazzumara* (what's the matter?), and *tamaniollo* (which, it seems, stood for the beer tankard that emissaries from Tammany Hall—the name given to the corruption-ridden headquarters of the Democratic Party in New York—offered newly arrived immigrants from Sicily in exchange for their vote); and above all, there were the Jews from Eastern Europe, who introduced the city's language to Yiddish terms like *schmaltz* (oversentimental), *allrightnik* (a Jew who is completely integrated), *chutzpa* (impudence), *shnorer* (professional beggar, or someone badly off), *meshumed* (apostate), *shlemiel* (poor wretch), and *bagel* (one of the essential ingredients of Sunday brunch in New York).

During this period between the end of the nineteenth and the beginning of the twentieth centuries, language was subjected to continual tension. That William D. Howells had understood this is evident from his review of Abraham Cahan's *Yekl*, when he spoke of "a New York jargon which shall be to English what the native Yiddish of [Cahan's] characters is to Hebrew, and it will be interlarded with Russian, Polish and German words, as their present jargon is with English vocables and with American slang." Henry James, albeit in a far more vexed and worried vein, had understood this, too. In *The American Scene*, the book that recorded his sense of wonder and disappointment on returning home to America, he wrote: "The accent of the very ultimate future, in the States, may be destined to become the most beautiful on the globe and the very music of humanity . . . ; but whatever we shall know it for, certainly, we shall not know it for English—in any sense for which there is an existing literary measure."

And it is a never-ending story, this one of the "accent of the very ultimate future," forever evolving and undergoing transformation. While walking around the metropolis, new and hybrid linguistic forms echo all around you, confirming the sensation that this is very much an ongoing process. It is the speech of Harlem: its tit-for-tat exchanges from windows and on the stoops, its noisy cries, its *dirty dozens*—those verbal challenges on the street consisting of twelve aggressive and insulting wisecracks aimed at the enemy's ancestors that only come to an end when one of the two challengers loses his cool . . . a whole universe that is not only linguistic but cultural, too. It is the Spanglish of Loisaida and the Barrio—a constant chipping away at the English block on the part of Caribbean Spanish, which not only imports terms like *arroz* (rice), *piraguero* (water ice seller), *bodega* (the local corner store that sells everything), *botánicas* (the store that sells religious articles), *bolitero* (the guy who collects clandestine bets), *jarana* (the wild party that lasts all night), *mofongo* (spicy snacks), and many, many more, but which also changes in alchemic fashion (almost as if it were simply a question of contact, proximity, and friction) both the languages. As Sandra María Esteves, a close friend and an excellent poet, writes: "We defy translation."

Now, there is something familiar about this dense universe of sounds that is New York, and I think I may have grasped what it is. On one of my departures from the city I sat down in one of the bars at JFK Airport to wait for my flight to be called. I was scribbling down my final notes and impressions for this book when the singer and performance artist Laurie Anderson (I recognized her immediately) waded in and sat down next to my table. A few minutes later we were chatting away. I must say that I don't like everything she does—some of it is a wee bit too cerebral for my liking, and I tend to prefer the rock music of Springsteen or Lou Reed. That said, she is definitely a genius in her field, blending together music and image, sound and the spoken word, song and monologue, and the

classical and the avant-garde in a way that is at once irresistible and very
New York. We spoke for a while about her concerts and my books, and
she wrote down a few lines in my notebook that I cherish to this very day.

When I got up to go toward my boarding gate, she smiled at me in that
typically idiosyncratic way of hers, something akin to the smile of a metropolitan elf: an Ariel-like figure who had just sprung out from the forests
and hills of Manhattan island. It was then that I understood what was so
familiar about the sounds of Manhattan. I couldn't help but think of
Caliban's words in Shakespeare's *The Tempest*: "Be not afeard; the isle is
full of noises. . . ."

*In the mornings, when the sky is still so clear, with only a glimmer in the east
beyond the river, I am sometimes awoken by a twittering sound on the win-
dowsill that seems to be saying, "Pretty soon, pretty soon, pretty soon," whatever that means. Then I get up and prepare my coffee, and I sit down to drink
it on the wide window ledge of the sitting room, knees tucked in beneath my chin,
a fresh October breeze blowing outside the window, and look down into the
street. At this time of the day, it's almost as if there are no sounds of the city:
perhaps they have all been carefully wrapped in the cotton wool of morning, or
hidden away somewhere beneath the sidewalk in their very own Pandora's box.
As Edna St. Vincent Millay wrote in "English Sparrow (Washington Square),"
"How sweet the sound in the city an hour before sunrise."*

*Then, as the eastern sides of the tall blocks gradually slip on their golden-tint-
ed attire, the cotton wool disappears and Pandora's box opens. Sounds burst
forth, they move in the streets, rebound off the walls, fill the houses. You can
almost touch them. The day will be full of them: the intermittent wail of fire trucks
rushing by, the screaming of police cars, the long, drawn-out screeching of brak-
ing yellow taxis, the dull thud of cars landing on the huge metal sheets thrown
down to cover up the roadworks, the obsessive chanting of antitheft devices, the
roaring of the subway, the machine gun–like chorus of jackhammers, the rhythmic pounding of drills tearing up the earth to lay the foundations of a new tower
block, the guttural shrieking of the poor wretch hobbling along the sidewalk, and
the vibrations emanating from a radio sitting on the shoulder of some ghetto boy.
And then maybe, at night, in the seething half-light of the Nuyorican Poets'
Café, the verses of the poets of Harlem, Spanish Harlem, the Bronx, and
Loisaida: verses steeped in anger and irony, a blend of longings and frustrations,
tenderness and harshness—less a contemporary babel (as one might be tempted
to conclude) than a polyphony—a concert of ostensibly discordant sounds that
eventually settles and amalgamates, and tells the metropolis.*

Hence, when I am at home in the evening, the windows tinged with red and yellow as the city at last cools down and catches its breath, I know that I will shortly hear the ice-cream truck coming from afar, almost as if in a dream. The sounds of the city continue to clash and overlap even at that hour, but the sweet melody of the approaching truck—like that of an immense music box—is a charm able to dialogue with these sounds, almost reconciling them one to the other. The truck reaches the corner, then it stops for a few minutes down below, filling my house with familiar notes and affectionate melodies, hypnotic in their undulating movement, and enfolding every other sound—every other noise—of the pulsating city at dusk.

At that moment I stop whatever I'm doing, and smile: that dainty music box melody is my very own private New York "Nocturne."

9

Prism

*T*he light of the street lamps is particularly warm and friendly, this fall night. It pours yellow from above and cuts out glowing islands in the darkness, but its halo seems neither cold nor artificial. The trees are all shadows and rustlings, the traffic is a river, white and yellow and orange, the faces of passersby are covered with reflections, and in the distance the towers of Manhattan loom in silence after the daytime noise and chaos . . . Strange to see how the city changes its skin at night, as darkness, dense and strange, gradually seeps its way into street after street, jostling aside the marine transparency of daytime.

I couldn't say which is more real: New York by day, or New York by night. Both contain within themselves something elusive that cannot always be traced back to the materiality of its origins. I love city nights for their unique charm and mystery, their way of saying yet not saying, but perhaps not even London is able to cast the same spell over me as New York. The latter walks a different walk as it enters darkness, and its nocturnal mode of being almost results in a different disposition of space, light, perspectives, and rhythms: another of the metropolis's many guises. The night and the city possess an almost irresistible magnetism that can be deceptive and, at times, dangerous: years ago it was precisely this magnetism—the irrepressible need to find myself out in the streets, crossing one after the other—that led to my being mugged in a place I knew full well I should have avoided at that time on my own, but which seemed to have taken on a magical appearance at night.

Anyway, this evening there is a large group of us walking across Manhattan from east to west in the direction of the Village. There are old friends from New York and newly arrived friends from Italy, and the lengthy stroll turns into one of those journeys where the city's various stories and many faces are assessed anew. Howard comments on the proliferation of iron railings surrounding the luxuriant gardens downtown, Marlis pauses at certain street corners and tells us how they've changed over the last twenty years, what direction the process of transformation in certain blocks and neighborhoods has taken . . .

Beyond Washington Square, we walk through the nighttime chaos and con-

fusion of Bleecker Street toward 86 Bedford Street, an anonymous-seeming
address, no sign, no name, which actually coincides with one of Manhattan's
most legendary and little-known places: Chumley's. During the Prohibition era,
Chumley's was among the most revered of speakeasies, and access was subject
to one's being recognized through a peephole at the entrance. The peephole is still
there today, because Chumley's has hardly changed in all these years. You go
through a heavy main door, up a couple of steps, down some others, and you
find yourself in a spacious wooden-floored room with rickety tables all around,
soft lighting, a huge blackboard carrying details of tonight's menu in colored
chalk, a few private rooms, and then the bar counter, more steps and another
smaller and more narrow room and, at the back, a second door (the old securi-
ty exit) that looks out onto a quiet courtyard in Barrow Street, right behind the
corner of Bedford.

The food is good at Chumley's, and they serve excellent beer. The music
doesn't jar and the old tables come complete with carved names and phrases that
tell their own stories. If you get there early enough, you can enjoy a good hour's
worth of peace and tranquility before the place fills up, and, while waiting for
your food and beverages, you can follow the frieze along walls made up of
framed dust jackets of early-twentieth-century classics . . . Indeed, besides
being one of the most famous speakeasies, and besides telling us so much about
the Prohibition era (few such places have survived: there is the 21 Club, at 21
West 52nd Street, and Palm Restaurant on Second Avenue and East 45th
Street, but this remains my first choice, and it is perhaps the most genuine of
them all), Chumley's was also one of the favorite meeting places of artists not
only from the Village but from all over the city (rumors even have Joyce writ-
ing some pages of Ulysses in the little room at the back).

While we sit down at a table large enough to accommodate all of us, in this
place that represents yet another of the many universes to be found in New York,
I hear Billy Joel singing Piano Man against the background hubbub of voices
and music—more metropolitan microstories.

Getting to know New York is not simply a question of poring over its in-
depth and in-width maps (its layers, its sections). No: its isolated faces, its
loose fragments and time warps surround us and (with their reserved
silences or boisterous chatterings) tell the city; and from these metropolitan hypertext windows one can observe important stories and inconse-
quential events, reasons and causes lost in time, revelations and
unexpected epiphanies. Perhaps it is precisely this alternation of continuity and discontinuity—of the overall picture and the separate parts that
go to make up that picture—that makes it so difficult to get a grasp of New

York and puzzle out what it really is. And so every departure from the city necessarily implies a return, for is there not always a niggling unconscious suspicion that something has been omitted? It is at this stage that the sides of the prism become as important to our understanding as the in-depth and in-width maps.

This is a city of many icons. But if I were forced to say which stand closest to my heart, I would have to opt for two skyscrapers and a railway station. One breezy, sunny morning (or one light, limpid evening), take Park Avenue from the south or from the north, and at 26th Street turn to your left or your right. Walking one block farther on you will find yourself on the corner of Madison Square Park, and there it is, poking out from among the trees—the beautiful, airy Flatiron Building. It was designed in 1902 by Daniel H. Burnham, one of America's greatest architects, shortly after his arrival in New York from Chicago, where he had worked on the creation of the 1893 World Columbian Exposition (the great fair that proved something of a watershed between the old America of the frontier and the prairies and the new America of technology and the metropolis).

The nineteen Italian Renaissance–style floors of "Burnham's Folly," as it almost immediately became known, were built onto a streamlined steel structure, with French Renaissance–style ornamentations and warmly colored, lightly undulating rustic terra-cotta walls. Originally called the Fuller Building, its striking resemblance to a towering, narrow iron means it is more widely known as the Flatiron. Its shape also recalls that of a majestic ship's prow plowing its way northward through the chaotic undercurrents of Broadway, almost as if it were signposting the direction taken by the city in those years as it moved up Manhattan.

This particular New York spot is extraordinary: conventional perspectives are thrown to the wind wherever you look, and it suddenly feels as if you are standing in the eye of a small storm. Streets converge and radiate outward, the traffic spins about giddily, and there before you rises up this splendid architectonic object, in perpetual motion, traveling through the urban maelstrom. Here, the wind, too, has something to say and contributes a few lines to the social history of the area: in city slang the cry "Twenty-Three Skidoo!" takes its origins from the corner of Broadway and 23rd Street, where the vortex of winds used to have unpredictable effects on long skirts at the beginning of the twentieth century. Albeit in a minor key, this was something of a foretaste of what would later happen to Marilyn Monroe in the famous scene where she stands on a subway grate in *The Seven Year Itch,* and used to arouse the interest of numerous male oglers (who, courtesy of precisely that sharp cry, were asked to move on).

That aside, the formal beauty, the changing colors, the gradual laying bare of particular details at different hours of the day and night, the lightness and the movement, the unique position in which the building stands, and the sheer imaginative energy it gives off mean that the Flatiron goes well beyond the conventional attributes of a historic landmark (and, personally speaking, one of my New York passions): such is its chosen status among painters and photographers that a whole microhistory of metropolitan art could be written on and around it.

So, it is not easy to take your eyes off the Flatiron, but when you finally *do* manage to take your leave, go back in the direction you came from, head up Lexington Avenue, and walk about fifteen blocks north (yes, one *does* walk a lot in New York). And, there before you, complete with its slender spire, stands the distinctive Chrysler Building. Designed by the architect William Van Alen, it was finally completed in 1930 and was (if only for a few months) the tallest building in the world at 1,048 feet: shortly afterward, the Empire State Building made its appearance, and that was that. But this particular metropolitan race was already under way at the time of the Chrysler when, with a view to breaking the record, the builders of another skyscraper at 40 Wall Street made the surprise decision to add an extra twenty-four inches at the last moment. Van Alen and company wasted no time: the famous stainless steel spire that, together with the decorative work, makes the Chrysler so easily recognizable from all over Manhattan was assembled secretly in great haste and hoisted from inside the building through the dome before being fixed on top during the night. The next morning, the city woke up to feast its eyes on a Chrysler Building that soared upward to the tune of another thirty yards or so.

This is a triumph of art deco, pleasantly and roguishly kitsch and, especially when it casts its loving look in the nighttime sky, irresistibly charming. It is the apotheosis of the Manhattan building industry in the 1920s, the jubilation of an artifact (the car) that was about to embark on its long irresistible journey (check out the endless play of mirrors in the decorative work on the interior, in the splendid African marble lobby with its immense mural fresco on the ceiling, and, on the outside of the building, in the shape of radiators, handles, hubs, and fenders!). The hour of the building industry and the automobile was literally exploding on the American scene in the brief temporal crossroads that closed the decade of easy money and opened that of the Great Depression.

Beneath the winking eye of the Chrysler, walk westward a couple of hundred yards along 42nd Street and you come to the Grand Central Terminal, whose name says it all, really, what with that *grand* (as in imposing, magnificent, supreme) and that *terminal* (railhead, end of the line) that seems to reinforce still further the preceding *central* (and which, in New York symbology, attributes to the metropolis a peremptory definitiveness—the place where journeys end). It's always so fascinating to watch, study, *feel* big-city stations: you get the pulse of the city there, you understand something of its character and its rhythm. Even if you only spend half an hour in these vast, imposing spaces, it will help you appreciate much of what New York and Manhattan are about.

Grand Central Terminal is one of the most incredible constructions to be built in Beaux Arts style. It was completed in 1913 and has survived numerous attempts to demolish it (or, if it comes to that, to dwarf it, as Walter Gropius in part managed to do with his vile MetLife Building, which towers just behind). Three huge arches on the south facade illuminate the interior, surmounted by an enormous clock and a group of sculptures representing Mercury, Hercules, and Minerva (classicism and technology). Below stands a statue of "Commodore" Vanderbilt, the ruthless railway magnate and one of the numerous robber barons who seemed to proliferate at the end of the nineteenth century. The surface area amounts to almost three blocks, with two underground levels (the lower-level ceiling is covered in magnificent tile decorations) that contain more than thirty miles of railway track, and a host of marble ramps connecting the various sectors of what literally amounts to a labyrinth. And the most overpowering thing of all is the central concourse: the lofty vault supported by forty-yard-high columns and decorated with illuminated decorations of zodiac constellations, the large thirty-yard-high windows lending the concourse (celebrated in many a film noir) a certain solemn cathedral-like feel.

Inside and all around this deeply symbolic metropolitan location, there is the concentrated frenzy of thousand upon thousand of commuters, the intense to-ing and fro-ing up ramps and down corridors, the motionless snakes of long trains in the station depths awaiting the signal to leave, and the eloquent silence of a homeless population that has transformed the sinuous recesses of the terminal into the final resting home of anonymous shattered lives. And, in the sprawling concourse, the niggling cinema-induced sensation that something is about to happen from one moment to the next: a chase along stretches of shining marble, a flight at breakneck speed down the stairways, a stealthy retreat along the narrow communication passages beneath the large windows . . .

Then there are some very special niches within the city, where time seems to slow down as if suspended, to allow you a moment to reflect anew on the paths you have already trodden, reorganize the sensations you have felt, and think over the faces, voices, and stories you've come across. And one of these niches is located right here in the depths of Grand Central Terminal, and the mazelike tangle of the station doesn't make it easy to find.

The Oyster Bar and Restaurant is on the lowest level of the station, right in front of the place where the trains depart. With its wide barrel vaults covered in white tiles, it bears a striking resemblance to a cellar (and in the summer of 1997 the whole thing nearly went up in flames: I shudder at the idea of one of the peaceful city spots I cherish most literally going up in smoke). Don't be taken in by the restaurant on the left— a somewhat snooty establishment that offers similar fare, but probably at a steeper price. No, just to the right of the entrance, sit down on one of the stools in front of the horseshoe counters where waitresses move inside as in a diner and rush to set you up with a paper placemat and cotton napkin. The menu comes complete with succulent, exotic-sounding dishes like Maryland SheCrab Soup, Poached North Atlantic Salmon Filet, Florida Stone Crab Claws with Mustard Mayonnaise, Arctic Char Filet with Red and Black Caviar, Cajun Grilled Catfish Filet with Salsa Verde and Hush Puppies. And then there are the oysters, of course. Oysters from all over the place—Blue Point from Long Island, Wellfleet from Massachusetts, Moonstone from Rhode Island, Bras d'Or from Nova Scotia . . .

But I have to recommend the clam chowder, because the Oyster Bar is renowned for this (as well as for its unusual atmosphere). Rather than the Manhattan clam chowder (a vegetable and seafood broth, served with plenty of tomato), which might seem a more logical choice, go for the New England clam chowder (a denser and more creamy soup also of seafood and vegetables, but with milk in place of the tomato): a filling enough dish on its own, and a genuine psychophysical panacea. Then you could always finish up with the excellent rice pudding, and savor one of the wonderfully named beers on offer—Blanche de Brooklyn, Pete's Wicked Oktoberfest Minnesota, Sierra Nevada Pale Ale . . .

I like to think that you go there when night is falling and the lights of the metropolis are coming on to cope with the growing darkness, with the Chrysler Building stretching into the violet-black sky, all pure lines and clear-cut contours. Because at this time of day it is much easier that, at the coiling counter of the Oyster Bar, beside you or in front of you, people sit that have to take the last train home. And so, while you taste your clam chowder, your rice pudding, and your Blanche de Brooklyn, you will have at hand (in the faces, in the voices, in the clothes, in the gestures) dozens of stories to imagine—rather like in a tale by O. Henry or Damon Runyon.

Then, inevitably, we come to McSorley's—McSorley's Old Ale House, an Irish saloon on East 7th Street, almost on the corner with Third Avenue and Cooper Square. The sign outside says "Founded in 1854," the writings painted onto the two windows to the side of the entrance are peeling slightly, and on entering the saloon you are greeted by sawdust on the wooden floor. One of the best things, early in the morning or midafternoon, is the sheer peacefulness of the place as you walk slowly into the growing semidarkness of the first room. To your left, rough-and-ready round tables, big and small, a large potbellied stove, and a couple of cats sleeping on the chairs; to your right, the solid bar counter in dark, aging wood, the nineteenth-century icebox with its invitation to "Be Good or Be Gone," the menu of the day scribbled in chalk on the blackboard, and dozens of objects hanging from the ceiling; and the other room at the back, darker and more spacious, dotted about with tables, an unused fireplace, and the kitchen and the narrow washrooms. Two waiters dressed in grey speed about the rooms, hurriedly taking orders and plucking change from a thick wad of banknotes; and behind the bar stands Geoffrey the poet-barman, and my friend Pepe (pronounced Peppi), an omnipotent godlike figure who knows and recognizes everyone, who relishes in telling you a thing or two about the history of the saloon—and without whom I'm convinced New York wouldn't be the same.

There is a veritable folklore about McSorley's. For a start, its walls are a kind of crash course in the history of the city and the Lower East Side and, if you are curious enough to examine them inch by inch, your patience really will be rewarded: yellowing newspaper cuttings, precariously framed antique prints, slightly crumpled sepia-colored photographs, fin-de-siècle theater playbills, maps of the area, sketches and drawings, front pages of century-old magazines featuring huge illustrations (later replaced by photographic prints), book covers, scraps of paper carrying typewritten messages and recipes, autographs of famous persons and anonymous customers, and an incredible variety of objects. All these things cover the saloon walls in a time-encrusted layer of local color, of cultural and material history.

For many decades McSorley's was the focal point of the Irish community in the neighborhood before becoming the haunt of the radical intelligentsia at the beginning of the twentieth century (from John Reed and Eugene O'Neill to Big Bill Haywood and John Sloan). And, up until 1970, the previous owner of the bar, an aging and somewhat obstinate fellow, forbade entrance to women. McSorley's has been immortalized in the written pages of Brendan Behan and Joseph Mitchell, in a series of beautiful paintings and drawings by John Sloan (and also in a scene from *Once Upon a Time in America*, directed by Sergio Leone); articles, essays, and documentaries have also pieced together the 150-year-old story of the place. And when I feel like reading or jotting down a few things in peace, or simply letting the myriad stimuli of the city filter through my being, there is nothing better than pushing open the wooden door, saying hello to Pepe, and looking around in hopeful anticipation that the tiny semicircular table near the two large windows on the left is free and bathed in sunlight. I'll take my seat, order the beers (exclusive to McSorley's, they always come in twos, and very good they are, too), and later, if I feel like it, a bite to eat (corned beef with Savoy cabbage, for example, or roast lamb with potatoes, stew, and vegetables, or just a simple dish of crackers and cheddar cheese, garnished with the hot mustard that sits in pots lying about the tables here and there). Then I'll just wait: for Pepe to finish polishing up the bar so he can sit down next to me for a chat, for the aging regulars to take their places at the back of the first room and read their newspapers, for Gene to tell an amusing tale from one side of the room to the other, and for the person I'm waiting for to arrive. Or simply for the light to slant in at a different angle through the window onto the carved names and words of my little table.

But perhaps the real suspension of time can be enjoyed in the small garden of St. Luke-in-the-Fields, on Hudson Street between Christopher Street and Barrow Street. I was first taken there by a friend, but we were refused entry because a movie was being shot with Al Pacino, and the crew told us to keep to the other side of the street. And when I went back there on my own some time later, it was not easy to retrace my steps in the maze-like tangle of the West Village. The church was built in 1821 (it was half destroyed by fire about fifteen years ago, but was promptly restored to its former glory), and at the time the area was one of the greenest and most agreeable places in Manhattan, and one of the most secluded: given the disastrous state of the roads at that time, one got there preferably by boat, and perhaps this is one of the reasons why it has maintained its air of separateness, suspended in time—getting there is still complicated, without precise directions.

This, too, is a corner of Manhattan steeped in history and stories. The first warden of the church was a certain Clement Clarke Moore, a man who has gone down in the city's history for having written the poem *A Visit from St. Nicholas*, which begins with the line "'Twas the night before Christmas . . ." That poem, and those lines in particular, somehow became a part of the American collective imagination, so much so that the visionary film director, Tim Burton, must surely have borne them in mind when thinking up a title for that minor masterpiece of melancholic irreverence, *The Nightmare Before Christmas*. The magnificent old houses in Federal style standing nearby (it was from right around there that Al Pacino crossed back and forth continually . . .) were built more or less at the same time as the church, and it was in one of these houses that the writer Bret Harte lived at the end of the nineteenth century—one of the little big names of American literature, the author of several celebrated stories set in the California of the gold rush era some decades earlier . . .

But the garden really is something else. There is nothing straightforward about actually getting there: you have to follow quite a devious
route, passing beneath an arch, walking beyond the adjacent courtyards
of the primary school, skirting past classrooms and the little outside theater. Suddenly, there it is, the garden, and it is something of a maze in
itself, appearing to unravel endlessly, behind the apse of the church,
behind the priory, behind old walls covered in creeping plants, behind the
street, behind the city. Silent little lanes beautifully kept, the area subdi-
vided (despite the much-reduced size of everything) into four zones dif-
fering in configuration and vegetation, plants that are rare and unusual for
this latitude (exposed in a southwesterly direction, and benefiting from
the warm bricks of the enclosing walls, the garden's microclimate is particularly favorable), an incredible variety of birds and butterflies (this little plot of land is, in fact, situated along one of their flyways and is an ideal
stopover point), spacious, welcoming benches—the sense of having left
everything else aside. You take a seat, look about you, pick up a book to
read or a letter to write, and the three or four persons on the benches
around cross time with you, in this niche hollowed out of the wild
metropolis.

Icons, niches . . . the city prism has many sides to it, and some of these
consist of genuine time warps in which time doesn't simply coagulate in
material artifacts or suspend itself in places of tranquility, but positively
seems to reel backward. This is what you may experience in Harlem.

You get there from the south, along St. Nicholas Avenue, running
almost the entire length of Manhattan, and it may well be that you've driven through the neighborhood with more than the usual caution to avoid
any mishaps or moments of tension (giving way at the intersection,
watching out for children crossing the street: routine administration anywhere you go, but not in Harlem, especially when the driver is white).
And maybe there is something odd about the day anyway, grey and driz-
zly, bordering on the unreal. You park your car on St. Nicholas Avenue
abreast of West 106th Street and, on the right, go up some steps only to
find yourself projected backward into another place (New Orleans perhaps?)—another dimension, certainly. You've ended up in Sylvan
Terrace, a short, narrow lane lined with about ten identical-looking little
houses on each side—late-nineteenth-century wooden houses featuring
high stoops positioned laterally onto the facades, decorated balustrades,
frame windows, corbels, and friezes. The beautiful cobblestone paving and
the street lamps marking this brief stretch of road all make for a timeless

atmosphere. Everything is tasteful, gaily colored, and well kept and has recently been restored by the New York City Landmarks Preservation Commission (it seems that only one of the lodgers living in the wooden houses refused the offer of restoration; I couldn't say why).

But don't stop here. Go farther on past the small court called Jumel Terrace and enter Roger Morris Park (perhaps it is fall for you now, too, and the ground is strewn with leaves and acorns), which stretches its way all around the Morris-Jumel Mansion, one of the most intriguing historic landmarks in Manhattan. This solid, Georgian-style white building, complete with a large Federal-style portico two stories high, was erected in 1776 by Colonel Roger Morris. For the month of September in 1776 it served as the general headquarters of George Washington before being occupied by the English. It then became a tavern and later a farm before finally being purchased by Stephen Jumel, a wine merchant, and his wife, Eliza Bowen, a splendid former prostitute (and, if the history books are right, the richest woman in America at the time). It seems that the Jumels were also friends of Napoleon Bonaparte, and that many of the items of furniture used by the couple to enrich this mansion on a small hill facing Harlem River originally belonged to him. Mr. Jumel died in 1835, and his widow married the politician and former vice president of the United States, Aaron Burr, now more than seventy years old. But the marriage soon went downhill, and the divorce came through on the same day Burr died.

Inside, you really do feel as if you are in a time warp: hand-painted tapestries, transparent porcelain, antique clocks, and an octagonal room with views over the garden (the first, it seems, in America)—all very late 1700s and early 1800s. Outside, the metropolis of the second millennium spins all around you: traffic rushing along the fast lane of the ring road, the silhouette of Macombs Dam Bridge, the tensions of Harlem. And perhaps it is exactly out of this gap in time that the legend comes: of ghosts in colonial garb apparently haunting the mansion day and night, insinuating that the death of Mr. Jumel was not quite as straightforward as it seemed . . .

The contrasts in New York certainly *are* remarkable, both for the contradictory nature of the city's stories and the cheek-by-jowlness of its extremes. As Theodore Dreiser wrote in *The Color of a Great City*: "The glory of the city is its variety. The drama of it lies in its extremes." Take the Bowery, for example: I've already mentioned it once or twice in this book, but the time has come to consider it more closely.

This mile or so that today links Chatham Square to Cooper Square began its life as an Indian trail before serving as the thoroughfare that connected the most important Dutch farms in the area. Later it was the main

road linking New York and Boston, and finally, in the first half of the
nineteenth century, it became the residential area of a New York that was
still very much confined to the tip of Manhattan—a wealthy and refined
area whose numerous magnificent theaters (like the Great Bowery
Theater, opened in 1826) dominated the arts scene of the metropolis
until about 1875.

It was about this time that the heart of wealthy New York shifted in the
direction of Fifth Avenue and Broadway, marking the beginning of the end
of the Bowery. Indeed, it was shortly to become the domain of opium dens,
criminal gang hideouts, saloons run by retired actors, small theaters whose
actors included champion boxers like Jim Corbett, German wine cellars,
dime museums, and cheap attractions like sword swallowers, lion tamers,
dwarfs, bearded ladies, and unlikely mermaids . . . a disturbing yet fascinating chapter in the history of popular entertainment in New York during the
Victorian era. The nail in the coffin was the construction of the Third
Avenue Elevated. Its tracks ran the whole length of the Bowery in both
directions, supported by steel scaffolding that was erected adjacent to the
sidewalk (the traffic of wagons, barrows, and horse-drawn trams flowed along
the central section), and which cut the facades of all the glorious theaters in
half (including that of the immaculate neoclassical Thalia Theater)—and
which shrouded every object and living soul in dense smoke, thick shadows,
and coal dust (and, often, flying sparks and drops of oil).

Immigrants from all over the world flocked to the Bowery, a volatile
popular neighborhood, which also counted outcasts, tramps, prostitutes,
alcoholics, and homeless people among its inhabitants. Even so, the theater flourished for some years yet: as I mentioned earlier, Shakespeare's
plays were staged alongside Buffalo Bill's "melodramas of the West," and
the Peking Opera took turns with Yiddish theater. This double-edged
character of the street remained well into the opening years of the twentieth century and was perfectly captured in the 1912 song by Charles
Hoyt, "The Bowery" ("The Bow'ry, the Bow'ry! / They say such things,
and they do strange things on the Bow'ry! / The Bow'ry! I'll never go
there anymore!"), the book by Hutchins Hapgood, *Types from City Streets*
(1910), or *Diamond Lil*, a play set in a saloon during the last decade of the
nineteenth century, written by the "scandalous" Mae West in 1928. The
Bowery could boast all-night bars, Salvation Army missions, cheap brothels, and cheap hotels and flophouses for the aged and homeless, and by
1907 there were 25,000 "irregular inhabitants" living in the area, a situation that only worsened in the decades between the Great Depression and
the 1950s—as is well documented by Lionel Rogosin's bleak documentary
film, *On the Bowery* (1956), and by two exhaustive books: Alvin Harlow's
Old Bowery Days (1931) and Benedict Giamo's *On the Bowery* (1989).

Very little has changed today. The Bowery remains suspended between different and opposing states of being and extremes. It is a wide derelict street whose past and present scars are visible to all, a series of shops and wholesale stores selling lamps, chandeliers, and secondhand restaurant equipment, rows of rough-looking, blackened old houses that readily call to mind the roguish life and ways of the late nineteenth century, squalid hotels and flophouses, abandoned parking lots, Salvation Army missions. Then, here and there, the odd small theater reminds us—obstinately, doggedly—of what this long, spacious thoroughfare (which, in spite of everything, I like to trod on a sunny day) used to be: like the Dixon Place (if it is still open) or the Bowery Lane Theater (whose program really is something to watch out for).

Then of course (and this is where I really wanted to get to), there is CBGB (& OMFUG) and the Amato Opera. The weird acronym stands for Country, Bluegrass, Blues and Other Music for Uplifting Gourmandizers—a haunt that replaced a somewhat disreputable bar at 315 Bowery in 1973, a meeting place for country musicians, which soon became a temple of rock, punk, and new wave: Patti Smith, Iggy Pop, David Byrne and the Talking Heads, Mink De Ville, Television, the Ramones, the B52s, the Voidoids, and other celebrated names in contemporary music kicked off right here in this dark, cavelike venue. Graffiti and slogans line the walls inside and out, and such is the increasingly run-down appearance of the place that it ends up resembling something between a community center and a squat house (you can read all about it in Roman Kozak's *This Ain't No Disco*, 1988).

Leave CBGB, pass in front of the Palace Hotel (probably the most well known of flophouses for the homeless in New York: a century ago, it was Alexander's Museum, a much-visited dime museum on the Bowery, where Steve Brodie—a hugely popular figure on New York's nighttime circuit—used to sing, dance and perform his "monologues"), and just a few yards farther on, at 319 Bowery, you will see a small white brick building. After the black punkishness of CBGB, the Amato Opera makes for a striking contrast: another pearl in this ruined thoroughfare, another jewel in a contrast-ridden Manhattan.

Anthony Amato and his late wife, Sally, founded this opera company in 1947. At that time they didn't own a fixed venue, but after checking out what was available in the Village (still very Italian-dominated during this period), they finally came across these premises—an old warehouse—on the Bowery. In the early 1950s it can't have been an easy decision to open a small theater for opera buffs in one of the most derelict and dangerous areas in New York. And yet the Amato Opera is still going strong, and after all this time (fifty years!) it has established itself as one of the

most interesting and original places in the variegated musical world of
New York and a recognized springboard for talented young singers and
stage designers.

I went to talk to Anthony Amato, a small, peppy, bright-eyed man in
his seventies, whose large feet seem to weld him to the stage. Indeed,
everything is in proportion at the Amato Opera: a hundred seats squeezed
into a tiny auditorium and gallery (secured with the demolition of an
entire wall of the two-story warehouse), a stage barely ten yards across, an
orchestra pit situated in a basement that is just about able to accommodate an electric piano and a couple of wind instruments (the conductor
has to stoop), a chocolate-box–sized bar where you can get a glass of wine
during the intermission (often served by the singers themselves) or enter
the lottery for a ticket for the next performance, changing rooms and
workshops for costume staff and stage designers on the upper floor
(expertly organized in order to exploit the limited spaces as much as possible). Surprisingly intelligent solutions have been found to cope with all
the difficulties involved in the organization of the stage settings: when the
lights go down, the two miniature chandeliers imitate the wealthy
grandeur of the Metropolitan by rising upward to announce the beginning
of the performance (an amused public invariably bursts into applause), and
the singers themselves bring the scenery onto the stage, magically opening and folding it up as they go—a real delight to see (not to mention a
pleasurable debunking of the cumbersomeness and pretensions of the
grand opera theater tradition).

Well, I spoke at length with Anthony and Sally Amato one Saturday
afternoon while they were busy dispatching letters, preparing press releas-
es, and putting the finishing touches on stage costumes. In the evening I
went to see Verdi's *Falstaff*, an outstanding and thoroughly enjoyable performance not only because the stage was for once so close, but also
because of the general atmosphere created between the singers and spectators. On leaving, with Anthony Amato's promise that elephants would
be brought on stage for next week's performance of *Aida* still ringing in
my ears, it was really strange to find myself on the accursed Bowery, outside the Palace Hotel and CBGB. More New York contrasts, and food for
thought.

Apropos of contrasts: Central Park. And what has Central Park got to
do with all this, you may well ask yourself, mindful of Holden Caulfield as
he emotionally watches his sister Phoebe grubbing about for the ring,
from one of the wooden horses in the park carousel? Or remembering
Harry and Sally hanging out at one of the tables of the Boathouse near
Fifth Avenue? Or recalling Marianne Moore's words: "Spring: masses of
bloom, white and pink cherry blossoms on trees given us by Japan.

Summer: fragrance of black locust and yellow-wood flowers. Autumn: a leaf rustles. Winter: one catches sight of a skater, arms folded, leaning to the wind—the very symbol of peaceful solitude, unimpaired freedom. We talk of peace. This is it." Contrasts? What has the park got to do with contrasts?

Quite a lot, actually. Originally designed by the two eminent landscape architects Frederick Law Olmsted and Calvert Vaux in 1856, the park was intended to be an area where the tensions of the growing city could weaken and dissolve, an environment that would be natural but controlled at the same time. The history of this park at the heart of Manhattan, from its initial planning stages to the torments of the present day, is of great interest to those wishing to learn about the history of the city as a whole, its hidden mechanisms, its character, and its moods. And it is a story that has been admirably recounted by Roy Rosenzweig and Elizabeth Blackmar in their fascinating book, *The Park and the People* (1992).

The idea for a park that would celebrate the city and, at the same time, lead to a significant rise in the value of surrounding land, was the brainchild of wealthy merchants and property owners living in mid-nineteenth-century New York. A fierce debate followed in the corridors of city power for a couple of years, but finally a decision was made to purchase the first lot of just over seven hundred acres of water meadows and craggy rocks spanning 106th Street, Fifth Avenue, 59th Street, and Eighth Avenue. In 1857 the project was put to tender and was won by Olmsted and Vaux with their "Greensward Plan," an English, romantic-style landscape that mixed in carefully measured doses the pastoral, the picturesque, and the architectonic, with two long promenades, a terraced hillside, two reservoirs, several elegant buildings, two small lakes, about forty small bridges to connect up the drops and rises in the land and four transversal thoroughfares (East Side-West Side) wedged some yards below ground level to give the impression of uninterrupted continuity to the green expanse . . .

The first real conflict occurred—as I mentioned earlier in the book— when efforts were made to clear settlements of African American, Irish, and German people who had been living in the area for decades: entire villages like Seneca Village, with its three churches, its school and cemetery, were swept away, regardless of the fact that the land had often been regularly purchased by its residents—an act of brute force. After this, work went ahead on the building of the park.

Between 1857 and 1859 about 20,000 laborers set about the task, using more gunpowder than was employed during the Battle of Gettysburg, carrying off something in the region of 71 million cubic feet of earth and rock, planting about 270,000 trees and shrubs, and digging out the massive, irregular, round reservoir to the side of the already existing rectangular one. Central Park was inaugurated in the winter of 1859, and four years later it moved farther north for a total of four blocks, up to 110th Street, now accounting for 843 acres of land. From that time on, a new phase opened in the park's history. The first decade was dominated by an air of exclusiveness, since only the wealthy New York elite (complete with its horse parades and carriages) were allowed access. Strict regulations were imposed to ensure that working-class people were excluded: collective picnics (a Sunday caprice among the Germans and the Irish) were forbidden, and wagons and carts (the main means of transportation for small shopkeepers taking their families to the park on Sunday outings) were denied entry. Only toward the end of the nineteenth century did the city's combative working-class movement succeed in gaining permission for concerts to be held in the park on Sunday morning, while at the beginning of the twentieth century the entire way of running and experiencing the park was modified following the emergence of sprawling immigrant quarters like Harlem and, later, Spanish Harlem, around its northern boundaries.

But the conflicts didn't finish there. Around the end of the 1920s, it was decided that the old rectangular reservoir should be drained, but there was less agreement over what should be put in its place: some favored the building of a sports complex complete with swimming pool and playgrounds, while others wanted the area transformed in compliance with the dictates of the "City Beautiful" movement, advocating the construction of a huge square and a promenade that would link it to the museums situated all around the park. The argument was settled by the arrival of a third faction made up of landscape architects and conservationists who imposed the creation of the so-called Great Lawn, in between the Ramble and the Reservoir (immortalized in many a film, *The Marathon Man* starring Dustin Hoffman to name but one). More tensions and more conflicts were to follow, including the debate over the opening up of further traffic thoroughfares and the building of parking lots inside the park. And, more serious and complex still, the problems deriving from the increasingly multiethnic composition of those frequenting the park during the day or at nighttime, or the grim metropolitan violence that sneaked its way in among the pathways, down beneath the bridges, along the lakeside . . .

While you wend your way about the woods, avenues, and lawns (but not after darkness falls, I beseech you!), between Harlem Meer with its peace-loving fishermen and the Rowboat Lake with its clumsy oarsmen, among the statues of Mother Goose or the heroic dog Balto (who managed to get some medicine to an ice-imprisoned village somewhere out in the sticks), and while you listen to the hypnotic music of the carousel or gaze idly at the winter ice rink, walk about the vivaciously colored Conservatory Garden or hasten your step through the unnerving Warriors' Gate (which warriors?)—while you wander about this boundless rural expanse, New York remains with you all the time, poking its head out from among the trees and hills, a constant and almost sentrylike presence reminding you that you are not in another (otherworldly?) world, but right *there*, in the heart of Manhattan. Then, try to *feel* its complex history, that interweaving of economic-financial interests and pressures from below, regulations imposed by powerful elites and attempts at negotiation on the part of the excluded majority. Try to *feel* the history of a "garden within the metropolis," which was created with a view to warding off the threat of tensions and social divisions: but which, during the past 150 years, has unpredictably and paradoxically come to be their dark mirror, in the depths of its green beauty. Because at times the city seems to shudder, swell out, and, in the end, explode. The contrasts and tensions turn into riots: the long sequence of clashes between groups, communities, and classes that has left its mark on New York over the last two hundred years, and—in the frenzied vertigo of few hours or days—does much to repudiate the notion of harmony and the surmounting of differences that lies at the heart of American ideology.

The history of the New York riots is a real history in itself, and each individual episode puts the metropolis in a new light. In April 1788: enraged at rumors that corpses were being removed from their graves to be used for anatomical dissections, five thousand people marched on New York Hospital: for two days laboratories and offices were thrown into total confusion before police fired on the crowd, killing three demonstrators. In 1793 and 1798: repeated protests against certain well-known brothels soon changed to something like a popular insurrection, in which—well beyond the fortuitous cause—merged widespread frustrations and discontent. Something similar occurred on Christmas Day 1806: a street fight between Catholics (mostly consisting of newly arrived immigrants from Ireland) and Protestants (mostly native New Yorkers) turned into an out-and-out battle. During the course of the 1800s, these riots took on an increasingly social character, even if this may not have been immediately apparent. There were the longshoremen strikes of 1825 and 1828 and those of the weavers in 1828 and the stonecutters in 1829; then there were the "flour riots" in 1837: and on all of these occasions, Manhattan streets swarmed with demonstrators who often ended up fighting the police and local militias.

Then came the famous Astor Place Riots of 10 and 11 March 1849. Supporters of the American Shakespearean actor, Edwin Forrest, interrupted the performance of his English counterpart, William McReady, at the Astor Place Opera House. Crowds thronged the square opposite the theater, and when skirmishes between opposing factions started to reach the boiling point, the police and local militia intervened, guns ablaze: thirty people were killed and fifty injured. In July 1857, on the other hand, the forces of law and order were obliged to back down in the wake of the furious violence unleashed by two enemy gangs—the Bowery Boys and the Dead Rabbits—as they brought downtown to its knees during two days of urban guerrilla warfare. Just a few days later the Kleindeutschland Riots broke out when police tried to quell a brawl in the German quarter of the Lower East Side: one person died and there were quite a few injured.

But the most frightening instance occurred between 13 and 17 July 1863, with the Draft Riots. In the middle of the Civil War, a new law was promulgated allowing those who were able to pay a tax of three hundred dollars to avoid the draft, and the Irish—the poorest and most heavily exploited community in New York—wasted no time in attacking police stations, arsenals, and wealthy citizens' houses. What began as a gut response to an openly class-biased law then turned into something far more race-oriented: the African Americans were attacked, beaten, and wounded around the city, some even lynched and hanged from trees and street lamps. Midtown Manhattan was in flames, and only the intervention of the police, militia, and heavy artillery prevented the situation from deteriorating further. In the end 125 people were killed, although some sources put the figure at closer to a thousand.

Post–Civil War disturbances took on an increasingly social character. In January 1874 various organizations, including the International Workingmen's Association (the First International), called for a mass demonstration in the heart of the working-class and immigrant Lower East Side: the meeting was broken up with incredible violence by horse-mounted policemen in what history books have called the "massacre of Tompkins Square." More violence followed during the strikes of sugar refinery workers (in Williamsburg) in 1886 and, between January and February 1895, of Brooklyn railroad workers (which probably inspired the long "strike chapters" in Theodore Dreiser's Sister Carrie, 1890). Clashes between strikers and the police were common throughout the opening decades of the twentieth century, culminating in the years of the Great Depression when numerous demonstrations of the unemployed were broken up in Union Square and the surrounding area.

The first racial disorders of the new century got under way in the Tenderloin in August 1900. As for Harlem, the ghetto exploded for the first time in 1935, and in a Nation report on those events (which concluded with three deaths), black poet Claude McKay wrote: "One Hundred and Twenty-fifth Street is Harlem's main street and the theatrical and shopping center of the colored thousands. Anything that starts there will flash through Harlem as quick as lightning. The alleged beating of a kid caught stealing a trifle in one of the stores merely served to explode the smoldering discontent of the colored people against the Harlem merchants." The ghetto was again engulfed in flames in 1943 (six people died during a revolt that probably inspired the closing apocalyptic scenes of Ralph Ellison's 1952 work, *Invisible Man*), and throughout the troubled 1960s: in 1964, 1965, and 1968, when widespread unrest in the area was accompanied by the Columbia University student riots. And at the time of the 1977 blackout: when the whole city was plunged into deep and symbolic darkness, and thefts, robberies, and property seizures occurred. Lastly, in more recent history: the veritable nighttime uprising in the summer of 1988, in Tompkins Square Park, as demonstrators protested against the expulsion of the homeless encamped there and the imposition of a curfew in the park, and were quashed by mounted policemen, badgeless agents, helicopters hovering overhead (a few years later, the decision to evacuate some East 13th Street squats led to the appearance of an armored vehicle, no less).

Complex, multifaceted situations buried in the depths of the city, its history, and its culture: that you cannot (must not) forget as you walk along Broadway or Fifth Avenue.

Robert Moses died in 1981, yet his presence continues to loom over the metropolis, rather like those cartoon characters astride building tops, legs apart and arms crossed—symbols of absolute power and of the nexus between politics and finance, and yet another side to this city's prism. It's worth reflecting on a moment.

With his appointment as parks commissioner of New York City in the 1930s, Moses began his own very personal rise to power: autocratic and centralizing in the extreme, at one time he held down no fewer than twelve public appointments. But he soon decided to branch out beyond the (undoubtedly meritorious) task of opening parks all over the metropolis, and turned his hand to bridges (like the Triborough Bridge), housing estates for middle-income families (like Stuyvesant Town), and, most importantly, from the Second World War onward, highways, ring roads, elevated trains, and expressways.

In 1946 Moses became the city's construction coordinator, and as such he set about revolutionizing and rebuilding Manhattan and its environs especially for the automobile, the new grand reality on the American landscape. In the years to follow he built the Brooklyn-Queens Expressway, the Cross Bronx Expressway, the Staten Island Expressway, and the

Verrazano-Narrows Bridge; then he added an extra level to the George Washington Bridge, and, if the locals had not protested, he would have cut a swathe through downtown Manhattan with an expressway abreast of Broome Street. His way of thinking was akin to that of Napoleon III's minister, Baron Haussmann, who gutted entire working-class districts only to replace them with wide tree-lined avenues where, in times of trouble, barricades were more difficult to erect and troops easier to maneuver.

Of course, Moses was not particularly worried about potential insurrections (even if, as we have seen, they weren't that rare); rather, his projects and megalomaniac visions were ruled by land rent and by the up-and-coming social role of the automobile—a triumphal view of post–Second World War America. Even so (or maybe even precisely because of this), he obtained results similar to those of Haussmann. Indeed, every ring road, bridge, and expressway implied the demolition of working-class and immigrant neighborhoods and the dispersion of their former tenants to the four winds; during succeeding decades a good part of the infamous slum clearances that did away with the sight (but the sight only!) of urban degradation was the work of Moses.

Understandably, the master builder of New York was never really a great favorite with the man on the street. The straw that broke the camel's back (provoking an extremely violent and ultimately victorious resistance) was the plan to cement over whole areas of Central Park to build mega parking lots (accompanied by repeated instances of contempt for Joseph Papp's staging of Shakespearean plays in precisely the area which had been targeted by Moses). In the final chapter of his *All That Is Solid Melts into Air* (1982), entitled "In the Forest of Symbols: Some Notes on Modernism in New York," Marshall Berman writes that, in reply to his numerous critics, "Moses appealed plaintively to us all: Am I not the man who blotted out the Valley of Ashes and gave mankind beauty in its place? It is true, and we owe him homage for it. And yet, he did not really wipe out the ashes, only moved them to another site. For the ashes are part of us, no matter how straight and smooth we make our beaches and freeways, no matter how fast we drive—or are driven—no matter how far out on Long Island we go."

And this, too, is part and parcel of the history and stories of Manhattan.

As are the sprawling murals, frescoes painted onto building walls all over Manhattan, but especially visible in those neighborhoods off the traditional tourist circuit—those awkward places of the metropolis you have probably been advised to steer clear of: the Lower East Side, Harlem, El

Barrio, the Bronx . . . Not a surprise, because it is precisely here, in the midst of urban degradation, that the undying vitality and will to survive of those who live there encouraged the creation of these incredible works: a triumphant blend of forms and colors climbing their way five or six stories up the side of crumbling tenement blocks or spreading themselves out for dozens of feet along the wall of some disused warehouse, telling a story as they go. Storytelling, yes, that passion for narration that is so much a part of American culture (and which doesn't involve narrating to an unknown or neutral public but, rather, to a community that can share the narrated experience or which, through the storytelling, is encouraged to share it), and which here is translated into magnificent murals. Once you are in New York, you simply cannot afford to miss them: because they tell you the story of the city—the arrival of the immigrants, the workers' struggles, daily life in the neighborhood, the difficult dialectic between origins and the New World, the dreams of the present and the memories of the past, the faces of those who have disappeared and the street crowds, the thousand-and-one odd jobs and the kids' games, the different languages and cultures, and survival in the metropolis . . .

Behind these murals is a long tradition stretching back to the 1930s and to the muralist schools of artists like Diego Rivera, Thomas Hart Benton, and Reginald Marsh. And they often are the product of a combined effort on the part of artists and ghetto kids, of community centers like Charas/El Bohio and specially created bodies like CityArts (whose murals have been beautifully examined in *Toward a People's Art* [1977], a volume by Eva Cockcroft, John Weber, and James Cockcroft). They have names like *New Birth, Women Hold Up Half the Sky, Seeds for Progressive Change, Afro-Latin Coalition, Chi Lai /Arriba /Rise Up!, Crear Una Sociedad Nueva, Arise from Oppression* . . . Or perhaps one should say they *had* names like this, because the history of murals in New York is not without its downside, rather like that of the city's gardens. It's the sad story of *La Lucha Continua,* one of the most fascinating murals I have ever seen, taking its origins from a creative vision of Maria Dominguez—an enormous fresco binding together New York and Puerto Rico, yearnings and disappointments, headstrong survival, the past and daily lives. It was brutally covered over with a coat of white paint when the building it graced (on Avenue C, on the corner with East 9th Street) was refurbished for its middle-to-high-income residents: further evidence of that arrogant process of gentrification that refuses to tolerate the historical memory of neighborhoods subjected to the whims of real estate.

As I put the finishing touches on this book, a number of beautiful 1930s murals by Hugo Gellert on the walls of the Seward Park Houses in the Lower East Side are at risk of being destroyed. Many local activists and historians of American art and culture have joined forces to save them,

and (who knows?) if you visit New York in the near future, you may well
make it in time to see them.

This story of disappearing murals is hardly new to the city: in 1931
Diego Rivera was hired to paint a large mural in the Rockefeller Center
lobby and came up with a sort of "dream of the millennium" (Peter
Conrad), a fresco that would narrate the Promethean human existence as
it emerges from darkness toward the future. Rivera launched himself into
the enterprise with great enthusiasm, and the mural grew and grew as it
made its way across the Rockefeller Center walls. But then, when the
mural was already completed, he made a blunder: in among the faces
known and unknown populating his work, he included a portrait of
Lenin. The people responsible for the project asked him to remove it, but
Rivera would not comply and was promptly invited to leave. His great
mural was immediately struck out: more New York stories.

There is always room for the odd bizarre coincidence in this maelstrom of
a city. The same afternoon I finally managed to find again the garden of
St. Luke-in-the-Fields, my obstinate wanderings led me to the red
Victorian Gothic-style castle of the Jefferson Market Library. It was built
according to the designs of Calvert Vaux and Frederick Clarke Withers in
1874–77, on Sixth Avenue abreast of West 9th Street—one of the key
corners in the Village—and was originally intended to be a law court,
complete with a built-in jail and, to the side, fireman's barracks and a
market.

A small exhibition of tiny art books by an artist called Susan Rotolo was
being held there on the ground floor: notebooks filled with inventions,
flickering memories, drawings, impressions, materials taken from everyday
life, tickets, and photographs that had been cut out, touched up, and glued
in. To my immense surprise, there in the middle of one of these books was
a photographic sequence whose final shot I instantly recognized: a young
couple, walking affectionately arm-in-arm down a small snowbound street
in New York, cars to the left and right, fire-escaped tenements in the background; he, with his light brown buckskin jacket, hands tucked into jean
pockets, head bowed slightly forward; she, dark coat, long reddish-brown
hair, a simple and slightly dazed smile on her face, huddled up against his
left arm and shoulder—the cover of Bob Dylan's second LP, *The
Freewheelin' Bob Dylan*. I went over the sequence again and realized that
the "she" nestling up to Dylan was not Joan Baez (as I had so often imagined in my youth when looking at the cover—so sweet and tender), but
probably the author of those small, magical art books.

A few evenings later I happened to go to a Tibetan restaurant on East 9th Street with my friend Arthur Tobier (a local historian of the Lower East Side), his wife, and a couple I had met briefly some years before: he, an Italian TV cameraman, she, an Italo-American artist. At a certain point of the evening we were talking about Queens ("nothing there . . . urban desolation . . . ," an impression confirmed by memories of the three days I had spent there many years ago), and the artist told us of how she was born there and fled the place as soon as she could, heading for the Village at the beginning of the 1960s. I asked her what the Village was like at that time, and she spoke to me about it at great length: the crooked lanes, the villagelike atmosphere, the tiny Italian stores, the gloomy, dusty cafés that Ginsberg, Corso, and Kerouac already haunted. And then, with great nonchalance, she added that she had been Bob Dylan's first fiancé—a rather strange feeling, to be told that, in a Tibetan restaurant, in October of 1997.

I looked at her, and then, only then did I actually recognize her. I started laughing and told her everything—the exhibition, the LP cover, my adolescent hypotheses on that "she" and the surprising New York coincidence. And so Susan Rotolo started telling me about that cold, snowy afternoon up and down Jones Street, taking photos for Dylan's album . . .

The many-sided prism, the myriad combinations: all of them, taken together, say, reveal, and tell. Of course, it isn't always easy to put them together, work out the right combinations or join up the dots. It isn't easy, but it is necessary if one wants them to make sense—as parts and as a whole—together with the maps in-depth and in-width. On writing these words, I am reminded of some lines from *Chinatown*, the long (and as yet unfinished) poem by Fay Chiang, a Chinese American poetess who lives and works in New York, and who is a very close friend of mine—lines that have accompanied me through these years of exploration all over the city:

> All hours of the day and night
> I have coursed these streets
> like the memories
> coursing through my veins
> holding on to them
> like charms—
> a child's wish—
> that someday they
> would make sense. . . .

Chumley's is by now packed, and it's time to leave. Outside, this New York Friday night is inundating the Village streets, and moving about as a group is like swimming against the current. We decide to go over to the Nuyorican Poets' Café, where the famous poetry slam takes place every Friday night. The poetry slam is an exhausting poetry competition that seeks to recapture the tradition of the juegos florales they used to hold in Puerto Rico—a runway show of local beauties and poets challenging one another. But we really can't face the idea of walking as far as Alphabet City on a night like tonight, and on the corner of Bedford Street and Seventh Avenue, we hail a couple of cabs.

They will lose sight of one another, these cabs, navigating their way through the nighttime rivers of Manhattan traffic, but then they will meet up again in the midst of an urban setting that, despite its desolation, is dear and familiar to me. And we will all meet in front of the ordinary-looking entrance and the scrawled sign of the café, founded in the mid-1970s by Miguel Algarín and Miguel Piñero, tutelary deities of the Nuyorican poets together with Pedro Pietri and the maestro of them all, Jorge Brandon, a genuine metropolitan bard, el coco que habla, "the talking coconut" (in order that his poetry—never handed over to the press—might continue to be heard, even when he was tired, Jorge had planted a tiny tape recorder inside a hollowed-out coconut). More than ten years ago, the Café moved to its present address here on East 3rd Street, between Avenue B and Avenue C—roomier and perhaps less adventurous than the original long, narrow bar on East 6th Street between Avenue A and Avenue B, which witnessed the birth and full flowering of Loisaida . . .

We will be welcomed by the offhand brusqueness of Julio, the stocky bouncer, and after handing him our five bucks we will exchange a few words about who's here, who's about to arrive, and how the evening's going . . . On entering, we will walk up to the massive wooden counter at the bar and say hello to Algarín and Lois Griffith, Steve Cannon and David Henderson, the protagonists of a poetry scene that, after rising first in the Lower East Side, Harlem, the Bronx, and Brooklyn, now envelops the whole of New York.

Then we will make inroads into the half-darkness of the large, high-ceilinged and bare-bricked room, where we will be immediately greeted by the unstoppable laughter of Pedro Pietri and the sweet smile of Sandra María Esteves. We will join them for a drink at one of the small tables, and wait for the poetry evening—the new poetry slam—to begin.

10

Bridges

I made a pact with myself some years ago, and every time I go back to New York I try to honor it: to walk the entire length of the Brooklyn Bridge. And so, this bright mid-September Saturday morning, I got up early and headed straight off toward the labyrinth raveling and unraveling its way around the approach roads situated at one end of the bridge, between Park Row, Police Plaza, and Centre Street. There weren't many people about, and by the time I at last reached the boardwalk that stretches out a few hundred yards midair in the direction of Brooklyn, I had only come across a few gasping joggers, a couple of aerodynamic cyclists, and the odd long-legged, long-haired roller skater. On the asphalt lanes below, cars were few and far between. Such tranquility, a diffused marine light, and the sun still low on the horizon in front of me: just the right moment to honor that pact.

Halfway along the bridge, the emotion comes rushing back, just like the very first time. It isn't simply a question of the city views that accompany me to the left and right: the outline of spires and pinnacles, the leaping of the other bridges, the river ribboning out to become sea, or the blemished outlines of distant islands. It is the lightness and solidity of the structures that support me, the technological naturalness of the cabled cobweb that envelops me, the fervent solemnity of the two giant stone towers with their Gothic cathedral-style pointed arches, the constant play of light and shade around me, the wind whistling among the cables and the parapet, the difference between one's eyes literally being filled with images of the bridge and the fact of actually walking along and inside it, the almost magical sensation that one is literally suspended in midair over the river, between Manhattan and Brooklyn. And again I think I understand what Hart Crane wished to say and do with his long poem, The Bridge (1930): exploit this admirable architectonic object as a symbol of a historical and cultural crossroads between past and present, east and west, stone and steel, center and periphery . . .

As I walk toward the tower looming darkly against the light, I think about the epic undertaking of the bridge's construction. I think about John Augustus Roebling, one of Hegel's pupils in Berlin, who came to the United States in 1831 *and settled down in Pennsylvania where he was employed as a civil engineer in the canal building project; he invented a metallic cable to replace its hemp counterpart in the towing of boats against the current and began building suspension bridges, and in 1867, he planned to build a steel suspension bridge over the East River between Manhattan and Brooklyn: the Brooklyn Bridge, of course; and he died in an accident, two years after work began. And I think about Roebling's son, Washington, who saw through his father's project: he, too, risking his life, when he fell sick with "the bends" after spending time underwater in one of the rudimentary caissons used for digging out the tower foundations from the river bedrock. And now a lifetime invalid, he followed the works from his apartment in Brooklyn with the help of a telescope and his wife, Emily, who acted as a go-between with the technicians and workers (many died during the construction of the bridge, as a result of fires breaking out in the caissons, "the bends," or the sudden collapse of a building).*

Then I think over the host of problems that young Roebling must have had to overcome, not all of a technical nature: these were the years of the Gilded Age—easy money and widespread corruption—and a project like the Brooklyn Bridge must have left many mouths watering. At a certain point Roebling also discovered that the steel wire that had been used to make the cables (already stretched to support the span) was defective, so he had to reinforce the cables by wrapping them with more wire (all this makes me shudder a little, and I move more quickly toward Brooklyn, wondering if the cable that snapped and killed a woman some years ago may possibly have been one of those).

I think about the panicking crowds of onlookers one week after the bridge's inauguration on 24 May 1883: all that screaming, the stampeding, and the deaths of twelve passersby. I think about all those suicide attempts, successful and not, that have marked the history of the bridge from the beginning. And I think of the contrasting reactions that this synthesis of technology and masonry have inspired over the years: the enthusiasm of Walt Whitman, the hostility of Henry James. And then all the paintings, drawings, photographs, films, and images that have taken the bridge as their darling subject for well over a century.

I am nearly at the end of the long boardwalk: I turn around for the last time to gaze at the tower receding in the distance through the pointed arches of the tower I have just walked beneath. Then I head off in the direction of the approach road that will take me down into Brooklyn.

❧

There are 2,027 of them, according to the bulky, authoritative *Encyclopedia of New York City* (edited by Kenneth T. Jackson, 1995). I mean bridges on active service in the city: 76 stretched over the waters, 1,011 on the terra firma, and the rest made up of railroad and subway bridges, overpasses for pedestrians, or purposely built structures for parks. The first bridge was built in 1693 and demolished in 1917: King's Bridge, used to connect Manhattan to the Bronx abreast of the sharp bend called Spuyten Duyvil; the most recent one (1966) is the Rikers Island Bridge, over Bowery Bay, which unites Queens to Rikers Island (housing a 1935 penitentiary that today counts 16,000 inmates—a 300 percent increase since 1984: prison populations are on the rise everywhere in the United States); and the oldest surviving bridge is High Bridge, built in 1848 to link Manhattan with the Bronx over the Harlem River.

Of course, the most famous bridges are those that radiate outward from Manhattan, like so many cutwaters that anchor this ship-island to the surrounding mainland. The Brooklyn Bridge, naturally, and then, counterclockwise, going up the East River and Harlem River, and coming back down the Hudson River: the Manhattan Bridge (opened in 1909), the Williamsburg Bridge (1903), the Queensboro Bridge (1909), the Triborough Bridge (1936), the Willis Avenue Bridge (1901), the Third Avenue Bridge (1889), the Madison Avenue Bridge (1910), the 145th Street Bridge (1905), the Macombs Dam Bridge (1895), the High Bridge (1848), the Alexander Hamilton Bridge (1963), the Washington Bridge (1888), the University Heights Bridge (1908), the Broadway Bridge (1962), the Hudson River Bridge (1936), and the George Washington Bridge (1931). An impressive list, it cannot be denied, and to think that each of these bridges has diverse origins, forms, and characteristics and its own special story to tell. But it would be too complex a matter to delve into this particular labyrinth now.

For it really is a labyrinth. Open up a map of greater New York and look carefully: the Dutch had every reason to call the city Nieuw Amsterdam—a name that inevitably conjures up images of bridges, islands, and canals—even if the city was confined to the southern tip of Manhattan at the time. Indeed, it is easy to forget that the *whole* of New York is an immense archipelago, and that Manhattan is not the only island. If the truth were told, only the Bronx can lay claim to terra firma status, since the rest of the city is made up of islands. Enormous islands, as in the famous case of Long Island, which, in its New York part, contains Brooklyn and Queens; or minuscule islands, like Rat Island in the waters of the Bronx, in Long Island Sound, already colonized by writers at the beginning of the twentieth century, and a favorite hideaway for the escaped prisoners of Hart Island . . .

So, bridges and islands. And as your journey is about to end, you might want to take this opportunity to actually get out of Manhattan—sure, the beating heart of New York, but sometimes also a bit too arrogant in its jealous, exclusive will to capture and possess those who set foot in a city that,

with the passing of time, has expanded well beyond the confines of the
"hilly island" . . .

We'll start off from the Bronx. I imagine you get there from Manhattan
and that you have wandered the length and breadth of Inwood Hill Park
on the trail of the native Weckweesgeeks or Reckgawancs; then you will
have crossed your first bridge, the University Heights Bridge, and headed
up Fordham Road until the crossroads with the Grand Concourse. So
you're right in the middle of the famous (and infamous) borough. When
the Dutch were here, it must have been truly remarkable to behold—dotted with hills and woods to the west and sloping toward the sea of Long
Island Sound among small valleys and plateaus. Yet, everything considered, even today these forty square miles are green and pleasant—
notwithstanding the reputation of an urban wilderness the area has
earned over previous decades. About 24 percent of the land in the Bronx
consists of parks and gardens, and one of the wonders of New York—the
New York Botanical Garden—includes all that remains of an ancient
Canadian fir forest (and rare Weckweesgeek artifacts, including the first
carved stone ever discovered—the image of a tortoise, a sacred animal for
one of the clans).

Early days in the Bronx were pretty tumultuous. Jonas Bronck, a
Swedish naval captain on the payroll of the Dutch, became an immensely powerful landowner and was forever quarreling and fighting with the
Weckweesgeeks (an otherwise peaceful tribe). This continued until the
massacre of Anne Hutchinson, the excommunicated heretic Puritan who,
after being banned from the colony of Massachusetts in 1637, had settled
in Pelham Bay (at the eastern extreme of the Dutch territory) with a
small band of followers. Then the territory fell into English hands, and the
first bridge to Manhattan (King's Bridge) was built, by merchant
Frederick Philipse, who obtained hereditary rights from the king to run it
by means of charging a toll. Then the blacks started arriving from the
Dutch East Indies, followed by the Irish (who undertook the building of
the New York and Harlem Railroad and the Croton Aqueduct, as well as
working in the ironworks of Mott Haven), and, from the 1840s on, the
Germans.

The Bronx developed as a territory on the edge of New York, with its
small industrial settlements and wide-ranging expanses of fertile ground
where fruit, vegetables, and dairy products could be grown for the metropolis; and in 1874 several locations within the area (Morrisania, West
Farms, Kingsbridge) achieved Annexed District status and became a part
of the metropolis, with other locations following suit in 1895. In the
meantime, around 1888, the 3rd Avenue Elevated was extended as far as
132nd Street, thus helping to propel the Bronx into a new phase of demo-

graphic and commercial growth. The Grand Boulevard and Concourse (or, more simply, the Grand Concourse), where you are standing at this moment, is a monument to this development: stretching from south to north in the heart of the western section of the Bronx, parallel to the Harlem River, it is a real Champs Elysées–style avenue, spacious and tree-lined, with pedestrian subways at the main intersections.

We are now well into the twentieth century. In the search for more dignified accommodation, large numbers of immigrants and second-generation immigrants—Italians, Jews, Slavs, and Armenians—started trickling in from the increasingly congested and brutally urbanized "hilly island." After the Lower East Side and Harlem, people started settling in the Bronx, especially the Italians and the Jews. These "ethnic" exoduses are repeated after the Second World War: the inhabitants of the southern quarters of the Bronx (Morrisania, Hunts Point, Mott Haven) push north in search of more modern dwellings, and their places were taken by blacks and Puerto Ricans escaping from the slum clearances of entire immigrant neighborhoods. In the wake of the financial crisis of the mid-1970s, these southern areas of the Bronx were dominated by absentee property owners who had no intention of looking after the buildings (indeed, many were burnt to the ground to get the insurance money), and increasingly became the object of desperation, poverty, and violence. It was during this period that these areas became—how can I put this?—the part that represented the whole? the symbol of an entire borough? Thanks also to Hollywood . . .

Yes, the sight is often of desolation, in this Bronx inhabited by blacks (about a third), Puerto Ricans and more generally speaking Caribbeans (another third), and whites and Asian Americans (the remaining third). A far cry from the celebratory tones of Joseph Rodman Drake's 1835 poem, "Bronx": "Yet I will look upon thy face again, / My own romantic Bronx, and it will be / A face more pleasant than the face of men." The Bronx is a place where the contingents of that veritable army of uprooted and homeless driven from the "face-lifted" streets of Manhattan keep arriving, but where, as often occurs in New York, a closer look around often reveals unsuspected places of aggregation and resistance.

So, if you still happen to be on the corner of Fordham Road and the Grand Concourse, a number of options are available: a walk around the Concourse, a visit to Fordham University, or a wander around the Bronx Zoo and the New York Botanical Garden. Or, just a few yards away, you might want to pay homage to one of the shrines of literary New York: Poe Park, which enfolds the tiny wooden cottage where Edgar Allan Poe lived between 1846 and 1849 (and where his child bride, Virginia, died of tuberculosis in 1847)—the last New York residence of the writer and poet. Or you could always cross the Bronx longitudinally in the direction of Pelham Bay Park and set off on your island-hopping tour: start with City Island, which is connected to the mainland by the City Island Bridge—another world altogether. The local Siwanoy tribes used to call it Minnewit before it took its present name in 1761 when a group of visionaries thought about setting up an alternative to the port of New York, which would spare ships the more difficult and intricate maneuvers involved in entering the bay through what was revealingly called Hell's Gate. It didn't work, but ever since that moment City Island has remained a splendid marine village, another suspension of time, with all the virtues of absolute tranquility, and all the vices of a somewhat jarring sense of exclusivity.

However, I would like to suggest another option. Continue walking east in the direction of Fordham Road until you get to the intersection with Arthur Avenue. Pause for a moment and wander around, look about you carefully, sniff the air, and take in the atmosphere: you are in New York's real Little Italy (which has absolutely nothing to do with its tourist-oriented counterpart in Mulberry Street). The neighborhood is called Belmont, an increasingly popular home to the Italian community ever since the end of the nineteenth century. This was the period in which the zoo was built, and much of the surrounding area was rebuilt: the city administration openly encouraged Italian bricklayers to come to the area and help in its restoration (and it is hardly a coincidence that the base-ball team of the Bronx, the New York Yankees—aka the Bronx Bombers, and fierce rivals to the Brooklyn Dodgers—could count on a champion like Joe DiMaggio).

Today, Belmont can boast an Enrico Fermi Cultural Center, a marvelous and much-frequented local library stacked with Italian classics from the past and present, and this magnificent Arthur Avenue with its Italian food stores (Tytell's), restaurants like Mario's (someone told me that whole scenes from *The Godfather,* set in the Little Italy of Manhattan at the turn of the century, were in fact shot here: the atmosphere was more authentic), and the huge covered market, a fascinating kaleidoscope of colors, smells, sounds, and words, with a tiny and pleasantly rough-and-ready *trattoria* wedged between the pasta and meat counters, where excellent regional dishes may be consumed. And in all this, there really is very little of the phoniness or chauvinistic show-offiness that often makes the downtown world of Little Italy so difficult to digest.

The time has now come to abandon the Bronx and terra firma as we head off toward the islands of New York. In *The Other Islands of New York City* (1996), an enjoyable book by Sharon Seitz and Stuart Miller, the authors have identified and described about forty islands, although (with the odd exception) I'm afraid you are only going to be able to visit the largest of these in my company. The best thing to do at this point is to forge ahead until you reach the southeastern tip of the Bronx, at Throgs Neck, and take the suspended bridge (which goes under the same name, and whose main span is some five hundred yards long) designed by the Swedish engineer Othmar Ammann. From here you will arrive on the enormous Long Island, where Queens and Brooklyn begin. Glance quickly over to your left, beyond Little Neck Bay toward Great Neck and Little Neck, if only to take in the area where Fitzgerald set *The Great Gatsby*, renaming the localities West Egg and East Egg: Jay Gatsby had his house here, as did the love of his life, Daisy, on the opposite side of the bay, complete with its distinctive "green light of desire"; and, walking still farther south, you will come across the Long Island Expressway, which runs right across the famous "valley of ashes" where the novel's first tragedy takes place . . .

So here we are in Queens. As I said, I cherish no great memories of this borough, but to tell the truth, I've only spent a few days here, in Jackson Heights to the north, next door to the reverberating scaffolding of the subway. Too few, perhaps. Whatever, Queens means certain things: to begin with, tennis in Flushing Meadow and Forest Hills (the Forest Hills Inn, which used to be much frequented by stars of the game, resembles an English village and was—once again—the creation of Frederick Law Olmsted: his contribution to the outlay of New York, together with that of Stanford White, really does deserve studied attention); then there is the anachronistic Alley Pond Park with its "Environmental Center" on the Northern Boulevard and, on Bayshore Boulevard, the sumptuously exclusive Douglas Manor, hidden away among oak and chestnut trees, overlooking Long Island Sound with all the required haughtiness. Plenty of green areas, then, and many residential areas, too—a borough that maybe lacks an overall identity, but which, as David Yeadon suggests in his *New York's Nooks and Crannies* (1986), possesses as many separate identities as its numerous neighborhoods.

For example, take Corona, the place in Queens where the colored glass of Tiffany lamps is produced, inhabited for the most part by Italians and Jews and famous mostly for the fact that Louis Armstrong lived there between 1943 and 1971. Or Astoria, once the heart of New York's cinematographic industry: "The Big House," the great studios much frequented by stars of the silent movies like Rudolph Valentino, the Marx Brothers, Ginger Rogers, Edward G. Robinson, and Tallulah Bankhead (who, legend has it, took her daily "milk-baths" here). The studios disappeared when Hollywood took over from New York (there is more light in California—you know, "it never rains . . ."), but they made a comeback in the opening years of the 1970s. To honor the past, the wonderful Museum of the Moving Image (which covers this particular history from beginning to end) was added later.

History . . . There's plenty of that to be had in Queens, as well. Here, too, Dutch domination led to frequent clashes with the Native American Matinecocs, especially during the aggressive governorship of William Kieft. Religion was the primary cause of tension with the English: the new governor, Peter Stuyvesant—he of the wooden leg and iron will—couldn't stand the newly arrived Quakers and did everything in his power to make their lives miserable. In 1657 a group of people living in Flushing presented Stuyvesant with a "letter of remonstrance," the Flushing Remonstrance, and Stuyvesant's immediate reaction was to arrest John Browne (who had invited the Quakers to use his kitchen as a meeting place) and banish him from the English colony. The stubborn Browne protested to the General Council of the Dutch West Indies Company in Amsterdam and won his case in the name of freedom of worship: in 1694 the first house for the Society of Friends was built in Flushing.

In the years to follow, the history of Queens took on a more tranquil character. A rural area, it was an important producer of the first American apples to be exported to England (the Newtown Pippins) and was the first place in America to establish nursery gardens dedicated to the cultivation of trees and flowers. About the middle of the nineteenth century, the arrival of the railroad and the construction of the first horse-racing courses marked the beginnings of a new phase in the borough's history, and the first seeds of land speculation were duly sown. At the same time, the Irish and the Germans started trickling into the area, William Steinway established his first piano empire here, and factories and laboratories sprang up like mushrooms. Ever since then, the history of Queens has been largely the history of the unstable equilibrium between industrialization and the countryside: by the end of the century, the expansion of nursery gardens and small farms run by the Chinese (to supply a small but overcrowded Chinatown in Manhattan) was accompanied by an alarming increase in pollution and cement. The opening of the Queensboro Bridge in 1909 only accelerated the process, gradually transforming the borough into a sprawling dormitory neighborhood in certain areas and a residential quarter in others. Today, 36 percent of the people living in Queens were born abroad: most of them are of Asian American origin or speak Spanish. There are many Greeks, too, especially in Astoria and Jackson Heights, and I can still remember the tiny food stores and the *tavernas* with their kebabs in the windows, sharing the sidewalk with gloomy Irish saloons and Dominican and Columbian bodegas beneath the scaffolding of the Elevated . . .

Now, if I suggest you cross Queens from north to south and go to Jamaica Bay, I do so for two reasons, first and foremost because this is one of the most natural and pleasant localities in New York (yes, the metropolis-metropolis!). Broad Channel, which really is the life and soul of the area, is also known as "the Venice of New York": islands sprinkled here, there, and everywhere, ponds and canebrakes farther inland, tiny gulfs and inlets, the pier complete with wooden cottages, the idle rocking of the boats, the long and meditative time of the fishermen, the Jamaica Bay Wildlife Refuge (a triumph of indigenous flora and fauna), and then the ibis, the dragonflies, and speckled tortoises—all just a stone's throw from the gigantic JFK Airport. The second reason I mention this place is because it provides an easy, gradual access point to Brooklyn, the borough next door.

And Brooklyn does present some problems. Narrating this "city within the metropolis" is no easy task, also because it has meant (and continues to mean) so many different things at once: literary names like Walt Whitman, Hart Crane, Thomas Wolfe, Arthur Miller, Norman Mailer, and Alfred Kazin; the ultraorthodox Hasidic Jews of Williamsburg with their ecstatic street dances and songs; Spike Lee and his sophisticated black movies; the "Brooklynese" of Italian immigrants; the acute social and racial tensions of Bedford-Stuyvesant, Howard Beach, and Bensonhurst; the waterfront on the riverside facing Manhattan; the immense area used as a cemetery but Pedro Pietri is even more scorching when he writes, in his "Telephone Booth number 48," referring to the *whole* of Long Island: "cemeteries to the right / cemeteries to the left / cemeteries in front of you / cemeteries in back of you / miles and miles and miles / of speechless tombstones / its impossible to get an erection / when you are in long island"); or the Brooklyn Dodgers, the other great baseball team that symbolized sport in New York, at least up until 1957 when they left the borough for Los Angeles, provoking a genuine culture shock (an event that crops up again and again in the two films of Wayne Wang and Paul Auster, *Smoke* and *Blue in the Face*) . . . No, it's not easy to narrate Brooklyn.

When Giovanni da Verrazzano landed here, followed by Henry Hudson and the Dutch of the West Indies Company, the area was inhabited by the Canarsie Indians (their village, Ihpetonga—the high sandy bank—occupied roughly the area now called Brooklyn Heights), and clashes were frequent here, too. The colonies used native wampum (strings of white shell beads) as their means of monetary exchange for some time, and, even before a plan or map of the area existed, the central nucleus of the town developed along the lines of already existing Indian trails (Fulton Street is a good example): together with the name of one of

Brooklyn's neighborhoods, that was all that remained of the Canarsie. Then the number of farms increased, the first blacks arrived to work the land and build the town (in comparison with the rest of New York, slavery was abolished later in Brooklyn), and at the beginning of the nineteenth century, following the introduction of Robert Fulton's steam ferry, the nucleus overlooking the East River opposite Manhattan, Brooklyn Heights, really took off.

The opening of the Brooklyn Bridge and the rapid fanning out of railroad and tram lines hastened the process, and the original nucleus spread like wildfire to encompass other villages and localities. Like Queens, the borough was poised precariously between countryside and industrial development. The first celebrated parks were built (Prospect Park, designed by—yes, you guessed it!—Olmsted and Vaux), neighborhoods like Williamsburg, Brighton Beach, and Manhattan Beach were extended, the glamorous world of amusement parks made its first explosive appearance on Coney Island, successive waves of immigrants arrived to occupy areas like Bedford-Stuyvesant, Bensonhurst, and Howard Beach, the port and shipyards started throwing their considerable weight around (until 1966, when they were closed down), and, with its dockers and railroaders, the working class of Brooklyn wrote some pretty memorable pages in the history of the borough between the 1800s and 1900s. Decline followed: the shipyards were closed, many inhabitants got up and left, entire zones and streets fell into a state of degradation, and tensions built up and exploded. Notwithstanding all this, a certain vitality remains, a peculiar Brooklynese character, the pride of being there, just in front of Manhattan, without paling or stooping. And many are still areas of great beauty, of great interest.

I would, for example, suggest that you dedicate at least an hour to Montague Street and the surrounding area, right there in the middle of Brooklyn Heights, and just a few yards away from the approach road to the bridge and the IRT and BMT subways. I love Montague Street and nearby Montague Terrace, Remsen Street, and Hunts Lane—little cobbled streets with tree-lined sidewalks, small courtyards that recall the Netherlands and England, Paris and Greenwich Village, the old Victorian Gothic-style buildings that used to house libraries, the Brooklyn Art Association, and the Brooklyn Academy of Music, the relaxing bars where you can sit down for a few minutes, the little shops and stores where you can browse at leisure, and once again that reassuring sensation of being suspended in time. And finally, when you reach the riverbank along the Esplanade, the breathtaking views of Manhattan and the bay . . .

Of course, I can't let you leave without a trip to Coney Island. Once upon a time it really was an island, the "island of rabbits"—indeed, *three* islands on the Atlantic Ocean, united by deposits left in the wake of repeated sea storms—and in 1918 it was at last connected up with Brooklyn. Up until the middle of the nineteenth century, Coney Island remained a long, barren beach, where Walt Whitman used to bathe, sun, and declaim Shakespeare and Homer to seagulls and waves, for hours. Toward the end of the century, the locality was discovered by certain unscrupulous individuals who dedicated their efforts to creating a place for gamblers, prostitutes, and swindlers on the extreme western point of the island. Later, on the opposite side, important hotels were built: the exclusive Manhattan Beach Hotel, the Oriental Hotel with its towers and minarets, and the less presumptuous Brighton Beach Hotel. Then came a horse-racing track, which fueled the development of numerous railroads bringing punters and spectators from far and wide to a leisure spot embracing the extremes of a somewhat gaudy refinement and the criminal underworld.

The completion of the Switchback Railway in 1884 marked the beginning of the race to invent ever-more sophisticated and thrilling mechanical-technological means of entertainment—Dragon's Gorge, Mile High Sky Chaser, Drop the Dip, Thunderbolt (immortalized by Woody Allen in *Annie Hall*), Cyclone, Shoot-the-Chutes . . . In 1894 the first amusement park (the Sea Lion Park) was opened, and three years later it was the turn of the Steeplechase Park, which boasted a replica of the Ferris wheel exhibited at the 1893 World's Trade Fair in Chicago as the American answer to the Eiffel Tower. Luna Park and Dreamland were the next in line, ever more convulsive realms of a mass entertainment that combined circus and technology, entrepreneurship and humbug, limitless fantasy and implausibility—a revealing window on American life in the years straddling the nineteenth and twentieth centuries. And it didn't end there, because the story of Coney Island, with all its attractions, rides, and pastimes, continued well into the 1950s when the rot set in following the arrival of the automobile, the charm of suburbia, and the new residential neighborhoods built for the burgeoning middle classes. And so, while its glorious achievements were celebrated in the splendid drawings of Reginald Marsh in the 1940s (the crowded beaches and the outlines of rides and amusements), perhaps its final epitaph was chiseled out by the director Morris Engel in his beautiful 1953 movie, *Little Fugitive*.

Yet Coney Island hasn't gone away: more languid and rust-encrusted than in its heyday, but full of life all the same. Go there on a Saturday morning and walk along the spacious wooden boardwalk that stretches out along the shore for a couple of miles (it always makes me feel like running), watch the crab fishermen as they throw their cages (complete with chicken thighs) into the sea from the jetty, tuck into a hot dog at

Nathan's (they say it was invented here on Coney Island, and Nathan's has become something of a living legend), cross the Bowery (a name that openly recalls its Manhattan counterpart and itself a location where popular entertainment reigned supreme), pass beneath the Wonder Wheel, and let yourself go with the Sideshows-by-the-Sea with its never-changing repertoire of tricks and attractions; and if you happen to be there at the beginning of the summer, enjoy the Mermaid Parade, a kind of Halloween parade where everyone gets dressed up as mermaids or King Neptunes. Then proceed to Brighton Beach, sit down at one of the oceanside tables outside Primorski or Gastronom Moscow and listen to the melodic rise and fall of the Russian language being spoken all around you; order some stuffed cabbage and vodka, and take in all there is to see because you are now in "Little Odessa," yet another world within the kaleidoscopic world of Brooklyn.

Just a few miles on from Coney Island you come to another bridge, and hence another island: the Verrazano-Narrows Bridge (the second "z" is missing in the American spelling) and Staten Island: the last borough that, together with Manhattan, the Bronx, Queens, and Brooklyn, goes to make up New York. Robert Moses was the man who wanted the bridge, even if its construction meant the forced eviction of about eight thousand people, and Othmar Ammann, again, was responsible for its design (the New York Marathon leaves from the extreme point of Staten Island).

So here you are, on Staten Island, which you have already read something about earlier on. Not that there is much to add: at sixty square miles, it is the most isolated borough in New York (and, as the disgruntled murmurings of those in favor of secession would seem to confirm, it is the borough most eagerly at war with Manhattan, some five miles away at the nearest point), as well as the least populous and densely populated. A circle of islands, with a strategic position at the entrance to the bay and facing the Atlantic, some of the highest hills in the area, fields, parks, and important hotels, it is considered a residential area inhabited for the most part by commuters who work in Manhattan offices. Its proud, detached position and less frenetic urbanization has facilitated the preservation of many archeological treasures belonging both to the era in which the rulers of the island were the native Raritan Indians (who called it Aquehonga Manacknong or Eghquahons) and to the seventeenth century: after the explorations of Verrazzano and Hudson, Dutch and French Huguenots and Walloons started arriving on the island, giving rise to a highly original cultural and linguistic culture that survived intact for many decades.

The Dutch called it Staten Eylandt (a name that referred to the States General, the parliament of their native country) and fought the first wars against the Native Americans who, some decades later, were forced to leave the island. Then, as we have seen in the history of the other boroughs, African slaves made their appearance, followed by the English and further waves of immigrants. Staten Island soon won fame for its marine activities (particularly its oyster cultivations, which formed the basis of a key sector in the foodstuffs industry of New York City), its agriculture, and its industry (shipyards and chemicals).

Rest houses for sailors (Sailor's Snug Harbor, Seaman's Retreat), the Sea View Hospital (for many years the biggest sanatorium in the world), a quarantine station (a real thorn in the community's side, it was set on fire at the end of 1857), important hotels for a wealthy clientele, summer retreats for the captains of industry and financiers, and museums like the Historic Richmond Town and Snug Harbor Cultural Center, the Staten Island Historical Society (featuring the photographic archives of Alice Austen), and the Garibaldi-Meucci Museum; the Greenbelt, New York's largest park, opened in 1984; and, to top it all off, a permanent score to settle with New Jersey and its pollution-ridden industries and the never-ending battle waged with New York City—*that* is Staten Island.

Cross the island in the direction of the Bayonne Bridge, another of Othmar Ammann's creations: one of the longest steel arch bridges in the world, it has an 88-yard arch with a mid-span clearance of 546 yards and no intermediate pylon supports, and, approach roads included, is one and a half miles in length. And there you are, in New Jersey, from where thousands of motorists set off via the Holland and Lincoln Tunnels every Friday evening to reach the glittering lights of Manhattan. Instead of taking the tunnels, travel just a wee bit farther north and enjoy the cityscape from the west, observe the immense Hudson River, and linger a while to contemplate the Palisades (the destination of many a boat trip).

Finally, take the last bridge—this time over the Hudson River: the George Washington Bridge, designed (again!) by Ammann. When it was inaugurated in 1931, it was the longest steel suspension bridge in the world, with a main span of 3,500 feet, 212 feet above the water, supported by four steel cables each a yard in diameter, and in 1962 Ammann ordered the building of a second level to cope with increasing volumes of traffic. And so, here you are again in Manhattan, on West 178th Street, right below Inwood Hill Park, where our long journey (and this book) began, just a few yards off Broadway. Hopping from one bridge to another, from one island to another, skirting around a host of different places, stories, scenarios, and kaleidoscopes, you have embraced the length and breadth of New York City, and you've finally come back to the island from whence you departed, the mother island.

It is already late afternoon, and the sun is setting behind your back: maybe you are leaving tomorrow and you still have to pack your bags.

And maybe you should start thinking about what to do on your last evening in New York.

I don't think there are many more moving descriptions of Manhattan than that contained in F. Scott Fitzgerald's The Great Gatsby: "Over the great bridge, with the sunlight through the girders making a constant flicker upon the moving cars, with the city rising up across the river in white heaps and sugar lumps all built with a wish out of non-olfactory money. The city seen from the Queensboro Bridge is always the city seen for the first time, in its first wild promise of all the mystery and the beauty in the world."

All this passed through my mind this morning, while I was packing my last suitcase and taking a final look around the sun-drenched apartment that had been home-away-from-home for so many weeks, and went downstairs, waiting for the taxi to take me to the airport. So I asked the titian-haired driver not to plunge in the subterranean Queens Midtown Tunnel, but to take the old, steel, castlelike Williamsburg Bridge (by now rather unsteady after almost a century's use). And to get there from afar ("don't worry if it takes a while longer") means taking a detour up broad and luminous Delancey Street—the cheerful witness to so many of my homecomings, day and night, and a place I had explored inside out—before venturing into the dark cobweb of the bridge, with all its strange vibrations and cracked views of the river.

Now, simply by glancing a little to the left or right, I can see the Manhattan I am leaving behind, captured like so many fast-running frames through the girders of the bridge: the old port, the bend of East River Park, the huge, square complexes of working-class apartment buildings, the packed anthills of the tenements, the Con Edison smokestacks at the beginning of East 14th Street, and then, gradually fading on the horizon, the proud, arrogant flight of the midtown skyscrapers.

The city I can see from the Williamsburg Bridge is for me (and for you, too, today) the city seen for the last time: pregnant with memories and nostalgia, joy, anger, and passion, doubt and uncertainty, enthusiasm and discovery, promises kept or to be kept, unresolved riddles. It is the "Manhattan Sphinx" that remains aloof exactly as I found her, watching me in silence as I leave.

Then, until I reach the airport, there is nothing to see. Well, almost nothing.

Appendix: The Sites

Abyssinian Baptist Church, *136–142 West 138th Street* (52)

Amato Opera, *319 Bowery* (11)

Apollo Theater, *253 West 125th Street* (50)

Armory (69th New York Regiment), *Lexington Avenue (between East 25th and East 26th Streets)* (34)

Audubon Ballroom, *West 166th Street (between Broadway and St. Nicholas Avenue)* (58)

Barnes & Noble, *Union Square North* (31)

Boat Basin, *on the Hudson River (at West 79th Street)* (39)

Bobst Library, *70 Washington Square South* (16)

Brooklyn Bridge (1)

Café Orlin, *St. Mark's Place (between Second and First Avenues)* (24)

Caffè Farinelli, *corner of Prince and Greene Streets* (7)

Casa Adela, *Avenue C (between East 4th and East 5th Streets)* (7)

CBGB (& OMFUG), *315 Bowery* (10)

Charas, *605 East 9th Street* (28) (*no longer exists*)

Christine's, *208 First Avenue (between East 12th and East 13th Streets)* (30)

Chrysler Building (35)

Chumley's, *86 Bedford Street* (17)

Congregation Anshei Slonim, *172 Norfolk Street* (8)

Congregation Chasam Sopher, *8 Clinton Street* (9)

Cooper Union (21)

Ebenezer Gospel Tabernacle, *225 Lenox Avenue* (47)

Flatiron Bulding (33)

Frick Collection, *1 East 70th Street* (37)

Gramercy Park (32)

Grand Central Terminal (36)

Hamilton Terrace (*between West 141st and West 144th Streets, Convent and St. Nicholas Avenues*) (54)

Inwood Hill Park (59)

Jefferson Market Library, *Sixth Avenue (between West 8th and West 9th Streets)* (20)

Jewish Museum, *1109 Fifth Avenue* (41)

La Marqueta, *Park Avenue (between East 110th and East 116th Street)* (45)

LaMama, *74A East 4th Street* (15)

Leshko Café, *Avenue A (corner of East 7th Street)* (26)

Life Café, *Avenue B (corner of East 10th Street)* (29)

Lower East Side Tenement Museum, *90 Orchard Street* (5)

McSorley's Old Ale House, *15 East 7th Street* (22)

Minton's Playhouse, *at the Cecil Hotel, West 118th Street* (46)

Morris-Jumel Mansion, *at Roger Morris Park* (57)

Mount Morris Park (48)

Museo del Barrio, *1230 Fifth Avenue* (44)

Museum of Chinese in the Americas, *70 Mulberry Street* (2)

Museum of the City of New York, *Fifth Avenue (at East 103rd Street)* (43)

New-York Historical Society, *2 West 77th Street* (38)

Nuyorican Poets' Café, *236 East 3rd Street* (12)

Orpheum Theatre, *Second Avenue (between East 7th Street and St. Mark's Place)* (23)

Our Lady of Lourdes, *West 142nd Street* (55)

Oyster Bar and Restaurant *(Grand Central Terminal)* (36)

Parque de le Tranquilidad, *at 310 East 4th Street* (13)

Petrella Point, *corner of the Bowery and Canal Street* (3)

Riverside Park (40)

Schomburg Center for Research in Black Culture, *515 Malcolm X Boulevard* (51)

St. Luke-in-the-Fields, *Hudson Street (between Christopher Street and Barrow Street)* (18)

Strivers' Row, *between Frederick Douglass Boulevard and Adam Clayton Powell Jr. Boulevard, West 138th and West 139th Streets* (53)

Studio Museum, *144 West 125th Street* (49)

Sylvan Terrace, *between St. Nicholas Avenue and Roger Morris Park* (56)

Tompkins Square Park (27)

Vejigante Café, *155 East 106th Street* (42)

Veselka, *144 Second Avenue (between St. Mark's Place and East 9th Street)* (25)

Wah Mei Bird Garden, *between Delancey, Broome, Forsyth and Chrystie Streets* (6)

White Horse Tavern, *567 Hudson Street* (19)

Williamsburg Bridge (4)

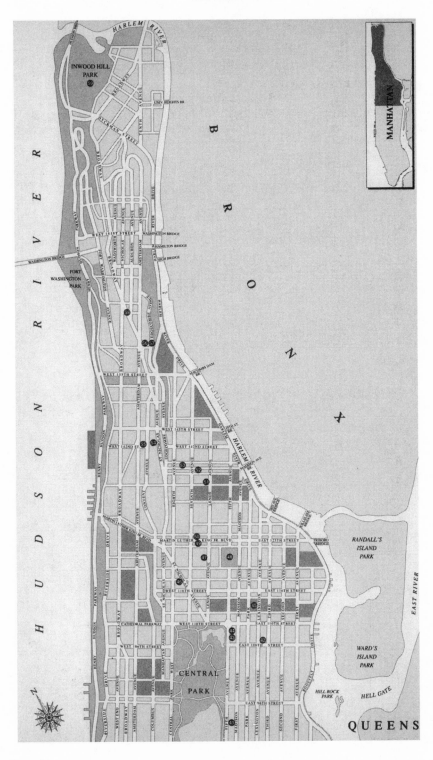

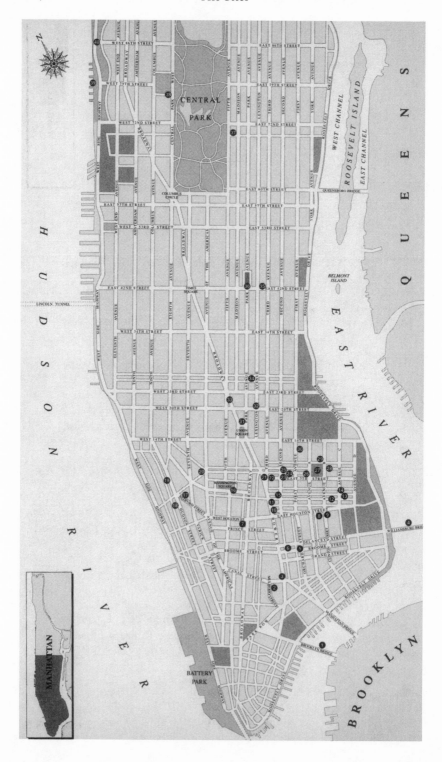

Bibliography

Abbott, Berenice. *Changing New York*. New York: Dutton, 1939.

Algarín, Miguel, and Miguel Piñero, eds. *Nuyorican Poetry: An Anthology of Puerto Rican Words and Feelings*. New York: William Morrow & Co., 1975.

Alleman, Richard. *The Movie Lover's Guide to New York*. New York: Harper & Row, 1988.

Allen, Irving Lewis. *The City in Slang: New York Life and Popular Speech*. New York: Oxford University Press, 1993.

Anbinder, Tyler. *Five Points*. New York: Free Press, 2001.

Asbury, Herbert. *The Gangs of New York: An Informal History of the Underworld*. 1927; New York: Paragon House, 1990.

Auster, Paul. *The New York Trilogy*. 1985–1986; Harmondsworth, Middlesex: Penguin Books, 1990.

Baldwin, James. *Notes of a Native Son*. New York: Beacon Press, 1954.

Beard, Rick, and Leslie Cohen Berlowitz, eds. *Greenwich Village: Culture and Counterculture*. New Brunswick, N.J.: Rutgers University Press, 1993.

Bender, Thomas. *New York Intellect*. Baltimore: Johns Hopkins University Press, 1987.

Benjamin, Walter. *The Arcades Project*. Cambridge, Mass: Belknap Press, 1999.

Berger, Meyer. *Meyer Berger's New York*. New York: Random House,1953.

Berman, Marshall. *All That Is Solid Melts into Air*. Harmondsworth, Middlesex: Penguin Books, 1988.

Botkin, B. A. *New York City Folklore*. New York: Random House, 1956.

Brennan, Joseph. "Fantasy in the Mole People." http://www.columbia.edu/~brennan/abandoned/mole-people.html.

Brooks, Michael W. *Subway City: Riding the Trains, Reading New York*. New Brunswick, N.J.: Rutgers University Press, 1997.

Burrows, Edwin G., and Mike Wallace. *Gotham: A History of New York City to 1898*. New York: Oxford University Press, 1999.

Cahan, Abraham. *The Rise of David Levinsky*. 1917; New York: Harper & Row, 1966.

———. *Yekl; and The Imported Bridegroom and Other Stories of Yiddish New York*. 1896; New York: Dover Publications, 1970.

Cantwell, Anne-Marie, and Diana diZerega Wall. *Unearthing Gotham: The Archaeology of New York City*. New Haven, Conn.: Yale University Press, 2001.

Castleman, Craig. *Getting Up: Subway Graffiti in New York*. Cambridge, Mass.: MIT Press, 1982.

Charnow, Sally, and Steven Zeitlin. *I've Been Working on the Subway: The Folklore and Oral History of Transit*. Brooklyn, N.Y.: New York Transit Museum, n.d.

Charyn, Jerome, *The Isaac Quartet*. London: Zomba Books, 1984.

———. *Metropolis*. New York: Avon Books, 1986.

———. *War Cries Over Avenue C*. Harmondsworth, Middlesex: Penguin Books, 1985.

Chiang, Fay. *Chinatown*. In Mario Maffi, ed., *Voci dal silenzio. Scrittori ai margini d'America*. Milan: Feltrinelli, 1996.

Chu, Louis. *Eat a Bowl of Tea*. Seattle: University of Washington Press, 1961.

Cockroft, Eva, John Weber, and James Cockroft, eds. *Toward a People's Art*. New York: E. P. Dutton, 1977.

Cohen, Barbara, Seymour Chwast, and Steven Heller, eds. *New York Observed: Artists and Writers Look at the City*. New York: Harry N. Abrams, 1987.

Cohen, Marilyn. *Reginald Marsh's New York: Paintings, Drawings, Prints and Photographs*. New York: Whitney Museum of American Art, in association with Dover Publications, Inc., 1983.

Cohen, Rose. *Out of the Shadow*. New York: George H. Doran, 1918.

Cohn, Nik. *The Heart of the World*. New York: Vintage Books, 1992.

Colon, Jesus. *A Puerto Rican in New York*. 1961; New York: International Publishers, 1982.

Conrad, Peter. *The Art of the City*. New York: Oxford University Press, 1984.

Cornwell, Patricia. *From Potter's Field*. New York: Scribner, 1995.

Cowley, Malcolm. *Exile's Return: A Literary Odyssey of the 1920s*. 1934; Harmondsworth, Middlesex: Penguin Books, 1994.

Crane, Hart. *The Bridge*. 1930; New York: Liveright, 1992.

Crane, Stephen. *Prose and Poetry*. New York: Library of America, 1984.

Crapsey, Edward. *The Nether Side of New York; or, The Vice, Crime and Poverty of the Great Metropolis*. 1872; Montclair, N.J.: Patterson Smith, 1969.

Cudahy, Brian J. *Under the Sidewalks of New York: The Story of the Greatest Subway System in the World*. New York: Fordham University Press, 1995.

DeLillo, Don. *Underworld*. New York: Scribner, 1997.

Dickens, Charles. *American Notes for General Circulation*. 1842; Harmondsworth, Middlesex: Penguin Books, 2001.

Doctorow, Edgar L. *Ragtime*. 1975; New York: Modern Library, 1997.

———. *World's Fair*. New York: Random House, 1985.

Dolkart, Andrew S., and Gretchen S. Sorin, *Touring Historic Harlem: Four*

Walks in Northern Manhattan. New York: New York Landmarks Conservancy, 1997.

D'Orsogna, Loretta M. *Il Bronx. Storia di un quartiere "malfamato."* Milan: Bruno Mondadori, 2002.

Dos Passos, John. *Manhattan Transfer*. 1922; Boston: Houghton Mifflin, n.d.

Douglass, Ann. *Terrible Honesty: Mongrel Manhattan in the 1920s*. New York: Farrar, Straus, Giroux, 1995.

Drake, Joseph Rodman. "Bronx." In *The Culprit Fay and Other Poems*. New York: George Dearborn, 1835.

Dreiser, Theodore. *The Color of a Great City*. 1923; Syracuse, N.Y.: Syracuse University Press, 1996.

———. *Sister Carrie*. 1900; New York: Penguin Books, 1994.

Drooker, Eric. *Flood!* New York: Four Walls Eight Windows, 1992.

Dunne, Finley Peter. Mr. *Dooley Remembers: The Informal Memoirs of F. P. Dunne*. Boston: Atlantic Monthly Press, 1963.

Edmiston, Susan, and Linda D. Cirino. *Literary New York*. New York: Peregrine Smith Books, 1976.

Ellison, Ralph. *Invisible Man*. 1952; New York: Random House, 2002.

———. *Shadow and Act*. New York: Random House, 1964.

Emerson, Ralph Waldo. *Essays and Lectures*. New York: Library of America, 1983.

Esteves, Sandra María. "Not Neither." In Sandra María Esteves, *Tropical Rains: A Bilingual Downpour*. Bronx, N.Y.: African Caribbean Poetry Theater, 1984.

Feirstein, Sanna. *Naming New York: Manhattan Places and How They Got Their Names*. New York: New York University Press, 2001.

Fitzgerald, F. Scott. *The Great Gatsby*. 1925; Harmondsworth, Middlesex: Penguin Books, 1967.

———. "My Lost City." In F. Scott Fitzgerald, *The Crack-Up*. 1932; Harmondsworth, Middlesex: Penguin Books, 1965.

Foster, George G. *New York by Gas-Light*. 1850; Berkeley: University of California Press, 1990.

Frisch, Michael. *A Shared Authority*. Albany: State University of New York Press, 1990.

Giamo, Benedict. *On the Bowery: Confronting Homelessness in American Society*. Iowa City: University of Iowa Press, 1989.

Ginsberg, Allen, and Eric Drooker. *Illuminated Poems*. New York: Four Walls Eight Windows, 1996.

Glickman, Toby, and Gene Glickman. *The New York Red Pages: A Radical Tourist Guide*. New York: Praeger, 1984.

Gold, Michael. *Jews Without Money*. 1930; New York: Carroll and Graf Publishers, 1984.

Goldberger, Paul. *The City Observed, New York: A Guide to the Architecture of Manhattan*. New York: Vintage Books, 1979.

Grafton, John. *New York in the Nineteenth Century*. New York: Dover Publications, 1980.

Granick, Harry. *Underneath New York*. 1947; New York: Fordham University Press, 1991.

Green, Martin. *New York 1913: The Armory Show and the Paterson Strike Pageant*. New York: Charles Scribner's Sons, 1988.

Halper, Albert. *Union Square*. 1933; New York: Belmont Books, 1962.

Hapgood, Hutchins. *The Spirit of the Ghetto*. 1902; Cambridge, Mass.: Harvard University Press, Belknap Press, 1967.

———. *Types from City Streets*. New York: Funk & Wagnalls, 1910.

Harlow, Alvin. *Old Bowery Days*. New York: D. Appleton & Co., 1931.

Henry, O. "The Last Leaf." In *Selected Stories of O. Henry*. New York: Modern Library, 1963.

Hine, Lewis. *Men at Work*. 1932; New York: Dover Publications, 1977.

The Historical Atlas of New York City. New York: Henry Holt & Co., 1994.

Homberger, Eric. *Scenes from the Life of a City*. New Haven, Conn.: Yale University Press, 1994.

Howells, William Dean. "An East Side Ramble." In *Impressions and Experiences*. New York: Harper, 1896.

———. "Editor's Study." *Harper's New Monthly Magazine* 63 (July 1866).

———. *A Hazard of New Fortunes*. 1890; New York: Meridian Books, 1994.

Hughes, Langston. "Harlem—A Dream Deferred." In *Collected Poems*. New York: Alfred A. Knopf, 1994.

"In Search of New York." *Dissent*, Special Issue (fall 1987).

Irving, Washington. *Diedrich Knickerbocker's History of New York*. 1809; Tarrytown, N.Y.: Sleepy Hollow Press, 1981.

Jackson, Kenneth T., ed. *The Encyclopedia of New York City*. New Haven, Conn.: Yale University Press, 1995.

Jacobs, Jane. *The Death and Life of Great American Cities*. 1961; Harmondsworth, Middlesex: Penguin Books, 1974.

James, Henry. *The American Scene*. 1907; London: Granville Publishing, 1987.

———. *Portrait of a Lady*. 1881; Harmondsworth, Middlesex: Penguin Classics, 1986.

———. *Washington Square*. 1880; New York: New American Library, 1964.

Johnson, James Weldon. "My City." 1928; in *The Norton Anthology of African American Literature*, edited by Henry Louis Gates Jr. and Nellie Y. McKay. New York: W. W. Norton, 1997.

Jones, LeRoi. *Dutchman and The Slave: Two Plays by LeRoi Jones*. New York: William Morrow and Company, 1964.

Klein, William. *New York*. 1956; Manchester: Dewi Lewis Publishing, 1995.

Koolhaas, Rem. *Delirious New York*. New York: Monacelli Press, 1994.

Kouwenhoven, John A. *The Columbia Historical Portrait of New York: An Essay in Graphic History*. New York: Harper & Row, 1972.

Kozac, Roman. *This Ain't No Disco: The Story of CBGB*. London and New York: Faber and Faber, 1988.

Kracauer, Sigfried. *Theory of Film*. New York: Oxford University Press, 1960.

Levine, Judy, and Nancy Jackson. *How to Speak New Yorkese*. Georgetown, Conn.: Spectacle Lane Press, 1988.

Liebling, A. J. *Back Where I Came From*. San Francisco: North Point Press, 1990.

Limmer, Ruth. *Six Heritage Tours of the Lower East Side: A Walking Guide*. New York: New York University Press, 1997.

Lopate, Phillip, ed. *Writing New York: A Literary Anthology*. New York: Library of America, 1998.

Maffi, Mario. *Gateway to the Promised Land: Ethnic Cultures on New York's Lower East Side*. New York: New York University Press, 1995.

———. *New York. L'isola delle colline*. Milan: Feltrinelli, 2003.

McCabe, James D., Jr. *New York by Gaslight*. 1882; New York: Greenwich House, 1984.

McInerney, Jay. *Bright Lights, Big City*. 1984; New York: Vintage Contemporaries, 1984.

McKay, Claude. "Harlem Runs Wild." *Nation*, April 3, 1935.

———. *Home to Harlem*. 1928; New York: Cardinal, 1965.

Melville, Herman. "Bartleby the Scrivener." 1853; New York: Library of America, 1984.

———. "Letter to Evert Duyckinck," November 7, 1851. Duyckinck Collection, New York Public Library.

Mencken, H. L. *The American Language: An Inquiry in the Development of English in the United States*. 1919; New York: Alfred A. Knopf, 1923.

Mitchell, Joseph. *Up in the Old Hotel*. New York: Vintage Books, 1993.

Mollenkopfs, John H., and Manuel Castells, eds. *Dual City: Restructuring New York*. New York: Russell Sage Foundation, 1991.

Moore, Marianne. "Introduction" to *Central Park Country: A Tune Within Us*. New York: Ballantine Books, 1968.

Morris, Jan. *The Great Port: A Passage Through New York*. 1965; New York: Oxford University Press, 1985.

Morton, Margaret. *The Tunnel: The Underground Homeless of New York*. New Haven, Conn.: Yale University Press, 1995.

New York Panorama. 1938; New York: Pantheon Books, 1984.

Nissenson, Hugh. *My Own Ground*. New York: Farrar, Straus and Giroux, 1976.

O'Connell, Shaun. *Remarkable, Unspeakable New York: A Literary History*. Boston: Beacon Press, 1995.

Odets, Clifford. *Waiting for Lefty*. New York: Covici-Friede [c1935]

O'Hara, Frank. "A Step Away from Them." 1956; In *The Collected Poems of Frank O'Hara*. Berkeley: University of California Press, 1995.

Osofsky, Gilbert. *Harlem: The Making of a Ghetto*. 1966; Chicago: Elephant Paperback, 1996.

Paley, Grace. "Enormous Changes at the Last Minute." 1974; New York: Noonday Press, 1985.

———. "The Little Disturbances of Man." 1959; New York: Viking Press, 1994.

Parry, Albert. *Garrets and Pretenders: A History of Bohemianism in America*. 1933; New York: Dover Publications, 1960.

Petry, Ann. *The Street*. 1946; Boston: Beacon Press, 1985.

Pietri, Pedro. *Out of Order/Fuori servizio*. Cagliari: CUEC, 2000.

———. *Prologue for Ode to Road Runners*. Typescript, n.d.

———. *Puerto Rican Obituary*. New York: Monthly Review Press, 1973.

Poe, Edgar Allan. *Poetry and Tales*. New York: The Library of America, 1984.

Pritchard, Evan T. *Native New Yorkers: The Legacy of the Algonquin People of New York*. San Francisco: Council Oak Books, 2002.

Ravage, Marcus. *An American in the Making: The Life History of an Immigrant*.1917; New York: Dover Publications, 1971.

Reed, John. "Almost Thirty." In *Adventures of a Young Man*. New York: International Publishers, 1963.

Rice, Elmer. *Street Scene*. 1929; New York: Samuel French, 1956.

Riis, Jacob. *How the Other Half Lives*. 1890; New York: Dover Publications, 1971.

Rosenzweig, Roy, and Elizabeth Blackmar. *The Park and the People*. New York: Henry Holt & Co., 1992.

Roth, Andrew. *Infamous Manhattan*. New York: Citadel Press, 1996.

Roth, Henry. *Call It Sleep*. 1934; Harmondsworth, Middlesex: Penguin Books, 1979.

———. *Mercy of a Rude Stream*. 4 vols. New York: St. Martin's Press, 1994–98.

Rukeyser, Muriel. "Study in a Late Subway." In *The Collected Poems*. New York: McGraw-Hill, 1978.

Runyon, Damon. *Broadway Stories*. Harmondsworth, Middlesex: Penguin Books, 1993.

Salinger, J. D. *The Catcher in the Rye*. 1951; Harmondsworth, Middlesex: Penguin Books, 1994.

Sante, Luc. *Low Life: Lures and Snares of Old New York*. New York: Farrar, Straus, Giroux, 1991.

Saroyan, William. *The Bicycle Rider in Beverly Hills*. New York: Charles Scribner's Sons, 1952.

Schoener, Allon, ed. *Portal to America: The Lower East Side, 1870–1925*. New York: Holt, Rinehart and Winston, 1967.

Scott, William B., and Peter M. Rutkoff. *New York Modern: The Arts and the City*. Baltimore and London: Johns Hopkins University Press, 1999.

Seitz, Sharon, and Stuart Miller. *The Other Islands of New York City*. Woodstock, Vt.: Countryman Press, 1996.

Selby, Hubert, Jr. *Last Exit to Brooklyn*. 1957; New York: Grove Press, 1965.

———. *Song of the Silent Snow*. 1986.

Silver, Nathan. *Lost New York*. New York: American Legacy Press, 1967.

Simon, Kate. *Bronx Primitive: Portraits in Childhood*. New York: Harper & Row, 1982.

Singer, Isaac Bashevis. *Enemies: A Love Story*. 1972; New York: Signet, 1989.

Sklar, Robert. *Movie-Made America*. 1975; New York: Vintage Books, 1994.

Snyder, Robert. *Transit Talk: New York's Bus and Subway Workers Tell Their Stories*. Brooklyn, N.Y.: New York Transit Museum, 1999.

———. *The Voice of the City: Vaudeville and Popular Culture in New York*. New York: Oxford University Press, 1989.

Sochen, June. *The New Woman in Greenwich Village, 1910–1920*. New York: Quadrangle/New York Times Book Co., 1972.

Sorkin, Michael, and Sharon Zukin, eds. *After the World Trade Center: Rethinking New York City*. New York: Routledge, 2002.

Soto, Pedro Juan. *Spiks*. 1970; New York: Monthly Review Press, 1973.

Steendam, Jacob. "The Complaint of New Amsterdam." In *Anthology of New Netherlands, or Translations from the Early Dutch Poets of New York*, edited by Henry C. Murphy. 1865; Port Washington, N.Y.: Ira J. Friedman, Inc., 1969.

Steinbeck, John. "Making of a New Yorker." *New York Times Magazine*, 1 February 1953.

Stern, Robert A. M., Gregory Gilmartin, and John Montegue Masengale, eds. *New York 1900: Metropolitan Architecture and Urbanism, 1890–1915*. New York: Rizzoli International, 1995.

Stern, Robert A. M., Gregory Gilmartin, and Thomas Mellins, eds., *New York 1930: Architecture and Urbanism Between the Two World Wars*. New York: Rizzoli International, 1994.

Sukenick, Ronald. *Down and In: Life in the Underground*. New York: William Morrow, 1987.

Tate, Allen. "The Subway." 1927; In *The Collected Poems, 1919–1976*. New York: Farrar, Straus and Giroux, 1977.

Taylor, William R. *In Pursuit of Gotham: Culture and Commerce in New York*. New York: Oxford University Press, 1992.

Thomas, Piri. *Down These Mean Streets*. 1967; New York: Vintage Books, 1974.

Thurber, James. *Writings and Drawings*. New York: Library of America, 1996.

Tobier, Arthur, ed. *Working at St. Mark's Preservation Youth Project: An Oral History*. New York: Community Documentation Workshop at St. Mark's Church-in-the-Bowery, 1978.

Toth, Jennifer. *The Mole People: Life in the Tunnels Beneath New York*. Chicago: Chicago Review Press, 1993.

Trachtenberg, Alan. *Brooklyn Bridge: Fact and Symbol*. Chicago: University of Chicago Press, 1965, 1979.

———. *The Incorporation of America: Culture and Society in the Golden Age*. New York: Hill and Wang, 1982.

Twelve Historical New York City Street and Transit Maps from 1860 to 1967. Flushing, N.Y.: H and M Productions, 1997.

Wakefield, Dan. *New York in the Fifties*. Boston and New York: Houghton Mifflin, 1992.

Wald, Alan M. *The New York Intellectuals: The Rise and Decline of the Anti-Stalinist Left from the 1930s to the 1980s*. Chapel Hill: University of North Carolina Press, 1987.

Wallock, Leonard, ed. *New York: Culture Capital of the World, 1940–1965*. New York: Rizzoli International, 1988.

Ward, David, and Olivier Zunz, eds. *The Landscape of Modernity: New York City, 1900–1940*. Baltimore: Johns Hopkins University Press, 1997.

Ware, Caroline. *Greenwich Village, 1920–1930: A Comment on American Civilization in the Post-War Years*. 1935; New York: Harper & Row, 1965.

Watson, Steven. *The Harlem Renaissance: Hub of African-American Culture, 1920–1930*. New York: Pantheon Books, 1995.

Wharton, Edith. *The Age of Innocence*. 1920; Harmondsworth, Middlesex: Penguin Books, 1974.

Whitman, Walt. "Crossing Brooklyn Ferry." 1860; In *Poetry and Prose*. New York: Library of America, 1982.

———. *Specimen Days*. 1882; in *Poetry and Prose*. New York: Library of America, 1982.

Wilentz, Sean. *Chants Democratic: New York City and the Rise of the American Working Class, 1788–1850*. New York: Oxford University Press, 1984.

Wilson, Edmund. *Apologies to the Iroquois*. 1960; Syracuse, N.Y.: Syracuse University Press, 1992.

Wolfe, Gerald D. *New York, A Guide to the Metropolis: Walking Tours of Architecture and History*. 1975; New York: McGraw-Hill, 1994.

Wolfe, Thomas. *Of Time and the River*. 1935; New York: Scribner, 1999.

The WPA Guide to New York City. 1939; New York: Pantheon Books, 1982.

Yeadon, David. *New York's Nooks and Crannies*. New York: Charles Scribner's Sons, 1986.

Yezierska, Anzia. *Bread Givers*. 1925; New York: Perseus Books, 1975.

———. *The Fat in the Land*. In Anzia Yezierska, *Hungry Hearts and Other Stories*. 1920; London: Virago Press, 1987.

Index

Lancaster, Ohio, 1800–2000: Frontier Town to Edge City
David R. Contosta

Suburb in the City: Chestnut Hill, Philadelphia, 1850–1990
David R. Contosta

Main Street Blues: The Decline of Small-Town America
Richard O. Davies

For the City as a Whole: Planning, Politics, and the Public Interest in Dallas, Texas, 1900–1965
Robert B. Fairbanks

Making Sense of the City: Local Government, Civic Culture, and Community Life in Urban America
Edited by Robert B. Fairbanks and Patricia Mooney-Melvin

The Mysteries of the Great City: The Politics of Urban Design, 1877–1937
John D. Fairfield

Faith and Action: A History of the Catholic Archdiocese of Cincinnati, 1821–1996
Roger Fortin

Cincinnati in 1840: The Social and Functional Organization of an Urban Community during the Pre–Civil War Period
Walter Stix Glazer

The Poetics of Cities: Designing Neighborhoods That Work
Mike Greenberg

History in Urban Places: The Historic Districts of the United States
David Hamer

The Failure of Planning: Permitting Sprawl in San Diego Suburbs, 1970–1999
Richard Hogan

Columbus, Ohio: A Personal Geography
Henry L. Hunker

Designing Modern America: The Regional Planning Association and Its Members
Edward K. Spann

Hopedale: From Commune to Company Town, 1840–1920
Edward K. Spann

Visions of Eden: Environmentalism, Urban Planning, and City Building in St. Petersburg, Florida, 1900–1995
R. Bruce Stephenson

Welcome to Heights High: The Crippling Politics of Restructuring America's Public Schools
Diana Tittle

Washing "The Great Unwashed": Public Baths in Urban America, 1840–1920
Marilyn Thornton Williams